Byron

CHILDE HAROLD'S PILGRIMAGE
AND OTHER ROMANTIC POEMS

Edited, with an introduction
and notes, by
JOHN D. JUMP
John Edward Taylor Professor of English Literature
in the University of Manchester

J. M. Dent & Sons Limited, London
Rowman and Littlefield, Totowa, N.J.

© Introduction and notes
J. M. Dent & Sons Ltd, 1975

All rights reserved
Printed in Great Britain
by Biddles Ltd, Guildford, Surrey.
Bound at the Aldine Press, Letchworth, Herts
for
J. M. DENT & SONS LTD
Aldine House . Albermarle Street . London
First published 1975

This book if bound as a paperback is
subject to the condition that it may not
be issued on loan or otherwise except in
its original binding

Dent edition
Hardback ISBN: 0 460 10005 x
Paperback ISBN: 0 460 11005 5

Rowman and Littlefield edition
Hardback ISBN 0 87471-626-8
Paperback ISBN 0 87471-639-x

CONTENTS

Introduction	vii
Select Bibliography	xxi
Childe Harold's Pilgrimage, I	1
Childe Harold's Pilgrimage, II	36
Childe Harold's Pilgrimage, III	62
Childe Harold's Pilgrimage, IV	93
The Giaour	141
The Prisoner of Chillon	173
Mazeppa	182
She Walks in Beauty	202
Oh! Snatch'd Away in Beauty's Bloom	202
The Destruction of Sennacherib	203
Stanzas for Music	204
When We Two Parted	205
Darkness	206
Epistle to Augusta	208
Lines on Hearing that Lady Byron Was Ill	212
So, We'll Go No More A Roving	213
Notes	214

INTRODUCTION

> He taught us little; but our soul
> Had *felt* him like the thunder's roll.

Matthew Arnold was speaking of Byron's poetry; others might have said much the same of the man himself; and still today avid readers of numerous accounts of his life can testify to the extraordinary power of his personality. Nor does the interest end with him. It spreads to all who were near to him, whether distinguished by their own achievements or not. As a result, we have full-length biographies, or substantial biographical essays, on his half-sister, his wife, several of his lovers, his daughters—not only the two he acknowledged but also a third he did not—and his chief male and female friends. To have known Byron at all well, or to have been closely related to him, is evidently to qualify for the attention of a biographer. Yet such interest merely reflects the irresistible fascination universally felt in the biographical, as once in the living, presence of the man himself.

He was born in 1788, the only child of an unstable marriage. His mother, widowed while he was still an infant, brought him up on a very modest income in Aberdeen in her native Scotland. Exposed there to the Calvinist doctrines of the innate evil of men and the predestined damnation of vast numbers of them, he developed emotional biases that were to remain with him for life. Then, in his eleventh year, the death of a great-uncle made him sixth Baron Byron of Rochdale. As a result, he and his mother moved to England, and he entered Harrow.

He came to regard his school with affection; but at home his relations with his mother grew less and less happy. She was an emotionally intemperate woman and alternated between indulging and abusing her son. When in one of her rages, she would even taunt him with his congenital lameness. By the time he went up to Trinity College, Cambridge, he was seeing as little as possible of her.

At the university he made a number of good friends, and with one of these, John Cam Hobhouse, he set off on a grand

Introduction

tour in 1809. The two young men sailed first to Portugal. There and in Spain, the French, who had for some time dominated the European mainland, were fighting a losing war against the British, who had established a bridgehead on the Iberian peninsula and were supporting the Spanish resistance with a view ultimately to overthrowing Napoleon I. Byron and Hobhouse spent nearly six weeks sightseeing. They toured battlefields; they witnessed a bullfight. Sailing from Gibraltar, they briefly visited Malta and eventually landed in the Ottoman Empire. They explored parts of what are now Albania and Greece before going on to Asia Minor and Constantinople (Istanbul). When Byron returned to Greece, Hobhouse went home. Nine months later, Byron followed him. He had been out of England for two years.

In 1812 he published *Childe Harold's Pilgrimage*, I and II, in which he sends his hero through the countries he had himself recently seen. It made him famous overnight. A few days earlier, he had delivered his maiden speech in the House of Lords in opposition to a Tory bill to make Luddite machine-breaking punishable by death. A few weeks later he again took a Whig line when he spoke in favour of Catholic Emancipation.

Naturally enough, the famous young poet became a welcome guest at the great Whig houses, and in one of these he met the sensitive, impetuous, and neurotic Lady Caroline Lamb. A stormy love-affair followed. This was very far indeed from being Byron's first, but it probably affected him more profoundly than any since 1803, when his Nottinghamshire neighbour Mary Chaworth had rejected his adolescent devotion. To Caroline Lamb there succeeded the mature and worldly Lady Oxford, and to her, in all probability, Byron's own half-sister Augusta. He and Augusta spent a very happy period together snowbound in Newstead Abbey, the family home of the Byrons, early in 1814. But the incestuous nature of this relationship made it dangerous for both parties. Perhaps people were beginning to talk. At all events, Byron decided to regularize his life by marriage.

The decision was unwise, and the choice of bride was disastrous—for her as for him. Byron was an eighteenth-century libertine aristocrat, Annabella Milbanke a Victorian Evangelical before her time. Crippled by the debts he had begun to accumulate while living extravagantly as an under-

Introduction

graduate, Byron was drinking heavily. The wonder is not that the marriage failed but that it lasted a whole year. When the end came early in 1816, hostility to the husband, though very far from unanimous, was widespread. It sufficed to make him leave England in April for the second and last time.

He crossed to Ostend and within a few days was visiting the field of Waterloo. There, less than a year previously, the French Empire had received its deathblow. Napoleon I himself always fascinated Byron. While not wishing him to invade England, he was happy to see him dominate the Continent. Regarding him as in some degree the agent of the French Revolution, and admiring him as a manifestation of relentless energy, he greatly preferred him to the 'legitimate-old-dynasty boobies of regular-bred sovereigns' (Journal, 17 November 1813) whom the French had routed in country after country. Byron had, moreover, his personal reasons for wishing to see the battlefield. Men whom he knew had fought and died there.

Continuing his journey, he travelled up the Rhine to Switzerland. He settled for some months beside the Lake of Geneva, where he saw a good deal of Shelley. The grief and humiliation consequent upon his separation from his wife, and the tender longing he still felt for Augusta, made him for a brief period susceptible to emotions to which he would yield less readily at other times. Shelley was even able to persuade him to take a more favourable view of Wordsworth. This lasted long enough to leave traces in *Childe Harold's Pilgrimage*, III, in which his hero follows him over the ground he had recently traversed.

In October 1816 he crossed the Alps into Italy. After a short stay in Milan, where he had his first opportunity of observing Austrian imperialism in action, he journeyed over the plain of Lombardy to Venice. This became his home for some years. The slow decadence of the city, its rich and sombre beauty, its momentous historical and literary past, and the opportunities it currently offered for the life of pleasure gave it a charm to which he was fully content to surrender. He formed numerous sexual associations, three of which lasted long enough to call for mention. Marianna Segati was the wife of the draper over whose shop he lodged during his earliest months in Venice. Her successor was the ferocious and passionate Margarita Cogni, a baker's wife. She took up

Introduction

residence with him for a time in the Palazzo Mocenigo on the Grand Canal, to which he moved in 1818. His last sexual attachment developed in 1819. In that year he became the *cavalier servente*, or sanctioned lover, of the Countess Teresa Guiccioli, the young wife of a wealthy husband forty years her senior.

Two years earlier, he had visited Rome with his old friend Hobhouse and had naturally glimpsed something of the other Italian cities through which he had to pass on his journeys between there and Venice. The melancholy beauty of the ruins of Rome appealed to him, as did also their powerful historical associations. A fourth and last canto of *Childe Harold's Pilgrimage* was the natural outcome. In this, the pilgrim broods upon many scenes in northern Italy but concerns himself mainly with Venice and Rome.

Byron found life in Italy extremely congenial, and, when he formed his stable relationship with Teresa Guiccioli, his whole existence grew much more settled. He had in any case reached what he considered middle age. The notion may surprise twentieth-century readers, but it would not have been thought extravagant during the earlier part of the nineteenth century. Twenty years later, a poetaster who evidently owed much to Byron could earnestly, if ludicrously, declare:

> . . . I cannot feel as I have felt
> Or sing as I have sung.
> Even to the verge of middle age
> I've brought my earthly pilgrimage;
> My heart's no longer young.
> In sooth, 'tis time, at twenty-seven,
> My Muse should be the bride of Heaven!

Byron at least deferred middle age to thirty.

As a middle-aged author, well-adjusted both socially and domestically, he relaxed from some of the more extreme Romantic attitudes characteristic of *Childe Harold's Pilgrimage*, of the Turkish tales composed during his years of fame in England, and of the metaphysical drama *Manfred*. The finest achievements of his later years were to be the serio-comic poems written in the octave stanza. From these, we know him as a worldly-wise commentator on human affairs, a sardonic observer of folly in all its forms, and a

Introduction

scornful opponent of hypocrisy and tyranny. He regards most things with a gay mockery, but he never loses his genial concern for his fellow men and his sheer enjoyment of living.

We must not allow ourselves to think of this well-adjusted, middle-aged man as quiescent or complacent. On the contrary, he remained actively committed to what he believed to be the cause of freedom. Teresa Guiccioli's father and brother were ardent liberals and members of the Carboneria, the secret society devoted to Italian unification and independence. Byron, too, became a Carbonaro.

The hopes of these republicans ran high in 1820. A wave of revolutionary unrest was sweeping over Europe. The success of the Neapolitans in forcing their tyrannical king to accept a more democratic constitution alarmed the absolutist powers of the Holy Alliance, and in 1821 an Austrian army marched south to suppress the popular movement. Byron hoped that the Carbonari would operate in the rear of the invaders. For some time he had been living in part of the palazzo of Count Guiccioli in Ravenna. He gave his comrades facilities for the storage of arms, and he was ready to go into action with them. But the Neapolitans collapsed, and the Carbonari did not budge.

Though the Austrian and Papal secret police had long been watching this notorious liberal and free-thinker, the authorities hesitated to act directly against a man whom they supposed highly influential. But when Count Gamba, Teresa's father, petitioned the Pope to separate the Guicciolis on account of the husband's misbehaviour, and when the Pope agreed to do so on condition that Teresa resided with her father, the authorities saw a way of proceeding indirectly. If they exiled the father from the territories they controlled, the troublesome English milord would certainly follow the daughter.

Things worked out as planned. The exiles withdrew to Tuscany, and Byron joined them there in the autumn of 1821. In Pisa and at the seaside he lived a quietly contented social life after the political anxieties and disappointments of the preceding period. Shelley was a much-loved member of the circle. His death by drowning in July 1822, and the repetition by the Tuscan government of the tactics which had dislodged Byron from the Papal States, brought this phase to a close. Teresa and her father withdrew to Genoa, and Byron followed them there in the autumn of 1822.

Introduction

One of the spies had noted in his diary:

> Lord Byron has finally decided to leave for Genoa. It is said that he is already sated or tired of his Favourite, the Guiccioli. He has, however, expressed his intention of not remaining in Genoa, but of going on to Athens in order to make himself adored by the Greeks.

Cynicism, a natural result of his contemptible calling, caused this agent to misunderstand his subject's motives. Byron remained deeply fond of Teresa, but was beginning to feel cramped in Italy. Since 1821 he had been noting with interest that the Greeks were rising in revolt against their Turkish masters; and in the spring of 1823 he accepted an invitation to become a member of the London Greek Committee. This body had a broadly liberal appearance. Not until later did Byron realize that it was administered exclusively by orthodox disciples of a theoretician, Jeremy Bentham, whom he found merely ridiculous. But already he showed a more realistic understanding of the Greeks' immediate needs than did the doctrinaire progressives in London. He suggested field guns, powder, and medical supplies; they were thinking primarily of representative government, education, and a free press.

He left Genoa for Greece in July 1823 and established himself initially on the island of Cephalonia, then under British protection. He wished to take stock of a confused situation before giving his support to any one of the rival nationalist movements on the mainland. His companion Trelawny, the bogus adventurer who had been a friend of Shelley, thought this unromantic and threw in his lot with the flamboyant and treacherous chieftain Androutsos ('Odysseus'); less predictably, the pedantic Benthamite Colonel Stanhope did likewise when Androutsos feigned an interest in utilitarianism. Having made his own more prudent choice, Byron proceeded to the mainland and began to form an artillery unit at Missolonghi. He was ready to go into action with this. But the obstacles were too great. The unit showed little sign of becoming an effective military instrument; the men who enlisted under him were turbulent and unreliable; he could have no confidence in Trelawny or Stanhope; and in the country generally the contending Greek factions seemed quite irreconcilable. Moreover, he was a sick man. Missolonghi was an unhealthy place, and Byron fell seriously ill

Introduction

after being caught in a rainstorm on 9 April 1824. Not until 15 April did his doctors appreciate how grave his condition was, and four days later he died.

His death attracted such publicity that it brought more aid to the Greek cause than he could himself have given by any imaginable military success.

Byron combined in himself a bewildering variety of attributes. In conversation with Lady Blessington, he admitted as much. He recognized that he could plausibly be regarded as 'a sort of sublime misanthrope, with moments of kind feeling', or as a cheerful mocker in the manner of his own *Don Juan*; and he hoped that it was also possible to see him as 'an *amiable*, ill-used gentleman, "more sinned against than sinning".' His own belief was that he had no character at all but was everything by starts and nothing long. He did claim, however, that there were two sentiments to which he was constant: 'a strong love of liberty, and a detestation of cant'.

* * *

Who were the two greatest English Romantic writers? A twentieth-century British reader would probably answer, 'Wordsworth and Keats'. If challenged to reconsider his choice, he might substitute Blake or Coleridge or Shelley for one or other of these. But a Continental reader, whether in the nineteenth or the twentieth century, would very likely reply, 'Byron and Scott', and leave it at that.

Many factors have contributed to this high estimate of Byron. The French have always taken a neighbourly pleasure in praising authors who can be depicted as victims of Anglo-Saxon puritanism and hypocrisy; a personal legend such as Byron inspired is more readily exportable than is poetry because it does not depend upon precise verbal formulation in a particular language; and Byron's poetry itself embodies thoughts and feelings more closely akin to those of the French and German Romantics than does that of any other important English writer of his time. Above all, however, even readers with an imperfect grasp of the language can sense in Byron's writings as in his life a natural force such as was expressed for Arnold by 'the thunder's roll'.

The kind of expression given to this force varies with the different phases of his literary career. The poems in the present selection illustrate some of its most openly, even extravagantly,

Introduction

Romantic manifestations. All of them were written by 1819, all except *Mazeppa* before Byron started work on *Don Juan*. Together with the Turkish tales that followed *The Giaour*, and with *Manfred* (1817), they are the poems that gave him his astounding contemporary and near-contemporary reputation, not only among his fellow-countrymen but among readers everywhere. They impressed once and for all upon men's imaginations the notion of 'the Byronic'.

Childe Harold's Pilgrimage dominates them. Each of its four cantos can be considered as an independent poem, or they can be taken together as a somewhat loosely organized whole. Byron shifts his position, even changes his mind, as he writes. At first he seems to be one more imitator of Spenser in the line of descent from James Thomson (1700–48), who describes his *Castle of Indolence* as 'writ in the manner of Spenser' and justifies 'the obsolete words, and a simplicity of diction in some of the lines which borders on the ludicrous' as 'necessary to make the imitation more perfect'. Accordingly, Byron, having invoked another eighteenth-century Spenserian in his preface, regales us with a quaint and affected jargon of 'whilome', 'wight', 'losel', 'eremite', 'ee', and so on.

But he cannot keep it up. His characteristic rhetoric in Canto I is that which we hear when he voices his hatred of war and his indignation against the French invaders of Spain. It is strong, assertive, ample, and unashamedly declamatory:

> Hark! heard you not those hoofs of dreadful note?
> Sounds not the clang of conflict on the heath?
> Saw ye not whom the reeking sabre smote;
> Nor saved your brethren ere they sank beneath
> Tyrants and tyrants' slaves?
> (*Childe Harold's Pilgrimage*, I. 414–18)

Neither here nor elsewhere does Byron's pacifism prevent him from acknowledging the possibility of a just war or from admiring the courage, energy, and high spirit that may be shown by persons engaged in combat. When he admires virtues similar to these in the doomed beast in the bull-ring,

> Here, there, he points his threatening front, to suit
> His first attack, wide waving to and fro
> His angry tail; red rolls his eye's dilated glow,
> (*Childe Harold's Pilgrimage*, I. 753–5)

Introduction

his rhetoric appropriately resumes its extraordinary resonance and power. At the close of the canto, admittedly, he seems to recollect that he is supposed to be imitating Spenser; so he tricks out the final stanza with 'fytte', 'moe', and 'Eld'. But there are few traces of Spenserian diction in the rest of *Childe Harold's Pilgrimage*. Although Byron continues to use the Spenserian stanza, it develops in his hands a vehemence, a capacity for emphasis, and an aggressive fervour that we do not find, and should indeed be disconcerted to find, in *The Faerie Queene*.

In Canto I, Byron professes to be tracing the pilgrimage of an imaginary character, whom he first describes with some care. From the beginning, however, Harold is liable to go missing. After his farewell to England, there follows a passage of more than a hundred lines, in which the poet approaches Lisbon; denounces the Portuguese; describes the landscape around Cintra; recalls William Beckford, the author of *Vathek*; and deplores the recent Convention of Cintra. 'So deem'd the Childe', he then declares (I. 315), as if these four words will suffice to impose Harold's point of view upon all that he has himself just told us. Canto II, similarly, opens with fifteen stanzas on the littleness of man and the decay of Athens, a decay recently accelerated by the depredations of Lord Elgin. 'But where is Harold?' asks the poet (II. 136), as if suddenly aware of having lost his hero. While Harold's appearances are distinctly erratic in Cantos I and II, he evaporates completely in the middle of Canto III, and the poet becomes undisguisedly the one who travels for the remainder of the poem. Nevertheless, he remembers to take courteous farewell of his Pilgrim in the stanzas which conclude the entire work.

Byron tried hard to separate Harold from himself. But the distinction was never sharp, and before long it became hopelessly blurred. As a result, we tend in reading *Childe Harold's Pilgrimage* to focus upon things seen and things encountered, and upon the rebellious attitudes voiced at critical points in the narrative, rather than upon the evasive and indeterminate tourist who has been alleged to move at its centre.

The main experiences and protests of Canto I have already been indicated. Certain of them recur in Canto II. Manifestations of energy and ferocity continue to fascinate Byron. He rejoices at the savagery of Albania:

Introduction

>Here roams the wolf, the eagle whets his beak,
>Birds, beasts of prey, and wilder men appear,
>And gathering storms around convulse the closing year.
>   (*Childe Harold's Pilgrimage*, II. 376–8)

But Canto II begins and ends in Greece. Byron's Classical education had prepared him to see this as a land 'of lost gods and godlike men' (II. 802); its actual population he found degraded by their long servitude to the conquering Turks. Some of them dreamed of regaining their freedom by 'foreign arms and aid'. But Byron warns them, 'Who would be free themselves must strike the blow' (II. 717–21). A decade later, when they struck the first blows in the Greek War of Independence, he was to bring them what assistance he could command. In the meantime, he rejoices in the enduring beauty of the country: 'The sun, the soil, but not the slave, the same' (II. 837).

Canto III is the most intimately personal of the four. Written while Byron's grief and mortification following the failure of his marriage were still acute, it testifies to Shelley's success in encouraging him to seek consolation in nature. Uncharacteristically imitating Wordsworth, Byron proclaims that

>   to me
>High mountains are a feeling, but the hum
>Of human cities torture.
>   (*Childe Harold's Pilgrimage*, III. 681–3)

Not only the Alps but the 'wide and winding Rhine' (III. 497) and the countryside closely associated with Rousseau evoke heartfelt responses.

His travels bring him to places where battles have been fought. As in Canto I, he deplores the cruelty and the destructiveness of war. At the same time, he is too honest to deny the fascination of its pageantry and too generous to scorn the military virtues of resolution and gallantry. But he reserves his full acclamation for those who fought for freedom. He sees Marathon as a glorious deliverance, Waterloo as an unnecessary carnage. Byron's stanzas on Waterloo are deservedly famous. He thrills to the pibroch, he grieves for 'the unreturning brave' (III. 238), and he asks indignantly what the world has gained by this 'first and last of fields! king-making Victory' (III. 153).

Introduction

Waterloo not only restored the legitimate monarchs whom Byron despised; it also deposed the self-made emperor whom he admired. Napoleon I was a further manifestation of the ferocious energy that he always valued so highly. Moreover, Byron's mobility of temperament, and his self-contradictions, made him unusually susceptible to the 'spirit antithetically mixt' of this great man of action who was 'Extreme in all things' (III. 317-20).

The fall of Napoleon is one among many reminders throughout *Childe Harold's Pilgrimage* of the instability and transitoriness of all that men value in this life. Whole 'nations, tongues, and worlds must sink beneath the stroke' (II. 477); nor has a creature as insignificant as man any grounds for complaint. Some of Byron's contemporaries held this a belittlement of the human race such as proved Byron an utter misanthropist. In saying so, they pushed matters too far. To be sure, Byron makes no lofty estimate either of his fellows or of himself. On both topics he can speak with ruthless cynicism. But in the end his attitude is easy, tolerant, kindly. Men fall tragically far short of the ideals they profess, and of the dignity they arrogate to themselves, but they can still surprise us by what they intermittently achieve. The situation in which we find ourselves, 'Swept into wrecks anon by Time's ungentle tide' (I. 287), ought surely to inspire in us only pity for one another.

Thoughts and feelings of this kind dominate much of Canto IV, in which the poet, a 'ruin amidst ruins' (IV. 219), contemplates the surviving traces of the dead empires of Venice and Rome. The palaces of the one 'are crumbling to the shore' (IV. 21), and in the other the Palatine Hill itself 'the Imperial Mount', is littered with

> what were chambers, arch crush'd, column strown
> In fragments, choked-up vaults, and frescos steep'd
> In subterranean damps.
> (*Childe Harold's Pilgrimage*, IV. 957-9)

Such sights, and the melancholy reflections they suggest, can easily lead to quietism or defeatism. Not in Byron, however. A profoundly rebellious impulse stirs throughout *Childe Harold's Pilgrimage*. Reading the opening stanzas of Canto II, contemporaries shrank from the poet's subversive speculations on death and the unlikelihood of immortality.

Introduction

Equally disturbing to them was his defiant declaration in Canto III of his sympathy with the French Revolution. Though he deplores its wanton destructiveness, he accepts the democratic principle that inspired it: 'Mankind have felt their strength, and made it felt' (III. 780). In Canto IV he recalls the American Revolution and asks whether the Europeans are now doomed forever to be subject to the despots reinstated in 1815. He denies the necessity of their servitude:

> Yet, Freedom! yet thy banner, torn, but flying,
> Streams like the thunder-storm *against* the wind;
> Thy trumpet voice, though broken now and dying,
> The loudest still the tempest leaves behind;
> Thy tree hath lost its blossoms, and the rind,
> Chopp'd by the axe, looks rough and little worth,
> But the sap lasts, and still the seed we find
> Sown deep, even in the bosom of the North;
> So shall a better spring less bitter fruit bring forth.
> (*Childe Harold's Pilgrimage*, IV. 874–82)

In these final cantos, Byron still writes with a good deal of his attention fixed upon the readers whom he wishes to persuade or dissuade. That is, he still writes as something of an orator. But he is now vastly more experienced in the art. He controls the pace, pitch, and volume of his lines with an almost unfailing skill. He moves assuredly, clause by clause and phrase by phrase, to each bold climax. Apostrophes and rhetorical questions—even sequences of rhetorical questions—bring emphasis where he requires it. Sudden hushed lines occur in poignant contrast with what precedes or follows them; indeed, antithetical effects of every kind are frequent and powerful. The Waterloo stanzas in Canto III and the address to the ocean at the end of Canto IV illustrate this impassioned rhetoric at its most overwhelming. Nor is the triumph merely rhetorical. What we have in these and other bravura passages in *Childe Harold's Pilgrimage* is an oratory that is brilliantly poetic.

The Giaour, which appeared in 1813, was the first of five Turkish tales that Byron published by 1816. It therefore relates more closely to the earlier cantos of *Childe Harold's Pilgrimage*, issued in 1812, than to the later cantos, issued in 1816 and 1818. In particular its hero is often said to bear a striking family likeness to Childe Harold.

Introduction

The Giaour is a remorseful and sympathetic variant of the currently fashionable Gothic villain. His pale and gloomy brow, his evil eye, his bitter smile, his air as of a fallen angel, and his customary attitude of 'mix'd defiance and despair' (l. 908) are all representative features. On his first appearance, Harold is something of a Gothic villain, too. But this is only part of the truth about him. High-born, proud, restless, solitary, sinful, sated, loving, and sad, he combines within himself the traits of several current hero types. Above all, he is a gloomy egoist and a man of feeling; and in the later cantos he develops into a Romantic hero of sensibility and becomes indistinguishable from the poet.

The heroes of the remaining Turkish tales, and the hero of *Manfred*, differ from one another as well as from Harold and the Giaour. Nevertheless, these various figures have enough in common for critics to have felt able to delineate a generalized 'Byronic hero'. Reviewing Moore's *Life of Byron* in 1831, Macaulay described this character as 'a man proud, moody, cynical, with defiance on his brow, and misery in his heart, a scorner of his kind, implacable in revenge, yet capable of deep and strong affection'. The fact that these words can apply to Emily Brontë's Heathcliff draws attention to just one of the Byronic hero's innumerable descendants.

But the most interesting feature of *The Giaour* is the way in which Byron presents his story. His friend Samuel Rogers had recently experimented with a fragmented narrative in *The Voyage of Columbus*. Byron followed his example but went further: he wrote his fragments from a variety of points of view, and he departed from a strictly chronological sequence.

He opens *The Giaour* from his own poetic point of view by contrasting the liberty and glory Greece once knew with the servitude and degradation which are hers as he writes. A Mohammedan fisherman then introduces to us the remorseful and vengeful Giaour. Having done so, he pushes forward in time and describes the desolation of the Turkish Hassan's hall after the Giaour has killed its owner. To account for the deed, he moves back in time and tells how Hassan drowned one of his women who had become the Giaour's lover. He then juxtaposes a description of this dead woman, Leila, with his narrative of the Giaour's violent revenge. Before withdrawing, this fisherman introduces the third narrator, a member of a religious community to which the Giaour has

Introduction

retired. The fourth and last point of view is that of the Giaour himself in a long unrepentant confession.

The deviousness of this enables Byron to provoke curiosity, heighten suspense, and suggest mystery. By deferring explanations and resolutions, he successfully keeps his reader on tenterhooks. It is regrettable that he never again employed techniques of this sort.

The Turkish tales evidently owed much of their contemporary appeal to their exhibition of sensational acts of human savagery in exotic settings of great natural beauty. For *The Prisoner of Chillon* and *Mazeppa*, which came shortly after the last of them, Byron abandoned the eastern Mediterranean but retained the human savagery. In the former, the victim's enemies confine him in the Castle of Chillon, at first with his brothers but after their deaths in solitude. In the latter, Mazeppa is tied to the back of a wild horse and sent to what is intended to be his death. Both men survive their ordeals and regain their freedom, Bonnivard 'with a sigh' (*The Prisoner of Chillon*, l. 392), Mazeppa to revenge himself on his foe. Byron's 'strong love of liberty' is fundamental to both works. The pathos of the earlier is characteristic of the Swiss period in which Byron wrote it. While Mazeppa's ferocious pride in action and in endurance relates him to the earlier Byronic heroes, the occasional comic and satirical touches in the poem remind us that Byron was writing it about the time he started *Don Juan*.

Byron wrote rapidly. More than that, he can be felt to have written rapidly. His impetuosity and copiousness contribute significantly to our aesthetic response as we read the longer poems on which his reputation mainly rests. The tale last discussed, *Mazeppa*, conveniently illustrates just this. But Byron composed also many successful lyrical and other shorter poems. A selection from these completes the present volume.

'When We Two Parted' voices a deeply grieved reproach, 'She Walks in Beauty' an awed, detached admiration, 'Oh! Snatch'd Away in Beauty's Bloom' a tender sorrow of bereavement, and 'Stanzas for Music' an utterly entranced devotion. All of these succeed precisely as songs. In contrast to them stands 'The Destruction of Sennacherib', a martial lyric so familiar that readers often have difficulty in seeing it clearly. But perhaps Byron's finest lyric is the poignant

Introduction

'So, We'll Go No More A Roving'—apparently an impromptu—which he sent to Moore on feeling the onset of middle age.

'Epistle to Augusta', 'Lines on Hearing that Lady Byron Was Ill', and 'Darkness' all belong to the months following the separation of Byron from his wife. Writing lovingly and gratefully to his half-sister, he acknowledges his errors with a humility that is the more moving for being exceptional in him. His lines to Lady Byron bitterly analyse what he had come to think the calculating disingenuousness shown by his 'moral Clytemnestra' (l. 37). In 'Darkness' he projects the emotions of this period into a vision of total disaster. He never came nearer absolute despair than in this account, shot through with cruel ironies, of the progressive extinction of all life on our planet.

Byron remains in conflict with himself to the end. He can find no solution to the strife of body and soul; he dreams of an ideal without believing that it can be realized; he yearns for a lost innocence but cannot repudiate the experience which has made it inaccessible; he grieves at the littleness of man and the transitoriness of earthly things, but he can at the same time recognize in the human spirit an ability to resist, and briefly to assert itself against, the forces which constantly operate to crush it. This precarious humanism underlies his hopes for liberty. It underlies also his sheer enjoyment, obvious throughout his writings, of the very processes of being alive.

SELECT BIBLIOGRAPHY

TEXTS

The Works of Lord Byron: Poetry, ed. E. H. Coleridge, 7 vols. (1898–1904); *Letters and Journals*, ed. R. E. Prothero, 6 vols (1898–1901). The standard edition; but its text of the prose is being superseded in the publication listed next.

Byron's Letters and Journals, ed. L. A. Marchand, probably about 10 vols (1973 onwards).

Byron: Poetical Works, ed. F. Page, revised J. D. Jump (1970). A convenient one-volume edition in the Oxford Standard Authors.

Select Bibliography

BIOGRAPHICAL AND CRITICAL STUDIES

John Buxton, *Byron and Shelley* (1968). An attractive history of the friendship between the two poets.

R. F. Gleckner, *Byron and the Ruins of Paradise* (Baltimore, 1967). A perceptive and sympathetic study of Byron's achievement prior to *Don Juan*.

M. K. Joseph, *Byron the Poet* (1964). A richly-informed general study.

J. D. Jump, *Byron* (1972). A general study of the poet in his historical setting.

J. D. Jump (ed.), *Byron: 'Childe Harold's Pilgrimage' and 'Don Juan': A Casebook* (1973). Short excerpts from nineteenth-century critics, longer pieces by twentieth-century critics.

L. A. Marchand, *Byron: A Biography*, 3 vols. (1957). The standard biography. Comprehensive and judicious.

L. A. Marchand, *Byron's Poetry: A Critical Introduction* (1965). Pays more attention to the poems prior to *Don Juan* than do the other authors of general studies listed here.

J. J. McGann, *Fiery Dust: Byron's Poetic Development* (Chicago, 1968). Treats most fully the period illustrated in the present volume.

Peter Quennell, *Byron: The Years of Fame; Byron in Italy* (1974). A lively and well-written biography, covering the period 1811–23. Before revision, its two parts had been published as two separate biographical sketches.

Andrew Rutherford, *Byron: A Critical Study* (Edinburgh and London, 1961). A judicious critical review.

P. L. Thorslev, *The Byronic Hero: Types and Prototypes* (Minneapolis, 1962). Usefully corrects excessively simple and generalized accounts of the Byronic hero.

Paul West (ed.), *Byron: A Collection of Critical Essays* (Englewood Cliffs, N.J., 1963). A valuable critical anthology.

Paul West, *Byron and the Spoiler's Art* (1960). A high-spirited and flamboyant general study.

CHILDE HAROLD'S PILGRIMAGE

A ROMAUNT

L'univers est une espéce de livre, dont on n'a lu que la première page quand on n'a vu que son pays. J'en ai feuilleté un assez grand nombre, que j'ai trouvé également mauvaises. Cet examen ne m'a point été infructueux. Je haïssais ma patrie. Toutes les impertinences des peuples divers, parmi lesquels j'ai vécu, m'ont reconcilié avec elle. Quand je n'aurais tiré d'autre bénéfice de mes voyages que celui-là, je n'en regretterais ni les frais ni les fatigues.

LE COSMOPOLITE.

ORIGINAL PREFACE

THE following poem was written, for the most part, amidst the scenes which it attempts to describe. It was begun in Albania; and the parts relative to Spain and Portugal were composed from the author's observations in those countries. Thus much it may be necessary to state for the correctness of the descriptions. The scenes attempted to be sketched are in Spain, Portugal, Epirus, Acarnania, and Greece. There, for the present, the poem stops: its reception will determine whether the author may venture to conduct his readers to the capital of the East, through Ionia and Phrygia: these two cantos are merely experimental.

A fictitious character is introduced for the sake of giving some connection to the piece; which, however, makes no pretension to regularity. It has been suggested to me by friends, on whose opinions I set a high value, that in this fictitious character, 'Childe Harold,' I may incur the suspicion of having intended some real personage: this I beg leave, once for all, to disclaim—Harold is the child of imagination, for the purpose I have stated. In some very trivial particulars, and those merely local, there might be grounds for such a notion; but in the main points, I should hope, none whatever.

It is almost superfluous to mention that the appellation 'Childe,' as 'Childe Waters,' 'Childe Childers,' etc., is used as more consonant with the old structure of versification which I have adopted. The 'Good Night,' in the beginning of the first canto, was suggested by 'Lord Maxwell's Good Night,' in the Border Minstrelsy, edited by Mr. Scott.

With the different poems which have been published on Spanish subjects, there may be found some slight coincidence in the first part, which treats of the Peninsula, but it can only be casual; as, with the exception of a few concluding stanzas, the whole of this poem was written in the Levant.

The stanza of Spenser, according to one of our most successful poets, admits of every variety. Dr. Beattie makes the following observation: 'Not long ago I began a poem in the style and stanza of Spenser, in which I propose to give full scope to my inclination, and be either droll or pathetic, descrip-

Original Preface

tive or sentimental, tender or satirical, as the humour strikes me; for, if I mistake not, the measure which I have adopted admits equally of all these kinds of composition.' Strengthened in my opinion by such authority, and by the example of some in the highest order of Italian poets, I shall make no apology for attempts at similar variations in the following composition; satisfied that, if they are unsuccessful, their failure must be in the execution rather than in the design sanctioned by the practice of Ariosto, Thomson, and Beattie.

London, February 1812.

ADDITION TO THE PREFACE

I HAVE now waited till almost all our periodical journals have distributed their usual portion of criticism. To the justice of the generality of their criticisms I have nothing to object: it would ill become me to quarrel with their very slight degree of censure, when, perhaps, if they had been less kind they had been more candid. Returning, therefore, to all and each my best thanks for their liberality, on one point alone shall I venture an observation. Amongst the many objections justly urged to the very indifferent character of the 'vagrant Childe' (whom, notwithstanding many hints to the contrary, I still maintain to be a fictitious personage), it has been stated, that, besides the anachronism, he is very *unknightly*, as the times of the Knights were times of Love, Honour, and so forth. Now, it so happens that the good old times, when 'l'amour du bon vieux tems, l'amour antique' flourished, were the most profligate of all possible centuries. Those who have any doubts on this subject may consult Sainte-Palaye, *passim*, and more particularly vol. ii. p. 69. The vows of chivalry were no better kept than any other vows whatsoever; and the songs of the Troubadours were not more decent, and certainly were much less refined, than those of Ovid. The 'Cours d'amour, parlemens d'amour, ou de courtesie et de gentilesse' had much more of love than of courtesy or gentleness. See Rolland on the same subject with Sainte-Palaye. Whatever other objection may be urged to that most unamiable personage Childe Harold, he was so far perfectly knightly in his attributes—'No waiter, but a knight templar.' By the by, I fear that Sir Tristrem and Sir Lancelot were no better than they should be, although very poetical personages and true knights 'sans peur,' though not 'sans reproche.' If the story of the institution of the 'Garter' be not a fable, the knights of that order have for several centuries borne the badge of a Countess of Salisbury, of indifferent memory. So much for chivalry. Burke need not have regretted that its days are over, though Marie-Antoinette was quite as chaste as most of those in whose honours lances were shivered, and knights unhorsed.

Before the days of Bayard, and down to those of Sir Joseph

Addition to Original Preface

Banks (the most chaste and celebrated of ancient and modern times), few exceptions will be found to this statement; and I fear a little investigation will teach us not to regret these monstrous mummeries of the Middle Ages.

I now leave 'Childe Harold' to live his day, such as he is; it had been more agreeable, and certainly more easy, to have drawn an amiable character. It had been easy to varnish over his faults, to make him do more and express less, but he never was intended as an example, further than to show, that early perversion of mind and morals leads to satiety of past pleasures and disappointment in new ones, and that even the beauties of nature and the stimulus of travel (except ambition, the most powerful of all excitements) are lost on a soul so constituted, or rather misdirected. Had I proceeded with the poem, this character would have deepened as he drew to the close; for the outline which I once meant to fill up for him was, with some exceptions, the sketch of a modern Timon, perhaps a poetical Zeluco.

TO IANTHE

Not in those climes where I have late been straying,
Though Beauty long hath there been matchless deem'd;
Not in those visions to the heart displaying
Forms which it sighs but to have only dream'd,
Hath aught like thee in truth or fancy seem'd:
Nor, having seen thee, shall I vainly seek
To paint those charms which varied as they beam'd—
To such as see thee not my words were weak;
To those who gaze on thee what language could they speak?

Ah! may'st thou ever be what now thou art, *10*
Nor unbeseem the promise of thy spring,
As fair in form, as warm yet pure in heart,
Love's image upon earth without his wing,
And guileless beyond Hope's imagining!
And surely she who now so fondly rears
Thy youth, in thee, thus hourly brightening,
Beholds the rainbow of her future years,
Before whose heavenly hues all sorrow disappears.

Young Peri of the West!—'tis well for me
My years already doubly number thine; *20*
My loveless eye unmoved may gaze on thee,
And safely view thy ripening beauties shine;
Happy, I ne'er shall see them in decline;
Happier, that while all younger hearts shall bleed,
Mine shall escape the doom thine eyes assign
To those whose admiration shall succeed,
But mix'd with pangs to Love's even loveliest hours decreed.

Oh! let that eye, which, wild as the Gazelle's,
Now brightly bold or beautifully shy,
Wins as it wanders, dazzles where it dwells, *30*
Glance o'er this page, nor to my verse deny
That smile for which my breast might vainly sigh,
Could I to thee be ever more than friend:
This much, dear maid, accord; nor question why
To one so young my strain I would commend,
But bid me with my wreath one matchless lily blend.

To Ianthe

Such is thy name with this my verse entwined;
And long as kinder eyes a look shall cast
On Harold's page, Ianthe's here enshrined
Shall thus be first beheld, forgotten last:
My days once number'd, should this homage past
Attract thy fairy fingers near the lyre
Of him who hail'd thee, loveliest as thou wast,
Such is the most my memory may desire;
Though more than Hope can claim, could Friendship less require?

CHILDE HAROLD'S PILGRIMAGE

CANTO THE FIRST

I

Oh, thou! in Hellas deem'd of heavenly birth,
Muse! form'd or fabled at the minstrel's will!
Since shamed full oft by later lyres on earth,
Mine dares not call thee from thy sacred hill:
Yet there I 've wander'd by thy vaunted rill;
Yes! sigh'd o'er Delphi's long deserted shrine,
Where, save that feeble fountain, all is still;
Nor mote my shell awake the weary Nine
To grace so plain a tale—this lowly lay of mine.

II

Whilome in Albion's isle there dwelt a youth,
Who ne in virtue's ways did take delight;
But spent his days in riot most uncouth,
And vex'd with mirth the drowsy ear of Night.
Ah, me! in sooth he was a shameless wight,
Sore given to revel and ungodly glee;
Few earthly things found favour in his sight
Save concubines and carnal companie,
And flaunting wassailers of high and low degree.

III

Childe Harold was he hight:—but whence his name
And lineage long, it suits me not to say;
Suffice it, that perchance they were of fame,
And had been glorious in another day:
But one sad losel soils a name for aye,
However mighty in the olden time;
Nor all that heralds rake from coffin'd clay,
Nor florid prose, nor honied lies of rhyme,
Can blazon evil deeds, or consecrate a crime.

IV

Childe Harold bask'd him in the noontide sun,
Disporting there like any other fly,
Nor deem'd before his little day was done   30
One blast might chill him into misery.
But long ere scarce a third of his pass'd by,
Worse than adversity the Childe befell;
He felt the fulness of satiety:
Then loathed he in his native land to dwell,
Which seem'd to him more lone than Eremite's sad cell.

V

For he through Sin's long labyrinth had run,
Nor made atonement when he did amiss,
Had sigh'd to many though he loved but one,
And that loved one, alas! could ne'er be his.   40
Ah, happy she! to 'scape from him whose kiss
Had been pollution unto aught so chaste;
Who soon had left her charms for vulgar bliss,
And spoil'd her goodly lands to gild his waste,
Nor calm domestic peace had ever deign'd to taste.

VI

And now Childe Harold was sore sick at heart,
And from his fellow bacchanals would flee;
'Tis said, at times the sullen tear would start,
But Pride congeal'd the drop within his ee:
Apart he stalk'd in joyless reverie,   50
And from his native land resolved to go,
And visit scorching climes beyond the sea;
With pleasure drugg'd, he almost long'd for woe,
And e'en for change of scene would seek the shades below.

VII

The Childe departed from his father's hall:
It was a vast and venerable pile;
So old, it seemed only not to fall,
Yet strength was pillar'd in each massy aisle.
Monastic dome! condemn'd to uses vile!
Where Superstition once had made her den   60
Now Paphian girls were known to sing and smile;
And monks might deem their time was come agen,
If ancient tales say true, nor wrong these holy men.

VIII

Yet oft-times in his maddest mirthful mood
Strange pangs would flash along Childe Harold's brow
As if the memory of some deadly feud
Or disappointed passion lurk'd below:
But this none knew, nor haply cared to know;
For his was not that open, artless soul
That feels relief by bidding sorrow flow, 70
Nor sought he friend to counsel or condole,
Whate'er this grief mote be, which he could not control.

IX

And none did love him—though to hall and bower
He gather'd revellers from far and near,
He knew them flatt'rers of the festal hour;
The heartless parasites of present cheer.
Yea! none did love him—not his lemans dear—
But pomp and power alone are woman's care,
And where these are light Eros finds a feere;
Maidens, like moths, are ever caught by glare, 80
And Mammon wins his way where Seraphs might despair.

X

Childe Harold had a mother—not forgot,
Though parting from that mother he did shun;
A sister whom he loved, but saw her not
Before his weary pilgrimage begun:
If friends he had, he bade adieu to none.
Yet deem not thence his breast a breast of steel:
Ye, who have known what 'tis to dote upon
A few dear objects, will in sadness feel
Such partings break the heart they fondly hope to heal. 90

XI

His house, his home, his heritage, his lands,
The laughing dames in whom he did delight,
Whose large blue eyes, fair locks, and snowy hands,
Might shake the saintship of an anchorite,
And long had fed his youthful appetite:
His goblets brimm'd with every costly wine,
And all that mote to luxury invite,
Without a sigh he left, to cross the brine,
And traverse Paynim shores, and pass Earth's central line.

XII

The sails were fill'd, and fair the light winds blew,
As glad to waft him from his native home;
And fast the white rocks faded from his view,
And soon were lost in circumambient foam:
And then, it may be, of his wish to roam
Repented he, but in his bosom slept
The silent thought, nor from his lips did come
One word of wail, whilst others sate and wept,
And to the reckless gales unmanly moaning kept.

XIII

But when the sun was sinking in the sea
He seized his harp, which he at times could string,
And strike, albeit with untaught melody,
When deem'd he no strange ear was listening:
And now his fingers o'er it he did fling,
And tuned his farewell in the dim twilight.
While flew the vessel on her snowy wing,
And fleeting shores receded from his sight,
Thus to the elements he pour'd his last 'Good Night.'

1

'Adieu, adieu! my native shore
Fades o'er the waters blue;
The Night-winds sigh, the breakers roar,
And shrieks the wild sea-mew.
Yon Sun that sets upon the sea
We follow in his flight;
Farewell awhile to him and thee,
My native Land—Good Night!

2

'A few short hours and He will rise
To give the morrow birth;
And I shall hail the main and skies,
But not my mother earth.
Deserted is my own good hall,
Its hearth is desolate;
Wild weeds are gathering on the wall;
My dog howls at the gate.

Childe Harold's Pilgrimage, I

3

'Come hither, hither, my little page!
Why dost thou weep and wail?
Or dost thou dread the billows' rage,
Or tremble at the gale?
But dash the tear-drop from thine eye;
Our ship is swift and strong:
Our fleetest falcon scarce can fly   *140*
More merrily along.'

4

'Let winds be shrill, let waves roll high,
I fear not wave nor wind;
Yet marvel not, Sir Childe, that I
Am sorrowful in mind;
For I have from my father gone,
A mother whom I love,
And have no friend, save these alone,
But thee—and one above.

5

'My father bless'd me fervently,   *150*
Yet did not much complain;
But sorely will my mother sigh
Till I come back again.'
'Enough, enough, my little lad!
Such tears become thine eye;
If I thy guileless bosom had,
Mine own would not be dry.

6

'Come hither, hither, my staunch yeoman,
Why dost thou look so pale?
Or dost thou dread a French foeman?   *160*
Or shiver at the gale?'
'Deem'st thou I tremble for my life?
Sir Childe, I'm not so weak;
But thinking on an absent wife
Will blanch a faithful cheek.

7

'My spouse and boys dwell near thy hall,
Along the bordering lake,
And when they on their father call,
What answer shall she make?'

'Enough, enough, my yeoman good,   *170*
Thy grief let none gainsay;
But I, who am of lighter mood,
Will laugh to flee away.

8

'For who would trust the seeming sighs
Of wife or paramour?
Fresh feres will dry the bright blue eyes
We late saw streaming o'er.
For pleasures past I do not grieve
Nor perils gathering near;
My greatest grief is that I leave   *180*
No thing that claims a tear.

9

'And now I'm in the world alone,
Upon the wide, wide sea:
But why should I for others groan,
When none will sigh for me?
Perchance my dog will whine in vain,
Till fed by stranger hands;
But long ere I come back again
He'd tear me where he stands.

10

'With thee, my bark, I'll swiftly go   *190*
Athwart the foaming brine;
Nor care what land thou bear'st me to,
So not again to mine.
Welcome, welcome, ye dark-blue waves!
And when you fail my sight,
Welcome, ye deserts, and ye caves!
My native Land—Good Night!'

XIV

On, on the vessel flies, the land is gone,
And winds are rude in Biscay's sleepless bay.
Four days are sped, but with the fifth, anon,   *200*
New shores descried make every bosom gay;
And Cintra's mountain greets them on their way,
And Tagus dashing onward to the deep,
His fabled golden tribute bent to pay;
And soon on board the Lusian pilots leap,
And steer 'twixt fertile shores where yet few rustics reap.

XV

Oh, Christ! it is a goodly sight to see
What Heaven hath done for this delicious land!
What fruits of fragrance blush on every tree!
What goodly prospects o'er the hills expand!   *210*
But man would mar them with an impious hand:
And when the Almighty lifts his fiercest scourge
'Gainst those who most transgress his high command,
With treble vengeance will his hot shafts urge
Gaul's locust host, and earth from fellest foemen purge.

XVI

What beauties doth Lisboa first unfold!
Her image floating on that noble tide,
Which poets vainly pave with sands of gold,
But now whereon a thousand keels did ride
Of mighty strength, since Albion was allied,   *220*
And to the Lusians did her aid afford:
A nation swoln with ignorance and pride,
Who lick yet loathe the hand that waves the sword
To save them from the wrath of Gaul's unsparing lord.

XVII

But whoso entereth within this town,
That, sheening far, celestial seems to be,
Disconsolate will wander up and down,
'Mid many things unsightly to strange ee;
For hut and palace show like filthily:
The dingy denizens are rear'd in dirt;   *230*
Ne personage of high or mean degree
Doth care for cleanness of surtout or shirt,
Though shent with Egypt's plague, unkempt, **unwash'd,
unhurt.**

XVIII

Poor, paltry slaves! yet born 'midst noblest scenes—
Why, Nature, waste thy wonders on such men?
Lo! Cintra's glorious Eden intervenes
In variegated maze of mount and glen.
Ah, me! what hand can pencil guide, or pen,
To follow half on which the eye dilates
Through views more dazzling unto mortal ken *240*
Than those whereof such things the bard relates,
Who to the awe-struck world unlock'd Elysium's gates?

XIX

The horrid crags, by toppling convent crown'd,
The cork-trees hoar that clothe the shaggy steep,
The mountain-moss by scorching skies imbrown'd,
The sunken glen, whose sunless shrubs must weep,
The tender azure of the unruffled deep,
The orange tints that gild the greenest bough,
The torrents that from cliff to valley leap,
The vine on high, the willow branch below, *250*
Mix'd in one mighty scene, with varied beauty glow.

XX

Then slowly climb the many-winding way,
And frequent turn to linger as you go,
From loftier rocks new loveliness survey,
And rest ye at 'Our Lady's house of woe;'
Where frugal monks their little relics show,
And sundry legends to the stranger tell:
Here impious men have punish'd been, and lo!
Deep in yon cave Honorius long did dwell,
In hope to merit Heaven by making earth a Hell. *260*

XXI

And here and there, as up the crags you spring,
Mark many rude-carved crosses near the path:
Yet deem not these devotion's offering—
These are memorials frail of murderous wrath:
For wheresoe'er the shrieking victim hath
Pour'd forth his blood beneath the assassin's knife,
Some hand erects a cross of mouldering lath;
And grove and glen with thousand such are rife
Throughout this purple land, where law secures not life.

XXII

On sloping mounds, or in the vale beneath,
Are domes where whilome kings did make repair;
But now the wild flowers round them only breathe;
Yet ruin'd splendour still is lingering there.
And yonder towers the Prince's palace fair:
There thou too, Vathek! England's wealthiest son,
Once form'd thy Paradise, as not aware
When wanton Wealth her mightiest deeds hath done,
Meek Peace voluptuous lures was ever wont to shun.

XXIII

Here didst thou dwell, here schemes of pleasure plan,
Beneath yon mountain's ever beauteous brow;
But now, as if a thing unblest by Man,
Thy fairy dwelling is as lone as thou!
Here giant weeds a passage scarce allow
To halls deserted, portals gaping wide;
Fresh lessons to the thinking bosom, how
Vain are the pleasaunces on earth supplied;
Swept into wrecks anon by Time's ungentle tide!

XXIV

Behold the hall where chiefs were late convened!
Oh! dome displeasing unto British eye!
With diadem hight foolscap, lo! a fiend,
A little fiend that scoffs incessantly,
There sits in parchment robe array'd, and by
His side is hung a seal and sable scroll,
Where blazon'd glare names known to chivalry,
And sundry signatures adorn the roll,
Whereat the Urchin points and laughs with all his soul.

XXV

Convention is the dwarfish demon styled
That foil'd the knights in Marialva's dome:
Of brains (if brains they had) he them beguiled,
And turn'd a nation's shallow joy to gloom.
Here Folly dash'd to earth the victor's plume,
And Policy regain'd what arms had lost:
For chiefs like ours in vain may laurels bloom!
Woe to the conqu'ring, not the conquer'd host,
Since baffled Triumph droops on Lusitania's coast!

XXVI

And ever since that martial synod met,
Britannia sickens, Cintra! at thy name;
And folks in office at the mention fret,
And fain would blush, if blush they could, for shame.
How will posterity the deed proclaim!   310
Will not our own and fellow nations sneer,
To view these champions cheated of their fame,
By foes in fight o'erthrown, yet victors here,
Where Scorn her finger points through many a coming year?

XXVII

So deem'd the Childe, as o'er the mountains he
Did take his way in solitary guise:
Sweet was the scene, yet soon he thought to flee,
More restless than the swallow in the skies:
Though here awhile he learn'd to moralize,
For Meditation fix'd at times on him;   320
And conscious Reason whisper'd to despise
His early youth, misspent in maddest whim;
But as he gazed on truth his aching eyes grew dim.

XXVIII

To horse! to horse! he quits, for ever quits
A scene of peace, though soothing to his soul:
Again he rouses from his moping fits,
But seeks not now the harlot and the bowl.
Onward he flies, nor fix'd as yet the goal
Where he shall rest him on his pilgrimage;
And o'er him many changing scenes must roll   330
Ere toil his thirst for travel can assuage,
Or he shall calm his breast, or learn experience sage.

XXIX

Yet Mafra shall one moment claim delay,
Where dwelt of yore the Lusians' luckless queen;
And church and court did mingle their array,
And mass and revel were alternate seen;
Lordlings and freres—ill-sorted fry I ween!
But here the Babylonian whore hath built
A dome, where flaunts she in such glorious sheen,
That men forget the blood which she hath spilt,   340
And bow the knee to Pomp that loves to varnish guilt.

Childe Harold's Pilgrimage, I

XXX

O'er vales that teem with fruits, romantic hills,
(Oh, that such hills upheld a freeborn race!)
Whereon to gaze the eye with joyaunce fills,
Childe Harold wends through many a pleasant place.
Though sluggards deem it but a foolish chase,
And marvel men should quit their easy chair,
The toilsome way, and long, long league to trace,
Oh! there is sweetness in the mountain air,
And life, that bloated Ease can never hope to share.   *350*

XXXI

More bleak to view the hills at length recede,
And, less luxuriant, smoother vales extend;
Immense horizon-bounded plains succeed!
Far as the eye discerns, withouten end,
Spain's realms appear whereon her shepherds tend
Flocks, whose rich fleece right well the trader knows—
Now must the pastor's arm his lambs defend:
For Spain is compass'd by unyielding foes,
And all must shield their all, or share Subjection's woes.

XXXII

Where Lusitania and her Sister meet,   *360*
Deem ye what bounds the rival realms divide?
Or ere the jealous queens of nations greet,
Doth Tayo interpose his mighty tide?
Or dark Sierras rise in craggy pride?
Or fence of art, like China's vasty wall?—
Ne barrier wall, ne river deep and wide,
Ne horrid crags, nor mountains dark and tall,
Rise like the rocks that part Hispania's land from Gaul:

XXXIII

But these between a silver streamlet glides,
And scarce a name distinguisheth the brook,   *370*
Though rival kingdoms press its verdant sides.
Here leans the idle shepherd on his crook,
And vacant on the rippling waves doth look,
That peaceful still 'twixt bitterest foemen flow;
For proud each peasant as the noblest duke:
Well doth the Spanish hind the difference know
'Twixt him and Lusian slave, the lowest of the low.

XXXIV

But ere the mingling bounds have far been pass'd,
Dark Guadiana rolls his power along
In sullen billows, murmuring and vast,
So noted ancient roundelays among.
Whilome upon his banks did legions throng
Of Moor and Knight, in mailed splendour drest:
Here ceased the swift their race, here sunk the strong;
The Paynim turban and the Christian crest
Mix'd on the bleeding stream, by floating hosts oppress'd.

XXXV

Oh, lovely Spain! renown'd, romantic land!
Where is that standard which Pelagio bore,
When Cava's traitor-sire first call'd the band
That dyed thy mountain streams with Gothic gore?
Where are those bloody banners which of yore
Waved o'er thy sons, victorious to the gale,
And drove at last the spoilers to their shore?
Red gleam'd the cross, and waned the crescent pale,
While Afric's echoes thrill'd with Moorish matrons' wail.

XXXVI

Teems not each ditty with the glorious tale?
Ah! such, alas! the hero's amplest fate!
When granite moulders and when records fail,
A peasant's plaint prolongs his dubious date.
Pride! bend thine eye from heaven to thine estate.
See how the Mighty shrink into a song!
Can Volume, Pillar, Pile, preserve thee great?
Or must thou trust Tradition's simple tongue,
When Flattery sleeps with thee, and History does thee wrong?

XXXVII

Awake, ye sons of Spain! awake! advance!
Lo! Chivalry, your ancient goddess, cries;
But wields not, as of old, her thirsty lance,
Nor shakes her crimson plumage in the skies:
Now on the smoke of blazing bolts she flies,
And speaks in thunder through yon engine's roar
In every peal she calls—'Awake! arise!'
Say, is her voice more feeble than of yore,
When her war-song was heard on Andalusia's shore?

Childe Harold's Pilgrimage, I

XXXVIII

Hark! heard you not those hoofs of dreadful note?
Sounds not the clang of conflict on the heath?
Saw ye not whom the reeking sabre smote;
Nor saved your brethren ere they sank beneath
Tyrants and tyrants' slaves?—the fires of death,
The bale-fires flash on high:—from rock to rock
Each volley tells that thousands cease to breathe; 420
Death rides upon the sulphury Siroc,
Red Battle stamps his foot, and nations feel the shock.

XXXIX

Lo! where the Giant on the mountain stands,
His blood-red tresses deep'ning in the sun,
With death-shot glowing in his fiery hands,
And eye that scorcheth all it glares upon;
Restless it rolls, now fix'd, and now anon
Flashing afar,—and at his iron feet
Destruction cowers, to mark what deeds are done;
For on this morn three potent nations meet, 430
To shed before his shrine the blood he deems most sweet.

XL

By Heaven! it is a splendid sight to see
(For one who hath no friend, no brother there)
Their rival scarfs of mix'd embroidery,
Their various arms that glitter in the air!
What gallant war-hounds rouse them from their lair,
And gnash their fangs, loud yelling for the prey!
All join the chase, but few the triumph share;
The Grave shall bear the chiefest prize away,
And Havoc scarce for joy can number their array. 440

XLI

Three hosts combine to offer sacrifice;
Three tongues prefer strange orisons on high;
Three gaudy standards flout the pale blue skies;
The shouts are France, Spain, Albion, Victory!
The foe, the victim, and the fond ally
That fights for all, but ever fights in vain,
Are met—as if at home they could not die—
To feed the crow on Talavera's plain,
And fertilize the field that each pretends to gain.

XLII

There shall they rot—Ambition's honour'd fools! 450
Yes, Honour decks the turf that wraps their clay!
Vain Sophistry! in these behold the tools,
The broken tools, that tyrants cast away
By myriads, when they dare to pave their way
With human hearts—to what?—a dream alone.
Can despots compass aught that hails their sway?
Or call with truth one span of earth their own,
Save that wherein at last they crumble bone by bone?

XLIII

Oh, Albuera, glorious field of grief!
As o'er thy plain the Pilgrim prick'd his steed, 460
Who could foresee thee, in a space so brief,
A scene where mingling foes should boast and bleed!
Peace to the perish'd! may the warrior's meed
And tears of triumph their reward prolong!
Till others fall where other chieftains lead,
Thy name shall circle round the gaping throng,
And shine in worthless lays, the theme of transient song.

XLIV

Enough of Battle's minions! let them play
Their game of lives, and barter breath for fame:
Fame that will scarce re-animate their clay, 470
Though thousands fall to deck some single name.
In sooth 'twere sad to thwart their noble aim
Who strike, blest hirelings! for their country's good,
And die, that living might have proved her shame;
Perish'd perchance, in some domestic feud,
Or in a narrower sphere wild Rapine's path pursued.

XLV

Full swiftly Harold wends his lonely way
Where proud Sevilla triumphs unsubdued:
Yet is she free—the spoiler's wish'd-for prey!
Soon, soon shall Conquest's fiery foot intrude, 480
Blackening her lovely domes with traces rude.
Inevitable hour! 'Gainst fate to strive
Where Desolation plants her famish'd brood
Is vain, or Ilion, Tyre might yet survive,
And Virtue vanquish all, and Murder cease to thrive.

Childe Harold's Pilgrimage, I

XLVI

But all unconscious of the coming doom,
The feast, the song, the revel here abounds;
Strange modes of merriment the hours consume,
Nor bleed these patriots with their country's wounds:
Nor here War's clarion, but Love's rebeck sounds;   *490*
Here Folly still his votaries inthralls;
And young-eyed Lewdness walks her midnight rounds:
Girt with the silent crimes of Capitals,
Still to the last kind Vice clings to the tott'ring walls.

XLVII

Not so the rustic—with his trembling mate
He lurks, nor casts his heavy eye afar,
Lest he should view his vineyard desolate,
Blasted below the dun hot breath of war.
No more beneath soft Eve's consenting star
Fandango twirls his jocund castanet: *500*
Ah, monarchs! could ye taste the mirth ye mar,
Not in the toils of Glory would ye fret;
The hoarse dull drum would sleep, and Man be happy yet!

XLVIII

How carols now the lusty muleteer?
Of love, romance, devotion is his lay,
As whilome he was wont the leagues to cheer,
His quick bells wildly jingling on the way?
No! as he speeds, he chants 'Vivā el Rey!'
And checks his song to execrate Godoy,
The royal wittol Charles, and curse the day   *510*
When first Spain's queen beheld the black-eyed boy,
And gore-faced Treason sprung from her adulterate joy.

XLIX

On yon long, level plain, at distance crown'd
With crags, whereon those Moorish turrets rest,
Wide scatter'd hoof-marks dint the wounded ground;
And, scathed by fire, the greensward's darken'd vest
Tells that the foe was Andalusia's guest:
Here was the camp, the watch-flame, and the host,
Here the bold peasant storm'd the dragon's nest;
Still does he mark it with triumphant boast,   *520*
And points to yonder cliffs, which oft were won and lost.

Childe Harold's Pilgrimage, I

L

And whomsoe'er along the path you meet
Bears in his cap the badge of crimson hue,
Which tells you whom to shun and whom to greet:
Woe to the man that walks in public view
Without of loyalty this token true:
Sharp is the knife, and sudden is the stroke;
And sorely would the Gallic foeman rue,
If subtle poniards, wrapt beneath the cloke,
Could blunt the sabre's edge, or clear the cannon's smoke.   530

LI

At every turn Morena's dusky height
Sustains aloft the battery's iron load;
And, far as mortal eye can compass sight,
The mountain-howitzer, the broken road,
The bristling palisade, the fosse o'erflow'd,
The station'd bands, the never-vacant watch,
The magazine in rocky durance stow'd,
The holster'd steed beneath the shed of thatch,
The ball-piled pyramid, the ever-blazing match,

LII

Portend the deeds to come:—but he whose nod   540
Has tumbled feebler despots from their sway,
A moment pauseth ere he lifts the rod;
A little moment deigneth to delay:
Soon will his legions sweep through these their way;
The West must own the Scourger of the world.
Ah! Spain! how sad will be thy reckoning-day,
When soars Gaul's Vulture, with his wings unfurl'd,
And thou shalt view thy sons in crowds to Hades hurl'd.

LIII

And must they fall? the young, the proud, the brave,
To swell one bloated Chief's unwholesome reign?   550
No step between submission and a grave?
The rise of rapine and the fall of Spain?
And doth the Power that man adores ordain
Their doom, nor heed the suppliant's appeal?
Is all that desperate Valour acts in vain?
And Counsel sage, and patriotic Zeal,
The Veteran's skill, Youth's fire, and Manhood's heart of steel?

LIV

Is it for this the Spanish maid, aroused,
Hangs on the willow her unstrung guitar,
And, all unsex'd, the anlace hath espoused,
Sung the loud song, and dared the deed of war?
And she, whom once the semblance of a scar
Appall'd, an owlet's larum chill'd with dread,
Now views the column-scattering bay'net jar,
The falchion flash, and o'er the yet warm dead
Stalks with Minerva's step where Mars might quake to tread.

LV

Ye who shall marvel when you hear her tale,
Oh! had you known her in her softer hour,
Mark'd her black eye that mocks her coal-black veil,
Heard her light, lively tones in Lady's bower,
Seen her long locks that foil the painter's power,
Her fairy form, with more than female grace,
Scarce would you deem that Saragoza's tower
Beheld her smile in Danger's Gorgon face,
Thin the closed ranks, and lead in Glory's fearful chase.

LVI

Her lover sinks—she sheds no ill-timed tear;
Her chief is slain—she fills his fatal post;
Her fellows flee—she checks their base career;
The foe retires—she heads the sallying host:
Who can appease like her a lover's ghost?
Who can avenge so well a leader's fall?
What maid retrieve when man's flush'd hope is lost?
Who hang so fiercely on the flying Gaul,
Foil'd by a woman's hand, before a batter'd wall?

LVII

Yet are Spain's maids no race of Amazons,
But form'd for all the witching arts of love:
Though thus in arms they emulate her sons,
And in the horrid phalanx dare to move,
'Tis but the tender fierceness of the dove,
Pecking the hand that hovers o'er her mate:
In softness as in firmness far above
Remoter females, famed for sickening prate;
Her mind is nobler sure, her charms perchance as great.

LVIII

The seal Love's dimpling finger hath impress'd
Denotes how soft that chin which bears his touch:
Her lips, whose kisses pout to leave their nest,
Bid man be valiant ere he merit such:
Her glance how wildly beautiful! how much
Hath Phoebus woo'd in vain to spoil her cheek,
Which glows yet smoother from his amorous clutch!   600
Who round the North for paler dames would seek?
How poor their forms appear! how languid, wan, and weak!

LIX

Match me, ye climes! which poets love to laud;
Match me, ye harams of the land! where now
I strike my strain, far distant, to applaud
Beauties that ev'n a cynic must avow:
Match me those Houries, whom ye scarce allow
To taste the gale lest Love should ride the wind,
With Spain's dark-glancing daughters—deign to know,
There your wise Prophet's paradise we find,   610
His black-eyed maids of Heaven, angelically kind.

LX

Oh, thou Parnassus! whom I now survey,
Not in the phrensy of a dreamer's eye,
Not in the fabled landscape of a lay,
But soaring snow-clad through thy native sky,
In the wild pomp of mountain majesty!
What marvel if I thus essay to sing?
The humblest of thy pilgrims passing by
Would gladly woo thine Echoes with his string,
Though from thy heights no more one Muse will wave her   620
   wing.

LXI

Oft have I dream'd of Thee! whose glorious name
Who knows not, knows not man's divinest lore:
And now I view thee, 'tis, alas! with shame
That I in feeblest accents must adore.
When I recount thy worshippers of yore
I tremble, and can only bend the knee;
Nor raise my voice, nor vainly dare to soar,
But gaze beneath thy cloudy canopy
In silent joy to think at last I look on Thee!

LXII

Happier in this than mightiest bards have been,   630
Whose fate to distant homes confined their lot,
Shall I unmoved behold the hallow'd scene,
Which others rave of, though they know it not?
Though here no more Apollo haunts his grot,
And thou, the Muses' seat, art now their grave,
Some gentle spirit still pervades the spot,
Sighs in the gale, keeps silence in the cave,
And glides with glassy foot o'er yon melodious wave.

LXIII

Of thee hereafter.—Ev'n amidst my strain
I turn'd aside to pay my homage here;   640
Forgot the land, the sons, the maids of Spain;
Her fate, to every freeborn bosom dear;
And hail'd thee, not perchance without a tear.
Now to my theme—but from thy holy haunt
Let me some remnant, some memorial bear;
Yield me one leaf of Daphne's deathless plant,
Nor let thy votary's hope be deem'd an idle vaunt.

LXIV

But ne'er didst thou, fair Mount! when Greece was young,
See round thy giant base a brighter choir,
Nor e'er did Delphi, when her priestess sung   650
The Pythian hymn, with more than mortal fire,
Behold a train more fitting to inspire
The song of love than Andalusia's maids,
Nurst in the glowing lap of soft desire:
Ah! that to these were given such peaceful shades
As Greece can still bestow, though Glory fly her glades.

LXV

Fair is proud Seville; let her country boast
Her strength, her wealth, her site of ancient days;
But Cadiz, rising on the distant coast,
Calls forth a sweeter, though ignoble praise.   660
Ah, Vice! how soft are thy voluptuous ways!
While boyish blood is mantling, who can 'scape
The fascination of thy magic gaze?
A Cherub-hydra round us dost thou gape,
And mould to every taste thy dear delusive shape.

LXVI

When Paphos fell by time—accursed Time!
The Queen who conquers all must yield to thee—
The Pleasures fled, but sought as warm a clime;
And Venus, constant to her native sea,
To nought else constant, hither deign'd to flee;   *670*
And fix'd her shrine within these walls of white;
Though not to one dome circumscribeth she
Her worship, but, devoted to her rite,
A thousand altars rise, for ever blazing bright.

LXVII

From morn till night, from night till startled Morn
Peeps blushing on the revel's laughing crew,
The song is heard, the rosy garland worn;
Devices quaint, and frolics ever new,
Tread on each other's kibes. A long adieu
He bids to sober joy that here sojourns;   *680*
Nought interrupts the riot, though in lieu
Of true devotion monkish incense burns,
And love and prayer unite, or rule the hour by turns.

LXVIII

The Sabbath comes, a day of blessed rest;
What hallows it upon this Christian shore?
Lo! it is sacred to a solemn feast;
Hark! heard you not the forest-monarch's roar?
Crashing the lance, he snuffs the spouting gore
Of man and steed, o'erthrown beneath his horn;
The throng'd arena shakes with shouts for more;   *690*
Yells the mad crowd o'er entrails freshly torn,
Nor shrinks the female eye, nor ev'n affects to mourn.

LXIX

The seventh day this; the jubilee of man.
London! right well thou know'st the day of prayer:
Then thy spruce citizen, wash'd artisan,
And smug apprentice gulp their weekly air:
Thy coach of hackney, whiskey, one-horse chair,
And humblest gig through sundry suburbs whirl;
To Hampstead, Brentford, Harrow make repair;
Till the tired jade the wheel forgets to hurl,   *700*
Provoking envious gibe from each pedestrian churl.

Childe Harold's Pilgrimage, I

LXX

Some o'er thy Thamis row the ribbon'd fair,
Others along the safer turnpike fly;
Some Richmond-hill ascend, some scud to Ware,
And many to the steep of Highgate hie.
Ask ye, Boeotian shades! the reason why?
'Tis to the worship of the solemn Horn,
Grasp'd in the holy hand of Mystery,
In whose dread name both men and maids are sworn,
And consecrate the oath with draught, and dance till morn. *710*

LXXI

All have their fooleries—not alike are thine,
Fair Cadiz, rising o'er the dark blue sea!
Soon as the matin bell proclaimeth nine,
Thy saint-adorers count the rosary:
Much is the VIRGIN teased to shrive them free
(Well do I ween the only virgin there)
From crimes as numerous as her beadsmen be;
Then to the crowded circus forth they fare:
Young, old, high, low, at once the same diversion share.

LXXII

The lists are oped, the spacious area clear'd, *720*
Thousands on thousands piled are seated round;
Long ere the first loud trumpet's note is heard,
Ne vacant space for lated wight is found:
Here dons, grandees, but chiefly dames abound,
Skill'd in the ogle of a roguish eye,
Yet ever well inclined to heal the wound;
None through their cold disdain are doom'd to die,
As moon-struck bards complain, by Love's sad archery.

LXXIII

Hush'd is the din of tongues—on gallant steeds,
With milk-white crest, gold spur, and light-pois'd lance *730*
Four cavaliers prepare for venturous deeds,
And lowly bending to the lists advance;
Rich are their scarfs, their chargers featly prance:
If in the dangerous game they shine to-day,
The crowd's loud shout and ladies' lovely glance,
Best prize of better acts, they bear away,
And all that kings or chiefs e'er gain their toils repay.

Childe Harold's Pilgrimage, I

LXXIV

In costly sheen and gaudy cloak array'd,
But all afoot, the light-limb'd Matadore
Stands in the centre, eager to invade 740
The lord of lowing herds; but not before
The ground, with cautious tread, is traversed o'er,
Lest aught unseen should lurk to thwart his speed:
His arms a dart, he fights aloof, nor more
Can man achieve without the friendly steed—
Alas! too oft condemn'd for him to bear and bleed.

LXXV

Thrice sounds the clarion; lo! the signal falls,
The den expands, and Expectation mute
Gapes round the silent circle's peopled walls.
Bounds with one lashing spring the mighty brute, 750
And, wildly staring, spurns, with sounding foot,
The sand, nor blindly rushes on his foe:
Here, there, he points his threatening front, to suit
His first attack, wide waving to and fro
His angry tail; red rolls his eye's dilated glow.

LXXVI

Sudden he stops: his eye is fix'd: away,
Away, thou heedless boy! prepare the spear:
Now is thy time, to perish, or display
The skill that yet may check his mad career.
With well-timed croupe the nimble coursers veer; 760
On foams the bull, but not unscathed he goes;
Streams from his flank the crimson torrent clear:
He flies, he wheels, distracted with his throes;
Dart follows dart; lance, lance; loud bellowings speak his woes.

LXXVII

Again he comes; nor dart nor lance avail,
Nor the wild plunging of the tortured horse;
Though man and man's avenging arms assail,
Vain are his weapons, vainer is his force.
One gallant steed is stretch'd a mangled corse;
Another, hideous sight! unseam'd appears, 770
His gory chest unveils life's panting source;
Though death-struck, still his feeble frame he rears;
Staggering, but stemming all, his lord unharm'd he bears.

LXXVIII

Foil'd, bleeding, breathless, furious to the last,
Full in the centre stands the bull at bay,
Mid wounds, and clinging darts, and lances brast,
And foes disabled in the brutal fray:
And now the Matadores around him play,
Shake the red cloak, and poise the ready brand:
Once more through all he bursts his thundering way—   *780*
Vain rage! the mantle quits the conynge hand,
Wraps his fierce eye—'tis past—he sinks upon the sand!

LXXIX

Where his vast neck just mingles with the spine,
Sheathed in his form the deadly weapon lies.
He stops—he starts—disdaining to decline:
Slowly he falls, amidst triumphant cries,
Without a groan, without a struggle dies.
The decorated car appears — on high
The corse is piled—sweet sight for vulgar eyes—
Four steeds that spurn the rein as swift as shy,   *790*
Hurl the dark bulk along, scarce seen in dashing by.

LXXX

Such the ungentle sport that oft invites
The Spanish maid, and cheers the Spanish swain.
Nurtured in blood betimes, his heart delights
In vengeance, gloating on another's pain.
What private feuds the troubled village stain!
Though now one phalanx'd host should meet the foe,
Enough, alas! in humble homes remain,
To meditate 'gainst friends the secret blow,
For some slight cause of wrath, whence life's warm stream   *800*
    must flow.

LXXXI

But Jealousy has fled: his bars, his bolts,
His wither'd centinel, Duenna sage!
And all whereat the generous soul revolts,
Which the stern dotard deem'd he could encage,
Have pass'd to darkness with the vanish'd age.
Who late so free as Spanish girls were seen,
(Ere War uprose in his volcanic rage,)
With braided tresses bounding o'er the green,
While on the gay dance shone Night's lover-loving Queen?

Childe Harold's Pilgrimage, I

LXXXII

Oh! many a time, and oft, had Harold loved,
Or dream'd he loved, since Rapture is a dream;
But now his wayward bosom was unmoved,
For not yet had he drunk of Lethe's stream;
And lately had he learn'd with truth to deem
Love has no gift so grateful as his wings:
How fair, how young, how soft soe'er he seem,
Full from the fount of Joy's delicious springs
Some bitter o'er the flowers its bubbling venom flings.

LXXXIII

Yet to the beauteous form he was not blind,
Though now it moved him as it moves the wise;
Not that Philosophy on such a mind
E'er deign'd to bend her chastely-awful eyes:
But Passion raves itself to rest, or flies;
And Vice, that digs her own voluptuous tomb,
Had buried long his hopes, no more to rise:
Pleasure's pall'd victim! life-abhorring gloom
Wrote on his faded brow curst Cain's unresting doom.

LXXXIV

Still he beheld, nor mingled with the throng;
But view'd them not with misanthropic hate:
Fain would he now have join'd the dance, the song;
But who may smile that sinks beneath his fate?
Nought that he saw his sadness could abate:
Yet once he struggled 'gainst the demon's sway,
And as in Beauty's bower he pensive sate,
Pour'd forth this unpremeditated lay,
To charms as fair as those that soothed his happier day.

TO INEZ

1

Nay, smile not at my sullen brow;
Alas! I cannot smile again:
Yet Heaven avert that ever thou
Shouldst weep, and haply weep in vain.

2

And dost thou ask, what secret woe
I bear, corroding joy and youth?
And wilt thou vainly seek to know
A pang, ev'n thou must fail to soothe?

3

It is not love, it is not hate,
Nor low Ambition's honours lost,
That bids me loathe my present state,
And fly from all I prized the most:

4

It is that weariness which springs
From all I meet, or hear, or see: 850
To me no pleasure Beauty brings;
Thine eyes have scarce a charm for me.

5

It is that settled, ceaseless gloom
The fabled Hebrew wanderer bore;
That will not look beyond the tomb,
But cannot hope for rest before.

6

What Exile from himself can flee?
To zones, though more and more remote,
Still, still pursues, where'er I be,
The blight of life—the demon Thought.   860

7

Yet others rapt in pleasure seem,
And taste of all that I forsake;
Oh! may they still of transport dream,
And ne'er, at least like me, awake!

8

Through many a clime 'tis mine to go,
With many a retrospection curst;
And all my solace is to know,
Whate'er betides, I've known the worst.

9

What is that worst? Nay, do not ask—
In pity from the search forbear: 870
Smile on—nor venture to unmask
Man's heart, and view the Hell that's there.'

LXXXV

Adieu, fair Cadiz! yea, a long adieu!
Who may forget how well thy walls have stood?
When all were changing thou alone wert true,
First to be free and last to be subdued:
And if amidst a scene, a shock so rude,

Some native blood was seen thy streets to dye;
A traitor only fell beneath the feud:
Here all were noble, save Nobility;
None hugg'd a conqueror's chain, save fallen Chivalry!

LXXXVI

Such be the sons of Spain, and strange her fate!
They fight for freedom who were never free;
A Kingless people for a nerveless state,
Her vassals combat when their chieftains flee,
True to the veriest slaves of Treachery:
Fond of a land which gave them nought but life,
Pride points the path that leads to Liberty;
Back to the struggle, baffled in the strife,
War, war is still the cry, 'War even to the knife!'

LXXXVII

Ye, who would more of Spain and Spaniards know
Go, read whate'er is writ of bloodiest strife:
Whate'er keen Vengeance urged on foreign foe
Can act, is acting there against man's life:
From flashing scimitar to secret knife,
War mouldeth there each weapon to his need—
So may he guard the sister and the wife,
So may he make each curst oppressor bleed,
So may such foes deserve the most remorseless deed!

LXXXVIII

Flows there a tear of pity for the dead?
Look o'er the ravage of the reeking plain;
Look on the hands with female slaughter red;
Then to the dogs resign the unburied slain,
Then to the vulture let each corse remain;
Albeit unworthy of the prey bird's maw,
Let their bleach'd bones, and blood's unbleaching stain,
Long mark the battle-field with hideous awe:
Thus only may our sons conceive the scenes we saw!

LXXXIX

Nor yet, alas! the dreadful work is done;
Fresh legions pour adown the Pyrenees:
It deepens still, the work is scarce begun,
Nor mortal eye the distant end foresees.
Fall'n nations gaze on Spain; if freed, she frees
More than her fell Pizarros once enchain'd:

Childe Harold's Pilgrimage, I

Strange retribution! now Columbia's ease
Repairs the wrongs that Quito's sons sustain'd,
While o'er the parent clime prowls Murder unrestrain'd.

XC

Not all the blood at Talavera shed,
Not all the marvels of Barossa's fight,
Not Albuera lavish of the dead,   *920*
Have won for Spain her well-asserted right.
When shall her Olive-Branch be free from blight?
When shall she breathe her from the blushing toil?
How many a doubtful day shall sink in night,
Ere the Frank robber turn him from his spoil,
And Freedom's stranger-tree grow native of the soil!

XCI

And thou, my friend!—since unavailing woe
Bursts from my heart, and mingles with the strain—
Had the sword laid thee with the mighty low,
Pride might forbid e'en Friendship to complain: *930*
But thus unlaurel'd to descend in vain,
By all forgotten, save the lonely breast,
And mix unbleeding with the boasted slain,
While Glory crowns so many a meaner crest!
What hadst thou done to sink so peacefully to rest?

XCII

Oh, known the earliest, and esteem'd the most!
Dear to a heart where nought was left so dear!
Though to my hopeless days for ever lost,
In dreams deny me not to see thee here!
And Morn in secret shall renew the tear   *940*
Of Consciousness awaking to her woes,
And Fancy hover o'er thy bloodless bier,
Till my frail frame return to whence it rose,
And mourn'd and mourner lie united in repose.

XCIII

Here is one fytte of Harold's pilgrimage:
Ye who of him may further seek to know,
Shall find some tidings in a future page,
If he that rhymeth now may scribble moe.
Is this too much? stern Critic! say not so:
Patience! and ye shall hear what he beheld   *950*
In other lands, where he was doom'd to go:
Lands that contain the monuments of Eld,
Ere Greece and Grecian arts by barbarous hands were quell'd.

Childe Harold's Pilgrimage, II

CANTO THE SECOND

I

Come, blue-eyed maid of heaven!—but thou, alas!
Didst never yet one mortal song inspire—
Goddess of Wisdom! here thy temple was,
And is, despite of war and wasting fire,
And years, that bade thy worship to expire:
But worse than steel, and flame, and ages slow,
Is the dread sceptre and dominion dire
Of men who never felt the sacred glow
That thoughts of thee and thine on polish'd breasts bestow.

II

Ancient of days! august Athena! where,
Where are thy men of might? thy grand in soul?
Gone—glimmering through the dream of things that were:
First in the race that led to Glory's goal,
They won, and pass'd away—is this the whole?
A schoolboy's tale, the wonder of an hour!
The warrior's weapon and the sophist's stole
Are sought in vain, and o'er each mouldering tower,
Dim with the mist of years, gray flits the shade of power.

III

Son of the morning, rise! approach you here!
Come—but molest not yon defenceless urn:
Look on this spot—a nation's sepulchre!
Abode of gods, whose shrines no longer burn.
Even gods must yield—religions take their turn:
'Twas Jove's—'tis Mahomet's—and other creeds
Will rise with other years, till man shall learn
Vainly his incense soars, his victim bleeds;
Poor child of Doubt and Death, whose hope is built on reeds.

IV

Bound to the earth, he lifts his eye to heaven—
Is 't not enough, unhappy thing! to know
Thou art? Is this a boon so kindly given,
That being, thou would'st be again, and go,
Thou know'st not, reck'st not to what region, so
On earth no more, but mingled with the skies?
Still wilt thou dream on future joy and woe?
Regard and weigh yon dust before it flies:
That little urn saith more than thousand homilies.

Childe Harold's Pilgrimage, II

V

Or burst the vanish'd Hero's lofty mound;
Far on the solitary shore he sleeps:
He fell, and falling nations mourn'd around;
But now not one of saddening thousands weeps,   40
Nor warlike worshipper his vigil keeps
Where demi-gods appear'd, as records tell.
Remove yon skull from out the scatter'd heaps:
Is that a temple where a God may dwell?
Why ev'n the worm at last disdains her shatter'd cell!

VI

Look on its broken arch, its ruin'd wall,
Its chambers desolate, and portals foul:
Yes, this was once Ambition's airy hall,
The dome of Thought, the palace of the Soul:
Behold through each lack-lustre, eyeless hole,   50
The gay recess of Wisdom and of Wit
And Passion's host, that never brook'd control:
Can all saint, sage, or sophist ever writ,
People this lonely tower, this tenement refit?

VII

Well didst thou speak, Athena's wisest son!
'All that we know is, nothing can be known.'
Why should we shrink from what we cannot shun?
Each hath his pang, but feeble sufferers groan
With brain-born dreams of evil all their own,
Pursue what Chance or Fate proclaimeth best;   60
Peace waits us on the shores of Acheron:
There no forced banquet claims the sated guest,
But Silence spreads the couch of ever welcome rest.

VIII

Yet if, as holiest men have deem'd, there be
A land of souls beyond that sable shore,
To shame the doctrine of the Sadducee
And sophists, madly vain of dubious lore;
How sweet it were in concert to adore
With those who made our mortal labours light!
To hear each voice we fear'd to hear no more!   70
Behold each mighty shade reveal'd to sight,
The Bactrian, Samian sage, and all who taught the right!

Childe Harold's Pilgrimage, II

IX

There, thou!—whose love and life together fled,
Have left me here to love and live in vain—
Twined with my heart, and can I deem thee dead
When busy Memory flashes on my brain?
Well—I will dream that we may meet again,
And woo the vision to my vacant breast:
If aught of young Remembrance then remain,
Be as it may Futurity's behest, 80
For me 'twere bliss enough to know thy spirit blest!

X

Here let me sit upon this massy stone,
The marble column's yet unshaken base;
Here, son of Saturn! was thy fav'rite throne:
Mightiest of many such!   Hence let me trace
The latent grandeur of thy dwelling-place.
It may not be: nor ev'n can Fancy's eye
Restore what Time hath labour'd to deface.
Yet these proud pillars claim no passing sigh;
Unmoved the Moslem sits, the light Greek carols by. 90

XI

But who, of all the plunderers of yon fane
On high, where Pallas linger'd, loth to flee
The latest relic of her ancient reign;
The last, the worst, dull spoiler, who was he?
Blush, Caledonia! such thy son could be!
England! I joy no child he was of thine:
Thy free-born men should spare what once was free;
Yet they could violate each saddening shrine,
And bear these altars o'er the long-reluctant brine.

XII

But most the modern Pict's ignoble boast, 100
To rive what Goth, and Turk, and Time hath spared:
Cold as the crags upon his native coast,
His mind as barren and his heart as hard,
Is he whose head conceived, whose hand prepared,
Aught to displace Athena's poor remains:
Her sons too weak the sacred shrine to guard,
Yet felt some portion of their mother's pains,
And never knew, till then, the weight of Despot's chains.

Childe Harold's Pilgrimage, II

XIII

What! shall it e'er be said by British tongue,
Albion was happy in Athena's tears?   *110*
Though in thy name the slaves her bosom wrung,
Tell not the deed to blushing Europe's ears;
The ocean queen, the free Britannia, bears
The last poor plunder from a bleeding land:
Yes, she, whose gen'rous aid her name endears,
Tore down those remnants with a harpy's hand,
Which envious Eld forbore, and tyrants left to stand.

XIV

Where was thine Aegis, Pallas! that appall'd
Stern Alaric and Havoc on their way?
Where Peleus' son? whom Hell in vain enthrall'd,   *120*
His shade from Hades upon that dread day
Bursting to light in terrible array!
What! could not Pluto spare the chief once more,
To scare a second robber from his prey?
Idly he wander'd on the Stygian shore,
Nor now preserved the walls he loved to shield before.

XV

Cold is the heart, fair Greece, that looks on thee,
Nor feels as lovers o'er the dust they loved;
Dull is the eye that will not weep to see
Thy walls defaced, thy mouldering shrines removed   *130*
By British hands, which it had best behoved
To guard those relics ne'er to be restored.
Curst be the hour when from their isle they roved,
And once again thy hapless bosom gored,
And snatch'd thy shrinking Gods to northern climes abhorr'd!

XVI

But where is Harold? shall I then forget
To urge the gloomy wanderer o'er the wave?
Little reck'd he of all that men regret;
No loved-one now in feign'd lament could rave;
No friend the parting hand extended gave,   *140*
Ere the cold stranger pass'd to other climes,
Hard is his heart whom charms may not enslave;
But Harold felt not as in other times,
And left without a sigh the land of war and crimes.

Childe Harold's Pilgrimage, II

XVII

He that has sail'd upon the dark blue sea
Has view'd at times, I ween, a full fair sight;
When the fresh breeze is fair as breeze may be,
The white sail set, the gallant frigate tight;
Masts, spires, and strand retiring to the right,
The glorious main expanding o'er the bow, *150*
The convoy spread like wild swans in their flight,
The dullest sailor wearing bravely now,
So gaily curl the waves before each dashing prow.

XVIII

And oh, the little warlike world within!
The well-reeved guns, the netted canopy,
The hoarse command, the busy humming din,
When, at a word, the tops are mann'd on high:
Hark, to the Boatswain's call, the cheering cry!
While through the seaman's hand the tackle glides;
Or schoolboy Midshipman that, standing by, *160*
Strains his shrill pipe as good or ill betides,
And well the docile crew that skilful urchin guides.

XIX

White is the glassy deck, without a stain,
Where on the watch the staid Lieutenant walks:
Look on that part which sacred doth remain
For the lone chieftain, who majestic stalks,
Silent and fear'd by all—not oft he talks
With aught beneath him, if he would preserve
That strict restraint, which broken, ever balks
Conquest and Fame: but Britons rarely swerve *170*
From law, however stern, which tends their strength to nerve.

XX

Blow! swiftly blow, thou keel-compelling gale!
Till the broad sun withdraws his lessening ray;
Then must the pennant-bearer slacken sail,
That lagging barks may make their lazy way.
Ah! grievance sore, and listless dull delay,
To waste on sluggish hulks the sweetest breeze!
What leagues are lost, before the dawn of day,
Thus loitering pensive on the willing seas,
The flapping sail haul'd down to halt for logs like these! *180*

XXI

The moon is up; by Heaven, a lovely eve!
Long streams of light o'er dancing waves expand;
Now lads on shore may sigh, and maids believe:
Such be our fate when we return to land!
Meantime some rude Arion's restless hand
Wakes the brisk harmony that sailors love;
A circle there of merry listeners stand,
Or to some well-known measure featly move,
Thoughtless, as if on shore they still were free to rove.

XXII

Through Calpe's straits survey the steepy shore; 190
Europe and Afric on each other gaze!
Lands of the dark-eyed Maid and dusky Moor
Alike beheld beneath pale Hecate's blaze:
How softly on the Spanish shore she plays,
Disclosing rock, and slope, and forest brown,
Distinct, though darkening with her waning phase;
But Mauritania's giant-shadows frown,
From mountain-cliff to coast descending sombre down.

XXIII

'Tis night, when Meditation bids us feel
We once have loved, though love is at an end: 200
The heart, lone mourner of its baffled zeal,
Though friendless now, will dream it had a friend.
Who with the weight of years would wish to bend,
When Youth itself survives young Love and Joy?
Alas! when mingling souls forget to blend,
Death hath but little left him to destroy!
Ah! happy years! once more who would not be a boy?

XXIV

Thus bending o'er the vessel's laving side,
To gaze on Dian's wave-reflected sphere,
The soul forgets her schemes of Hope and Pride, 210
And flies unconscious o'er each backward year.
None are so desolate but something dear,
Dearer than self, possesses or possess'd
A thought, and claims the homage of a tear;
A flashing pang! of which the weary breast
Would still, albeit in vain, the heavy heart divest.

Childe Harold's Pilgrimage, II

XXV

To sit on rocks, to muse o'er flood and fell,
To slowly trace the forest's shady scene,
Where things that own not man's dominion dwell,
And mortal foot hath ne'er or rarely been;
To climb the trackless mountain all unseen,
With the wild flock that never needs a fold;
Alone o'er steeps and foaming falls to lean,
This is not solitude; 'tis but to hold
Converse with Nature's charms, and view her stores unroll'd.

XXVI

But midst the crowd, the hum, the shock of men,
To hear, to see, to feel, and to possess,
And roam along, the world's tired denizen,
With none who bless us, none whom we can bless;
Minions of splendour shrinking from distress!
None that, with kindred consciousness endued,
If we were not, would seem to smile the less
Of all that flatter'd, follow'd, sought, and sued;
This is to be alone; this, this is solitude!

XXVII

More blest the life of godly eremite,
Such as on lonely Athos may be seen,
Watching at eve upon the giant height,
Which looks o'er waves so blue, skies so serene,
That he who there at such an hour hath been
Will wistful linger on that hallow'd spot;
Then slowly tear him from the witching scene,
Sigh forth one wish that such had been his lot,
Then turn to hate a world he had almost forgot.

XXVIII

Pass we the long, unvarying course, the track
Oft trod, that never leaves a trace behind;
Pass we the calm, the gale, the change, the tack,
And each well-known caprice of wave and wind;
Pass we the joys and sorrows sailors find,
Coop'd in their winged sea-girt citadel;
The foul, the fair, the contrary, the kind,
As breezes rise and fall and billows swell,
Till on some jocund morn—lo, land! and all is well.

Childe Harold's Pilgrimage, II

XXIX

But not in silence pass Calypso's isles,
The sister tenants of the middle deep;
There for the weary still a haven smiles,
Though the fair goddess long hath ceased to weep,
And o'er her cliffs a fruitless watch to keep
For him who dared prefer a mortal bride:
Here, too, his boy essay'd the dreadful leap
Stern Mentor urged from high to yonder tide;   *260*
While thus of both bereft, the nymph-queen doubly sigh'd.

XXX

Her reign is past, her gentle glories gone:
But trust not this; too easy youth, beware!
A mortal sovereign holds her dangerous throne,
And thou may'st find a new Calypso there.
Sweet Florence! could another ever share
This wayward, loveless heart, it would be thine:
But check'd by every tie, I may not dare
To cast a worthless offering at thy shrine,
Nor ask so dear a breast to feel one pang for mine.   *270*

XXXI

Thus Harold deem'd, as on that lady's eye
He look'd, and met its beam without a thought,
Save Admiration glancing harmless by:
Love kept aloof, albeit not far remote,
Who knew his votary often lost and caught,
But knew him as his worshipper no more,
And ne'er again the boy his bosom sought:
Since now he vainly urged him to adore,
Well deem'd the little God his ancient sway was o'er.

XXXII

Fair Florence found, in sooth with some amaze,   *280*
One who, 'twas said, still sigh'd to all he saw,
Withstand, unmoved, the lustre of her gaze,
Which others hail'd with real or mimic awe,
Their hope, their doom, their punishment, their law;
All that gay Beauty from her bondsmen claims:
And much she marvell'd that a youth so raw
Nor felt, nor feign'd at least, the oft-told flames,
Which, though sometimes they frown, yet rarely anger dames.

43

XXXIII

Little knew she that seeming marble heart,
Now mask'd in silence or withheld by pride,
Was not unskilful in the spoiler's art,
And spread its snares licentious far and wide;
Nor from the base pursuit had turn'd aside,
As long as aught was worthy to pursue:
But Harold on such arts no more relied;
And had he doted on those eyes so blue,
Yet never would he join the lover's whining crew.

XXXIV

Not much he kens, I ween, of woman's breast,
Who thinks that wanton thing is won by sighs;
What careth she for hearts when once possess'd?
Do proper homage to thine idol's eyes;
But not too humbly, or she will despise
Thee and thy suit, though told in moving tropes:
Disguise ev'n tenderness, if thou art wise;
Brisk Confidence still best with woman copes;
Pique her and soothe in turn, soon Passion crowns thy hopes.

XXXV

'Tis an old lesson; Time approves it true,
And those who know it best, deplore it most;
When all is won that all desire to woo,
The paltry prize is hardly worth the cost:
Youth wasted, minds degraded, honour lost,
These are thy fruits, successful Passion! these!
If, kindly cruel, early Hope is crost,
Still to the last it rankles, a disease,
Not to be cured when Love itself forgets to please.

XXXVI

Away! nor let me loiter in my song,
For we have many a mountain-path to tread,
And many a varied shore to sail along;
By pensive Sadness, not by Fiction, led—
Climes, fair withal as ever mortal head
Imagined in its little schemes of thought;
Or e'er in new Utopias were ared,
To teach man what he might be, or he ought;
If that corrupted thing could ever such be taught.

XXXVII

Dear Nature is the kindest mother still,
Though always changing, in her aspect mild;
From her bare bosom let me take my fill,
Her never-wean'd, though not her favour'd child.
Oh! she is fairest in her features wild,
Where nothing polish'd dares pollute her path: 330
To me by day or night she ever smiled,
Though I have mark'd her when none other hath,
And sought her more and more, and loved her best in wrath.

XXXVIII

Land of Albania! where Iskander rose,
Theme of the young, and beacon of the wise,
And he his namesake, whose oft-baffled foes
Shrunk from his deeds of chivalrous emprise;
Land of Albania! let me bend mine eyes
On thee, thou rugged nurse of savage men!
The cross descends, thy minarets arise, 340
And the pale crescent sparkles in the glen,
Through many a cypress grove within each city's ken.

XXXIX

Childe Harold sail'd, and pass'd the barren spot
Where sad Penelope o'erlook'd the wave;
And onward view'd the mount, not yet forgot,
The lover's refuge, and the Lesbian's grave.
Dark Sappho! could not verse immortal save
That breast imbued with such immortal fire?
Could she not live who life eternal gave?
If life eternal may await the lyre, 350
That only heaven to which Earth's children may aspire.

XL

'Twas on a Grecian autumn's gentle eve
Childe Harold hail'd Leucadia's cape afar;
A spot he longed to see, nor cared to leave:
Oft did he mark the scenes of vanish'd war,
Actium, Lepanto, fatal Trafalgar;
Mark them unmoved, for he would not delight
(Born beneath some remote inglorious star)
In themes of bloody fray, or gallant fight,
But loathed the bravo's trade, and laughed at martial wight. 360

XLI

But when he saw the evening star above
Leucadia's far-projecting rock of woe,
And hail'd the last resort of fruitless love,
He felt, or deem'd he felt, no common glow:
And as the stately vessel glided slow
Beneath the shadow of that ancient mount,
He watch'd the billows' melancholy flow,
And, sunk albeit in thought as he was wont,
More placid seem'd his eye, and smooth his pallid front.

XLII

Morn dawns; and with it stern Albania's hills,   *370*
Dark Suli's rocks, and Pindus' inland peak,
Robed half in mist, bedewed with snowy rills,
Array'd in many a dun and purple streak,
Arise; and, as the clouds along them break,
Disclose the dwelling of the mountaineer:
Here roams the wolf, the eagle whets his beak,
Birds, beasts of prey, and wilder men appear,
And gathering storms around convulse the closing year.

XLIII

Now Harold felt himself at length alone,
And bade to Christian tongues a long adieu;   *380*
Now he adventured on a shore unknown,
Which all admire, but many dread to view:
His breast was arm'd 'gainst fate, his wants were few;
Peril he sought not, but ne'er shrank to meet:
The scene was savage, but the scene was new:
This made the ceaseless toil of travel sweet,
Beat back keen winter's blast, and welcomed summer's heat.

XLIV

Here the red cross, for still the cross is here,
Though sadly scoff'd at by the circumcised,
Forgets that pride to pamper'd priesthood dear;   *390*
Churchman and votary alike despised.
Foul Superstition! howsoe'er disguised,
Idol, saint, virgin, prophet, crescent, cross,
For whatsoever symbol thou art prized,
Thou sacerdotal gain, but general loss!
Who from true worship's gold can separate thy dross?

Childe Harold's Pilgrimage, II

XLV

Ambracia's gulf behold, where once was lost
A world for woman, lovely, harmless thing!
In yonder rippling bay, their naval host
Did many a Roman chief and Asian king   400
To doubtful conflict, certain slaughter bring:
Look where the second Caesar's trophies rose:
Now, like the hands that reared them, withering:
Imperial anarchs, doubling human woes!
God! was thy globe ordain'd for such to win and lose?

XLVI

From the dark barriers of that rugged clime,
Ev'n to the centre of Illyria's vales,
Childe Harold pass'd o'er many a mount sublime,
Through lands scarce noticed in historic tales;
Yet in famed Attica such lovely dales   410
Are rarely seen; nor can fair Tempe boast
A charm they know not; loved Parnassus fails,
Though classic ground and consecrated most,
To match some spots that lurk within this lowering coast.

XLVII

He pass'd bleak Pindus, Acherusia's lake,
And left the primal city of the land,
And onwards did his further journey take
To greet Albania's chief, whose dread command
Is lawless law; for with a bloody hand
He sways a nation, turbulent and bold: 420
Yet here and there some daring mountain-band
Disdain his power, and from their rocky hold
Hurl their defiance far, nor yield, unless to gold.

XLVIII

Monastic Zitza! from thy shady brow,
Thou small, but favour'd spot of holy ground!
Where'er we gaze, around, above, below,
What rainbow tints, what magic charms are found!
Rock, river, forest, mountain, all abound,
And bluest skies that harmonize the whole:
Beneath, the distant torrent's rushing sound   430
Tells where the volumed cataract doth roll
Between those hanging rocks, that shock yet please the soul.

47

XLIX

Amidst the grove that crowns yon tufted hill,
Which, were it not for many a mountain nigh
Rising in lofty ranks, and loftier still,
Might well itself be deem'd of dignity,
The convent's white walls glisten fair on high:
Here dwells the caloyer, nor rude is he,
Nor niggard of his cheer; the passer by
Is welcome still; nor heedless will he flee 440
From hence, if he delight kind Nature's sheen to see.

L

Here in the sultriest season let him rest,
Fresh is the green beneath those aged trees;
Here winds of gentlest wing will fan his breast,
From heaven itself it may inhale the breeze:
The plain is far beneath—oh! let him seize
Pure pleasure while he can; the scorching ray
Here pierceth not, impregnate with disease:
Then let his length the loitering pilgrim lay,
And gaze, untired, the morn, the noon, the eve away. 450

LI

Dusky and huge, enlarging on the sight,
Nature's volcanic amphitheatre,
Chimaera's alps extend from left to right:
Beneath, a living valley seems to stir;
Flocks play, trees wave, streams flow, the mountain-fir
Nodding above; behold black Acheron!
Once consecrated to the sepulchre.
Pluto! if this be hell I look upon,
Close shamed Elysium's gates, my shade shall seek for none.

LII

No city's towers pollute the lovely view; 460
Unseen is Yanina, though not remote,
Veil'd by the screen of hills: here men are few,
Scanty the hamlet, rare the lonely cot:
But peering down each precipice, the goat
Browseth; and, pensive o'er his scatter'd flock,
The little shepherd in his white capote
Doth lean his boyish form along the rock,
Or in his cave awaits the tempest's short-lived shock.

Childe Harold's Pilgrimage, II

LIII

Oh! where, Dodona! is thine aged grove,
Prophetic fount, and oracle divine? *470*
What valley echo'd the response of Jove?
What trace remaineth of the Thunderer's shrine?
All, all forgotten—and shall man repine
That his frail bonds to fleeting life are broke?
Cease, fool! the fate of gods may well be thine:
Wouldst thou survive the marble or the oak?
When nations, tongues, and worlds must sink beneath the stroke!

LIV

Epirus' bounds recede, and mountains fail;
Tired of up-gazing still, the wearied eye
Reposes gladly on as smooth a vale *480*
As ever Spring yclad in grassy dye:
Ev'n on a plain no humble beauties lie,
Where some bold river breaks the long expanse,
And woods along the banks are waving high,
Whose shadows in the glassy waters dance,
Or with the moonbeam sleep in midnight's solemn trance.

LV

The sun had sunk behind vast Tomerit,
And Laos wide and fierce came roaring by;
The shades of wonted night were gathering yet,
When, down the steep banks winding warily, *490*
Childe Harold saw, like meteors in the sky,
The glittering minarets of Tepalen,
Whose walls o'erlook the stream; and drawing nigh,
He heard the busy hum of warrior-men
Swelling the breeze that sigh'd along the lengthening glen.

LVI

He pass'd the sacred Haram's silent tower,
And underneath the wide o'er-arching gate
Survey'd the dwelling of this chief of power,
Where all around proclaim'd his high estate.
Amidst no common pomp the despot sate, *500*
While busy preparation shook the court,
Slaves, eunuchs, soldiers, guests, and santons wait;
Within, a palace, and without, a fort:
Here men of every clime appear to make resort.

LVII

Richly caparison'd, a ready row
Of armed horse, and many a warlike store,
Circled the wide extending court below;
Above, strange groups adorn'd the corridore;
And oft-times through the area's echoing door,
Some high-capp'd Tartar spurr'd his steed away: 510
The Turk, the Greek, the Albanian, and the Moor,
Here mingled in their many-hued array,
While the deep war-drum's sound announced the close of day.

LVIII

The wild Albanian kirtled to his knee,
With shawl-girt head and ornamented gun,
And gold-embroider'd garments, fair to see:
The crimson-scarfed men of Macedon;
The Delhi with his cap of terror on,
And crooked glaive; the lively, supple Greek:
And swarthy Nubia's mutilated son; 520
The bearded Turk, that rarely deigns to speak,
Master of all around, too potent to be meek,

LIX

Are mix'd conspicuous: some recline in groups,
Scanning the motley scene that varies round;
There some grave Moslem to devotion stoops,
And some that smoke, and some that play, are found;
Here the Albanian proudly treads the ground;
Half whispering there the Greek is heard to prate;
Hark! from the mosque the nightly solemn sound,
The Muezzin's call doth shake the minaret, 530
'There is no god but God!—to prayer—lo! God is great!'

LX

Just at this season Ramazani's fast
Through the long day its penance did maintain:
But when the lingering twilight hour was past,
Revel and feast assumed the rule again:
Now all was bustle, and the menial train
Prepared and spread the plenteous board within;
The vacant gallery now seem'd made in vain,
But from the chambers came the mingling din,
As page and slave anon were passing out and in. 540

Childe Harold's Pilgrimage, II

LXI

Here woman's voice is never heard: apart,
And scarce permitted, guarded, veil'd, to move,
She yields to one her person and her heart,
Tamed to her cage, nor feels a wish to rove:
For, not unhappy in her master's love,
And joyful in a mother's gentlest cares,
Blest cares! all other feelings far above!
Herself more sweetly rears the babe she bears,
Who never quits the breast, no meaner passion shares.

LXII

In marble-paved pavilion, where a spring *550*
Of living water from the centre rose,
Whose bubbling did a genial freshness fling,
And soft voluptuous couches breathed repose,
ALI reclined, a man of war and woes:
Yet in his lineaments ye cannot trace,
While Gentleness her milder radiance throws
Along that aged venerable face,
The deeds that lurk beneath, and stain him with disgrace.

LXIII

It is not that yon hoary lengthening beard
Ill suits the passions which belong to youth; *560*
Love conquers age—so Hafiz hath averr'd,
So sings the Teian, and he sings in sooth—
But crimes that scorn the tender voice of ruth,
Beseeming all men ill, but most the man
In years, have mark'd him with a tiger's tooth;
Blood follows blood, and, through their mortal span,
In bloodier acts conclude those who with blood began.

LXIV

'Mid many things most new to ear and eye
The pilgrim rested here his weary feet,
And gazed around on Moslem luxury, *570*
Till quickly wearied with that spacious seat
Of Wealth and Wantonness, the choice retreat
Of sated Grandeur from the city's noise:
And were it humbler it in sooth were sweet;
But Peace abhorreth artificial joys,
And Pleasure, leagued with Pomp, the zest of both destroys.

LXV

Fierce are Albania's children, yet they lack
Not virtues, were those virtues more mature.
Where is the foe that ever saw their back?
Who can so well the toil of war endure? 580
Their native fastnesses not more secure
Than they in doubtful time of troublous need:
Their wrath how deadly! but their friendship sure,
When Gratitude or Valour bids them bleed,
Unshaken rushing on where'er their chief may lead.

LXVI

Childe Harold saw them in their chieftain's tower
Thronging to war in splendour and success;
And after view'd them, when, within their power,
Himself awhile the victim of distress;
That saddening hour when bad men hotlier press: 590
But these did shelter him beneath their roof,
When less barbarians would have cheer'd him less,
And fellow-countrymen have stood aloof —
In aught that tries the heart how few withstand the proof!

LXVII

It chanced that adverse winds once drove his bark
Full on the coast of Suli's shaggy shore,
When all around was desolate and dark;
To land was perilous, to sojourn more;
Yet for a while the mariners forbore,
Dubious to trust where treachery might lurk: 600
At length they ventured forth, though doubting sore
That those who loathe alike the Frank and Turk
Might once again renew their ancient butcher-work.

LXVIII

Vain fear! the Suliotes stretch'd the welcome hand,
Led them o'er rocks and past the dangerous swamp,
Kinder than polish'd slaves though not so bland,
And piled the hearth, and wrung their garments damp,
And fill'd the bowl, and trimm'd the cheerful lamp,
And spread their fare; though homely, all they had:
Such conduct bears Philanthropy's rare stamp— 610
To rest the weary and to soothe the sad,
Doth lesson happier men, and shames at least the bad.

Childe Harold's Pilgrimage, II

LXIX

It came to pass, that when he did address
Himself to quit at length this mountain-land,
Combined marauders half-way barr'd egress,
And wasted far and near with glaive and brand;
And therefore did he take a trusty band
To traverse Acarnania's forest wide,
In war well season'd, and with labours tann'd,
Till he did greet white Achelous' tide,   620
And from his further bank Aetolia's wolds espied.

LXX

Where lone Utraikey forms its circling cove,
And weary waves retire to gleam at rest,
How brown the foliage of the green hill's grove,
Nodding at midnight o'er the calm bay's breast,
As winds come lightly whispering from the west,
Kissing, not ruffling, the blue deep's serene:—
Here Harold was received a welcome guest;
Nor did he pass unmoved the gentle scene,
For many a joy could he from Night's soft presence glean.   630

LXXI

On the smooth shore the night-fires brightly blazed,
The feast was done, the red wine circling fast,
And he that unawares had there ygazed
With gaping wonderment had stared aghast;
For ere night's midmost, stillest hour was past,
The native revels of the troop began;
Each Palikar his sabre from him cast,
And bounding hand in hand, man link'd to man,
Yelling their uncouth dirge, long daunced the kirtled clan.

LXXII

Childe Harold at a little distance stood   640
And view'd, but not displeased, the revelrie,
Nor hated harmless mirth, however rude:
In sooth, it was no vulgar sight to see
Their barbarous, yet their not indecent, glee;
And, as the flames along their faces gleam'd,
Their gestures nimble, dark eyes flashing free,
The long wild locks that to their girdles stream'd,
While thus in concert they this lay half sang, half scream'd:—

Childe Harold's Pilgrimage, II

1

TAMBOURGI! Tambourgi! thy 'larum afar
Gives hope to the valiant, and promise of war;   650
All the sons of the mountains arise at the note,
Chimariot, Illyrian, and dark Suliote!

2

Oh! who is more brave than a dark Suliote,
In his snowy camese and his shaggy capote?
To the wolf and the vulture he leaves his wild flock,
And descends to the plain like the stream from the rock.

3

Shall the sons of Chimari, who never forgive
The fault of a friend, bid an enemy live?
Let those guns so unerring such vengeance forego?
What mark is so fair as the breast of a foe?   660

4

Macedonia sends forth her invincible race;
For a time they abandon the cave and the chase:
But those scarfs of blood-red shall be redder, before
The sabre is sheathed and the battle is o'er.

5

Then the pirates of Parga that dwell by the waves,
And teach the pale Franks what it is to be slaves,
Shall leave on the beach the long galley and oar,
And track to his covert the captive on shore.

6

I ask not the pleasures that riches supply,
My sabre shall win what the feeble must buy;   670
Shall win the young bride with her long flowing hair,
And many a maid from her mother shall tear.

7

I love the fair face of the maid in her youth,
Her caresses shall lull me, her music shall soothe;
Let her bring from the chamber her many-toned lyre,
And sing us a song on the fall of her sire.

8

Remember the moment when Previsa fell,
The shrieks of the conquer'd, the conquerors' yell;
The roofs that we fired, and the plunder we shared,
The wealthy we slaughter'd, the lovely we spared.   680

9

I talk not of mercy, I talk not of fear;
He neither must know who would serve the Vizier:
Since the days of our prophet the Crescent ne'er saw
A chief ever glorious like Ali Pashaw.

10
Dark Muchtar his son to the Danube is sped,
Let the yellow-hair'd Giaours view his horse-tail with dread;
When his Delhis come dashing in blood o'er the banks,
How few shall escape from the Muscovite ranks!

11
Selictar! unsheathe then our chief's scimitar:
Tambourgi! thy 'larum gives promise of war. *690*
Ye mountains, that see us descend to the shore,
Shall view us as victors, or view us no more!

LXXIII
Fair Greece! sad relic of departed worth!
Immortal, though no more; though fallen, great!
Who now shall lead thy scatter'd children forth,
And long accustom'd bondage uncreate?
Not such thy sons who whilome did await,
The hopeless warriors of a willing doom,
In bleak Thermopylae's sepulchral strait—
Oh! who that gallant spirit shall resume, *700*
Leap from Eurotas' banks, and call thee from the tomb?

LXXIV
Spirit of freedom! when on Phyle's brow
Thou sat'st with Thrasybulus and his train,
Couldst thou forebode the dismal hour which now
Dims the green beauties of thine Attic plain?
Not thirty tyrants now enforce the chain,
But every carle can lord it o'er thy land;
Nor rise thy sons, but idly rail in vain,
Trembling beneath the scourge of Turkish hand
From birth till death enslaved; in word, in deed, unmann'd. *710*

LXXV
In all save form alone, how changed! and who
That marks the fire still sparkling in each eye,
Who but would deem their bosoms burn'd anew
With thy unquenched beam, lost Liberty!
And many dream withal the hour is nigh
That gives them back their fathers' heritage:
For foreign arms and aid they fondly sigh,
Nor solely dare encounter hostile rage,
Or tear their name defiled from Slavery's mournful page.

LXXVI

Hereditary bondsmen! know ye not
Who would be free themselves must strike the blow?
By their right arms the conquest must be wrought?
Will Gaul or Muscovite redress ye? no!
True, they may lay your proud despoilers low,
But not for you will Freedom's altars flame.
Shades of the Helots! triumph o'er your foe!
Greece! change thy lords, thy state is still the same;
Thy glorious day is o'er, but not thy years of shame.

LXXVII

The city won for Allah from the Giaour,
The Giaour from Othman's race again may wrest;
And the Serai's impenetrable tower
Receive the fiery Frank, her former guest;
Or Wahab's rebel brood who dared divest
The prophet's tomb of all its pious spoil,
May wind their path of blood along the West;
But ne'er will freedom seek this fated soil,
But slave succeed to slave through years of endless toil.

LXXVIII

Yet mark their mirth—ere lenten days begin,
That penance which their holy rites prepare
To shrive from man his weight of mortal sin,
By daily abstinence and nightly prayer;
But ere his sackcloth garb Repentance wear,
Some days of joyaunce are decreed to all,
To take of pleasaunce each his secret share,
In motley robe to dance at masking ball,
And join the mimic train of merry Carnival.

LXXIX

And whose more rife with merriment than thine,
Oh Stamboul! once the empress of their reign?
Though turbans now pollute Sophia's shrine,
And Greece her very altars eyes in vain:
(Alas! her woes will still pervade my strain!)
Gay were her minstrels once, for free her throng,
All felt the common joy they now must feign,
Nor oft I've seen such sight, nor heard such song,
As woo'd the eye, and thrill'd the Bosphorus along.

Childe Harold's Pilgrimage, II

LXXX

Loud was the lightsome tumult on the shore,
Oft Music changed, but never ceased her tone,
And timely echo'd back the measured oar,
And rippling waters made a pleasant moan:
The Queen of tides on high consenting shone,   760
And when a transient breeze swept o'er the wave,
'Twas, as if darting from her heavenly throne,
A brighter glance her form reflected gave,
Till sparkling billows seem'd to light the banks they lave.

LXXXI

Glanced many a light caique along the foam,
Danced on the shore the daughters of the land,
Ne thought had man or maid of rest or home,
While many a languid eye and thrilling hand
Exchanged the look few bosoms may withstand,
Or gently prest, return'd the pressure still: 770
Oh Love! young Love! bound in thy rosy band,
Let sage or cynic prattle as he will,
These hours, and only these, redeem Life's years of ill!

LXXXII

But, midst the throng in merry masquerade,
Lurk there no hearts that throb with secret pain,
Even through the closest searment half betray'd?
To such the gentle murmurs of the main
Seem to re-echo all they mourn in vain;
To such the gladness of the gamesome crowd
Is source of wayward thought and stern disdain: 780
How do they loathe the laughter idly loud,
And long to change the robe of revel for the shroud!

LXXXIII

This must he feel, the true-born son of Greece,
If Greece one true-born patriot still can boast:
Not such as prate of war, but skulk in peace,
The bondsman's peace, who sighs for all he lost,
Yet with smooth smile his tyrant can accost,
And wield the slavish sickle, not the sword:
Ah! Greece! they love thee least who owe thee most;
Their birth, their blood, and that sublime record   790
Of hero sires, who shame thy now degenerate horde!

LXXXIV

When riseth Lacedemon's hardihood,
When Thebes Epaminondas rears again,
When Athens' children are with hearts endued,
When Grecian mothers shall give birth to men,
Then may'st thou be restored; but not till then.
A thousand years scarce serve to form a state;
An hour may lay it in the dust: and when
Can man its shatter'd splendour renovate,
Recall its virtues back, and vanquish Time and Fate?   800

LXXXV

And yet how lovely in thine age of woe,
Land of lost gods and godlike men! art thou!
Thy vales of evergreen, thy hills of snow,
Proclaim thee Nature's varied favourite now;
Thy fanes, thy temples to thy surface bow,
Commingling slowly with heroic earth,
Broke by the share of every rustic plough:
So perish monuments of mortal birth,
So perish all in turn, save well-recorded Worth;

LXXXVI

Save where some solitary column mourns   810
Above its prostrate brethren of the cave;
Save where Tritonia's airy shrine adorns
Colonna's cliff, and gleams along the wave;
Save o'er some warrior's half-forgotten grave,
Where the gray stones and unmolested grass
Ages, but not oblivion, feebly brave,
While strangers only not regardless pass,
Lingering like me, perchance, to gaze, and sigh 'Alas!'

LXXXVII

Yet are thy skies as blue, thy crags as wild;
Sweet are thy groves, and verdant are thy fields,   820
Thine olive ripe as when Minerva smiled,
And still his honied wealth Hymettus yields;
There the blithe bee his fragrant fortress builds,
The freeborn wanderer of thy mountain-air;
Apollo still thy long, long summer gilds,
Still in his beam Mendeli's marbles glare;
Art, Glory, Freedom fail, but Nature still is fair.

Childe Harold's Pilgrimage, II

LXXXVIII.

Where'er we tread 'tis haunted, holy ground,
No earth of thine is lost in vulgar mould,
But one vast realm of wonder spreads around,   *830*
And all the Muse's tales seem truly told,
Till the sense aches with gazing to behold
The scenes our earliest dreams have dwelt upon:
Each hill and dale, each deepening glen and wold
Defies the power which crush'd thy temples gone:
Age shakes Athena's tower, but spares gray Marathon.

LXXXIX

The sun, the soil, but not the slave, the same;
Unchanged in all except its foreign lord—
Preserves alike its bounds and boundless fame
The Battle-field, where Persia's victim horde   *840*
First bow'd beneath the brunt of Hellas' sword,
As on the morn to distant Glory dear,
When Marathon became a magic word;
Which utter'd, to the hearer's eye appear
The camp, the host, the fight, the conqueror's career,

XC

The flying Mede, his shaftless broken bow;
The fiery Greek, his red pursuing spear;
Mountains above, Earth's, Ocean's plain below;
Death in the front, Destruction in the rear!
Such was the scene—what now remaineth here?   *850*
What sacred trophy marks the hallow'd ground,
Recording Freedom's smile and Asia's tear?
The rifled urn, the violated mound,
The dust thy courser's hoof, rude stranger! spurns around.

XCI

Yet to the remnants of thy splendour past
Shall pilgrims, pensive, but unwearied, throng;
Long shall the voyager, with th' Ionian blast,
Hail the bright clime of battle and of song;
Long shall thine annals and immortal tongue
Fill with thy fame the youth of many a shore;   *860*
Boast of the aged! lesson of the young!
Which sages venerate and bards adore,
As Pallas and the Muse unveil their awful lore.

XCII

The parted bosom clings to wonted home,
If aught that's kindred cheer the welcome hearth;
He that is lonely, hither let him roam,
And gaze complacent on congenial earth.
Greece is no lightsome land of social mirth:
But he whom Sadness sootheth may abide,
And scarce regret the region of his birth,   *870*
When wandering slow by Delphi's sacred side,
Or gazing o'er the plains where Greek and Persian died.

XCIII

Let such approach this consecrated land,
And pass in peace along the magic waste;
But spare its relics—let no busy hand
Deface the scenes, already how defaced!
Not for such purpose were these altars placed:
Revere the remnants nations once revered:
So may our country's name be undisgraced,
So may'st thou prosper where thy youth was rear'd,   *880*
By every honest joy of love and life endear'd!

XCIV

For thee, who thus in too protracted song
Hast soothed thine idlesse with inglorious lays,
Soon shall thy voice be lost amid the throng
Of louder minstrels in these later days:
To such resign the strife for fading bays—
Ill may such contest now the spirit move
Which heeds nor keen reproach nor partial praise,
Since cold each kinder heart that might approve,
And none are left to please when none are left to love.   *890*

XCV

Thou too art gone, thou loved and lovely one!
Whom youth and youth's affections bound to me;
Who did for me what none beside have done,
Nor shrank from one albeit unworthy thee.
What is my being? thou hast ceased to be!
Nor staid to welcome here thy wanderer home,
Who mourns o'er hours which we no more shall see—
Would they had never been, or were to come!
Would he had ne'er return'd to find fresh cause to roam!

Childe Harold's Pilgrimage, II

XCVI

Oh! ever loving, lovely, and beloved! 900
How selfish Sorrow ponders on the past,
And clings to thoughts now better far removed!
But Time shall tear thy shadow from me last,
All thou couldst have of mine, stern Death! thou hast:
The parent, friend, and now the more than friend:
Ne'er yet for one thine arrows flew so fast,
And grief with grief continuing still to blend,
Hath snatch'd the little joy that life had yet to lend.

XCVII

Then must I plunge again into the crowd,
And follow all that Peace disdains to seek? 910
Where Revel calls, and Laughter, vainly loud,
False to the heart, distorts the hollow cheek,
To leave the flagging spirit doubly weak;
Still o'er the features, which perforce they cheer,
To feign the pleasure or conceal the pique;
Smiles form the channel of a future tear,
Or raise the writhing lip with ill-dissembled sneer.

XCVIII

What is the worst of woes that wait on age?
What stamps the wrinkle deeper on the brow?
To view each loved one blotted from life's page, 920
And be alone on earth, as I am now.
Before the Chastener humbly let me bow,
O'er hearts divided and o'er hopes destroy'd:
Roll on, vain days! full reckless may ye flow,
Since Time hath reft whate'er my soul enjoy'd,
And with the ills of Eld mine earlier years alloy'd.

Childe Harold's Pilgrimage, III

CANTO THE THIRD

Afin que cette application vous forçât à penser à autre chose; il n'y a en vérité de remède que celui-là et le temps.—Lettre du Roi de Prusse à D'Alembert, 7th September 1776.

I

Is thy face like thy mother's, my fair child!
ADA! sole daughter of my house and heart?
When last I saw thy young blue eyes they smiled,
And then we parted,—not as now we part,
But with a hope.—
        Awaking with a start,
The waters heave around me; and on high
The winds lift up their voices: I depart,
Whither I know not; but the hour 's gone by,
When Albion's lessening shores could grieve or glad mine eye.

II

Once more upon the waters! yet once more!   10
And the waves bound beneath me as a steed
That knows his rider. Welcome to their roar!
Swift be their guidance, wheresoe'er it lead!
Though the strain'd mast should quiver as a reed,
And the rent canvas fluttering strew the gale,
Still must I on; for I am as a weed,
Flung from the rock, on Ocean's foam, to sail
Where'er the surge may sweep, the tempest's breath prevail.

III

In my youth's summer I did sing of One,
The wandering outlaw of his own dark mind;   20
Again I seize the theme, then but begun,
And bear it with me, as the rushing wind
Bears the cloud onwards: in that Tale I find
The furrows of long thought, and dried-up tears,
Which, ebbing, leave a sterile track behind,
O'er which all heavily the journeying years
Plod the last sands of life,—where not a flower appears.

Childe Harold's Pilgrimage, III

IV

Since my young days of passion—joy, or pain,
Perchance my heart and harp have lost a string,
And both may jar: it may be, that in vain
I would essay as I have sung to sing.
Yet, though a dreary strain, to this I cling
So that it wean me from the weary dream
Of selfish grief or gladness—so it fling
Forgetfulness around me—it shall seem
To me, though to none else, a not ungrateful theme.

V

He, who grown aged in this world of woe,
In deeds, not years, piercing the depths of life,
So that no wonder waits him; nor below
Can love, or sorrow, fame, ambition, strife,
Cut to his heart again with the keen knife
Of silent, sharp endurance: he can tell
Why thought seeks refuge in lone caves, yet rife
With airy images, and shapes which dwell
Still unimpair'd, though old, in the soul's haunted cell.

VI

'Tis to create, and in creating live
A being more intense, that we endow
With form our fancy, gaining as we give
The life we image, even as I do now.
What am I? Nothing: but not so art thou,
Soul of my thought! with whom I traverse earth,
Invisible but gazing, as I glow
Mix'd with thy spirit, blended with thy birth,
And feeling still with thee in my crush'd feelings' dearth.

VII

Yet must I think less wildly:—I *have* thought
Too long and darkly, till my brain became,
In its own eddy boiling and o'erwrought,
A whirling gulf of phantasy and flame:
And thus, untaught in youth my heart to tame,
My springs of life were poison'd. 'Tis too late!
Yet am I changed; though still enough the same
In strength to bear what time can not abate,
And feed on bitter fruits without accusing Fate.

Childe Harold's Pilgrimage, III

VIII

Something too much of this:—but now 'tis past
And the spell closes with its silent seal.
Long absent HAROLD re-appears at last;
He of the breast which fain no more would feel,
Wrung with the wounds which kill not, but ne'er heal;
Yet Time, who changes all, had alter'd him
In soul and aspect as in age: years steal   70
Fire from the mind as vigour from the limb;
And life's enchanted cup but sparkles near the brim.

IX

His had been quaff'd too quickly, and he found
The dregs were wormwood: but he fill'd again,
And from a purer fount, on holier ground,
And deemed its spring perpetual; but in vain!
Still round him clung invisibly a chain
Which gall'd for ever, fettering though unseen,
And heavy though it clank'd not; worn with pain,
Which pined although it spoke not, and grew keen,   80
Entering with every step he took through many a scene.

X

Secure in guarded coldness, he had mix'd
Again in fancied safety with his kind,
And deem'd his spirit now so firmly fix'd
And sheath'd with an invulnerable mind,
That, if no joy, no sorrow lurk'd behind;
And he, as one, might 'midst the many stand
Unheeded, searching through the crowd to find
Fit speculation; such as in strange land
He foun' in wonder-works of God and Nature's hand.   90

XI

But who can view the ripen'd rose, nor seek
To wear it? who can curiously behold
The smoothness and the sheen of beauty's cheek,
Nor feel the heart can never all grow old?
Who can contemplate Fame through clouds unfold
The star which rises o'er her steep, nor climb?
Harold, once more within the vortex, roll'd
On with the giddy circle, chasing Time,
Yet with a nobler aim than in his youth's fond prime.

Childe Harold's Pilgrimage, III

XII

But soon he knew himself the most unfit
Of men to herd with Man; with whom he held
Little in common; untaught to submit
His thoughts to others, though his soul was quell'd
In youth by his own thoughts; still uncompell'd,
He would not yield dominion of his mind
To spirits against whom his own rebell'd;
Proud though in desolation; which could find
A life within itself, to breathe without mankind.

XIII

Where rose the mountains, there to him were friends;
Where roll'd the ocean, thereon was his home;
Where a blue sky, and glowing clime, extends,
He had the passion and the power to roam;
The desert, forest, cavern, breaker's foam,
Were unto him companionship; they spake
A mutual language, clearer than the tome
Of his land's tongue, which he would oft forsake
For Nature's pages glass'd by sunbeams on the lake.

XIV

Like the Chaldean, he could watch the stars,
Till he had peopled them with beings bright
As their own beams; and earth, and earth-born jars,
And human frailties, were forgotten quite:
Could he have kept his spirit to that flight
He had been happy; but this clay will sink
Its spark immortal, envying it the light
To which it mounts, as if to break the link
That keeps us from yon heaven which woos us to its brink.

XV

But in Man's dwellings he became a thing
Restless and worn, and stern and wearisome,
Droop'd as a wild-born falcon with clipt wing,
To whom the boundless air alone were home:
Then came his fit again, which to o'ercome,
As eagerly the barr'd-up bird will beat
His breast and beak against his wiry dome
Till the blood tinge his plumage, so the heat
Of his impeded soul would through his bosom eat.

XVI

Self-exiled Harold wanders forth again,
With nought of hope left, but with less of gloom;
The very knowledge that he lived in vain,
That all was over on this side the tomb,
Had made Despair a smilingness assume,   140
Which, though 'twere wild,—as on the plunder'd wreck,
When mariners would madly meet their doom
With draughts intemperate on the sinking deck,—
Did yet inspire a cheer, which he forbore to check.

XVII

Stop!—for thy tread is on an Empire's dust!
An Earthquake's spoil is sepulchred below!
Is the spot mark'd with no colossal bust?
Nor column trophied for triumphal show?
None; but the moral's truth tells simpler so,
As the ground was before, thus let it be;—   150
How that red rain hath made the harvest grow!
And is this all the world has gained by thee,
Thou first and last of fields! king-making Victory?

XVIII

And Harold stands upon this place of skulls,
The grave of France, the deadly Waterloo;
How in an hour the power which gave annuls
Its gifts, transferring fame as fleeting too!
In 'pride of place' here last the eagle flew,
Then tore with bloody talon the rent plain,
Pierced by the shaft of banded nations through;   160
Ambition's life and labours all were vain;
He wears the shatter'd links of the world's broken chain.

XIX

Fit retribution! Gaul may champ the bit
And foam in fetters;—but is Earth more free?
Did nations combat to make *One* submit;
Or league to teach all kings true sovereignty?
What! shall reviving Thraldom again be
The patch'd-up idol of enlighten'd days?
Shall we, who struck the Lion down, shall we
Pay the Wolf homage? proffering lowly gaze   170
And servile knees to thrones? No; *prove* before ye praise!

Childe Harold's Pilgrimage, III

XX

If not, o'er one fallen despot boast no more!
In vain fair cheeks were furrow'd with hot tears
For Europe's flowers long rooted up before
The trampler of her vineyards; in vain years
Of death, depopulation, bondage, fears,
Have all been borne, and broken by the accord
Of roused-up millions: all that most endears
Glory, is when the myrtle wreathes a sword
Such as Harmodius drew on Athens' tyrant lord.   *180*

XXI

There was a sound of revelry by night,
And Belgium's capital had gather'd then
Her Beauty and her Chivalry, and bright
The lamps shone o'er fair women and brave men;
A thousand hearts beat happily; and when
Music arose with its voluptuous swell,
Soft eyes look'd love to eyes which spake again,
And all went merry as a marriage-bell;
But hush! hark! a deep sound strikes like a rising knell!

XXII

Did ye not hear it?—No; 'twas but the wind   *190*
Or the car rattling o'er the stony street;
On with the dance! let joy be unconfined;
No sleep till morn, when Youth and Pleasure meet
To chase the glowing Hours with flying feet—
But, hark!—that heavy sound breaks in once more
As if the clouds its echo would repeat;
And nearer, clearer, deadlier than before!
Arm! Arm! it is—it is—the cannon's opening roar!

XXIII

Within a window'd niche of that high hall
Sate Brunswick's fated chieftain; he did hear   *200*
That sound the first amidst the festival,
And caught its tone with Death's prophetic ear;
And when they smiled because he deem'd it near,
His heart more truly knew that peal too well
Which stretch'd his father on a bloody bier,
And roused the vengeance blood alone could quell:
He rush'd into the field, and, foremost fighting, fell.

Childe Harold's Pilgrimage, III

XXIV

Ah! then and there was hurrying to and fro,
And gathering tears, and tremblings of distress,
And cheeks all pale, which but an hour ago   210
Blush'd at the praise of their own loveliness;
And there were sudden partings, such as press
The life from out young hearts, and choking sighs
Which ne'er might be repeated; who could guess
If ever more should meet those mutual eyes,
Since upon night so sweet such awful morn could rise!

XXV

And there was mounting in hot haste: the steed,
The mustering squadron, and the clattering car,
Went pouring forward with impetuous speed,
And swiftly forming in the ranks of war;   220
And the deep thunder peal on peal afar;
And near, the beat of the alarming drum
Roused up the soldier ere the morning star;
While throng'd the citizens with terror dumb,
Or whispering, with white lips—'The foe! they come! they come!'

XXVI

And wild and high the 'Cameron's gathering' rose!
The war-note of Lochiel, which Albyn's hills
Have heard, and heard, too, have her Saxon foes:—
How in the noon of night that pibroch thrills,
Savage and shrill! But with the breath which fills   230
Their mountain-pipe, so fill the mountaineers
With the fierce native daring which instils
The stirring memory of a thousand years,
And Evan's, Donald's fame rings in each clansman's ears!

XXVII

And Ardennes waves above them her green leaves,
Dewy with nature's tear-drops, as they pass,
Grieving, if aught inanimate e'er grieves,
Over the unreturning brave,—alas!
Ere evening to be trodden like the grass
Which now beneath them, but above shall grow   240
In its next verdure, when this fiery mass
Of living valour, rolling on the foe
And burning with high hope shall moulder cold and low.

XXVIII

Last noon beheld them full of lusty life,
Last eve in Beauty's circle proudly gay,
The midnight brought the signal-sound of strife,
The morn the marshalling in arms,—the day
Battle's magnificently stern array!
The thunder-clouds close o'er it, which when rent
The earth is cover'd thick with other clay,   *250*
Which her own clay shall cover, heap'd and pent,
Rider and horse,—friend, foe,—in one red burial blent!

XXIX

Their praise is hymn'd by loftier harps than mine;
Yet one I would select from that proud throng,
Partly because they blend me with his line,
And partly that I did his sire some wrong,
And partly that bright names will hallow song;
And his was of the bravest, and when shower'd
The death-bolts deadliest the thinn'd files along,
Even where the thickest of war's tempest lower'd,   *260*
They reach'd no nobler breast than thine, young, gallant Howard!

XXX

There have been tears and breaking hearts for thee,
And mine were nothing, had I such to give;
But when I stood beneath the fresh green tree,
Which living waves where thou didst cease to live,
And saw around me the wide field revive
With fruits and fertile promise, and the Spring
Come forth her work of gladness to contrive,
With all her reckless birds upon the wing,
I turn'd from all she brought to those she could not bring.   *270*

XXXI

I turn'd to thee, to thousands, of whom each
And one as all a ghastly gap did make
In his own kind and kindred, whom to teach
Forgetfulness were mercy for their sake;
The Archangel's trump, not Glory's, must awake
Those whom they thirst for; though the sound of Fame
May for a moment soothe, it cannot slake
The fever of vain longing, and the name
So honour'd but assumes a stronger, bitterer claim.

XXXII

They mourn, but smile at length; and, smiling, mourn:
The tree will wither long before it fall;
The hull drives on, though mast and sail be torn;
The roof-tree sinks, but moulders on the hall
In massy hoariness; the ruin'd wall
Stands when its wind-worn battlements are gone;
The bars survive the captive they enthral;
The day drags through though storms keep out the sun;
And thus the heart will break, yet brokenly live on:

XXXIII

Even as a broken mirror, which the glass
In every fragment multiplies; and makes
A thousand images of one that was,
The same, and still the more, the more it breaks;
And thus the heart will do which not forsakes,
Living in shatter'd guise, and still, and cold,
And bloodless, with its sleepless sorrow aches,
Yet withers on till all without is old,
Showing no visible sign, for such things are untold.

XXXIV

There is a very life in our despair,
Vitality of poison,—a quick root
Which feeds these deadly branches; for it were
As nothing did we die; but Life will suit
Itself to Sorrow's most detested fruit,
Like to the apples on the Dead Sea's shore,
All ashes to the taste: Did man compute
Existence by enjoyment, and count o'er
Such hours 'gainst years of life,—say, would he name threescore?

XXXV

The Psalmist number'd out the years of man:
They are enough; and if thy tale be *true*,
Thou, who didst grudge him even that fleeting span,
More than enough, thou fatal Waterloo!
Millions of tongues record thee, and anew
Their children's lips shall echo them, and say—
'Here, where the sword united nations drew,
Our countrymen were warring on that day!'
And this is much, and all which will not pass away.

Childe Harold's Pilgrimage, III

XXXVI

There sunk the greatest, nor the worst of men,
Whose spirit antithetically mixt
One moment of the mightiest, and again
On little objects with like firmness fixt,
Extreme in all things! hadst thou been betwixt, *320*
Thy throne had still been thine, or never been;
For daring made thy rise as fall: thou seek'st
Even now to re-assume the imperial mien,
And shake again the world, the Thunderer of the scene!

XXXVII

Conqueror and captive of the earth art thou!
She trembles at thee still, and thy wild name
Was ne'er more bruited in men's minds than now
That thou art nothing, save the jest of Fame,
Who woo'd thee once, thy vassal, and became
The flatterer of thy fierceness, till thou wert *330*
A god unto thyself; nor less the same
To the astounded kingdoms all inert,
Who deem'd thee for a time whate'er thou didst assert.

XXXVIII

Oh, more or less than man—in high or low,
Battling with nations, flying from the field;
Now making monarchs' necks thy footstool, now
More than thy meanest soldier taught to yield:
An empire thou couldst crush, command, rebuild,
But govern not thy pettiest passion, nor,
However deeply in men's spirits skill'd, *340*
Look through thine own, nor curb the lust of war,
Nor learn that tempted Fate will leave the loftiest star.

XXXIX

Yet well thy soul hath brook'd the turning tide
With that untaught innate philosophy,
Which, be it wisdom, coldness, or deep pride,
Is gall and wormwood to an enemy.
When the whole host of hatred stood hard by,
To watch and mock thee shrinking, thou hast smiled
With a sedate and all-enduring eye;—
When Fortune fled her spoil'd and favourite child, *350*
He stood unbow'd beneath the ills upon him piled.

XL

Sager than in thy fortunes: for in them
Ambition steel'd thee on too far to show
That just habitual scorn, which could contemn
Men and their thoughts; 'twas wise to feel, not so
To wear it ever on thy lip and brow,
And spurn the instruments thou wert to use
Till they were turn'd unto thine overthrow;
'Tis but a worthless world to win or lose;
So hath it proved to thee, and all such lot who choose.   360

XLI

If, like a tower upon a headlong rock,
Thou hadst been made to stand or fall alone,
Such scorn of man had help'd to brave the shock;
But men's thoughts were the steps which paved thy throne,
Their admiration thy best weapon shone;
The part of Philip's son was thine, not then
(Unless aside thy purple had been thrown)
Like stern Diogenes to mock at men;
For sceptred cynics earth were far too wide a den.

XLII

But quiet to quick bosoms is a hell,   370
And *there* hath been thy bane; there is a fire
And motion of the soul which will not dwell
In its own narrow being, but aspire
Beyond the fitting medium of desire;
And, but once kindled, quenchless evermore,
Preys upon high adventure, nor can tire
Of aught but rest; a fever at the core,
Fatal to him who bears, to all who ever bore.

XLIII

This makes the madmen who have made men mad
By their contagion; Conquerors and Kings,   380
Founders of sects and systems, to whom add
Sophists, Bards, Statesmen, all unquiet things
Which stir too strongly the soul's secret springs,
And are themselves the fools to those they fool;
Envied, yet how unenviable! what stings
Are theirs!   One breast laid open were a school
Which would unteach mankind the lust to shine or rule:

XLIV

Their breath is agitation, and their life
A storm whereon they ride, to sink at last,
And yet so nursed and bigoted to strife, 390
That should their days, surviving perils past,
Melt to calm twilight, they feel overcast
With sorrow and supineness, and so die;
Even as a flame unfed, which runs to waste
With its own flickering, or a sword laid by,
Which eats into itself, and rusts ingloriously.

XLV

He who ascends to mountain-tops, shall find
The loftiest peaks most wrapt in clouds and snow.
He who surpasses or subdues mankind,
Must look down on the hate of those below. 400
Though high *above* the sun of glory glow,
And far *beneath* the earth and ocean spread,
Round him are icy rocks, and loudly blow
Contending tempests on his naked head,
And thus reward the toils which to those summits led.

XLVI

Away with these! true Wisdom's world will be
Within its own creation, or in thine,
Maternal Nature! for who teems like thee,
Thus on the banks of thy majestic Rhine?
There Harold gazes on a work divine, 410
A blending of all beauties; streams and dells,
Fruit, foliage, crag, wood, cornfield, mountain, vine,
And chiefless castles breathing stern farewells
From gray but leafy walls, where Ruin greenly dwells.

XLVII

And there they stand, as stands a lofty mind,
Worn, but unstooping to the baser crowd,
All tenantless, save to the crannying wind,
Or holding dark communion with the cloud.
There was a day when they were young and proud,
Banners on high, and battles pass'd below; 420
But they who fought are in a bloody shroud,
And those which waved are shredless dust ere now,
And the bleak battlements shall bear no future blow.

Childe Harold's Pilgrimage, III

XLVIII

Beneath these battlements, within those walls,
Power dwelt amidst her passions; in proud state
Each robber chief upheld his armed halls,
Doing his evil will, nor less elate
Than mightier heroes of a longer date.
What want these outlaws conquerors should have?
But History's purchased page to call them great? *430*
A wider space, an ornamented grave?
Their hopes were not less warm, their souls were full as brave.

XLIX

In their baronial feuds and single fields,
What deeds of prowess unrecorded died!
And Love, which lent a blazon to their shields,
With emblems well devised by amorous pride,
Through all the mail of iron hearts would glide;
But still their flame was fierceness, and drew on
Keen contest and destruction near allied,
And many a tower for some fair mischief won, *440*
Saw the discolour'd Rhine beneath its ruin run.

L

But thou, exulting and abounding river!
Making thy waves a blessing as they flow
Through banks whose beauty would endure for ever
Could man but leave thy bright creation so,
Nor its fair promise from the surface mow
With the sharp scythe of conflict,—then to see
Thy valley of sweet waters, were to know
Earth paved like Heaven; and to seem such to me,
Even now what wants thy stream?—that it should Lethe be. *450*

LI

A thousand battles have assail'd thy banks,
But these and half their fame have pass'd away,
And Slaughter heap'd on high his weltering ranks;
Their very graves are gone, and what are they?
Thy tide wash'd down the blood of yesterday,
And all was stainless, and on thy clear stream
Glass'd with its dancing light the sunny ray;
But o'er the blacken'd memory's blighting dream
Thy waves would vainly roll, all sweeping as they seem.

LII

Thus Harold inly said, and pass'd along,
Yet not insensibly to all which here
Awoke the jocund birds to early song
In glens which might have made even exile dear:
Though on his brow were graven lines austere,
And tranquil sternness which had ta'en the place
Of feelings fierier far but less severe,
Joy was not always absent from his face,
But o'er it in such scenes would steal with transient trace.

LIII

Nor was all love shut from him, though his days
Of passion had consumed themselves to dust.
It is in vain that we would coldly gaze
On such as smile upon us; the heart must
Leap kindly back to kindness, though disgust
Hath wean'd it from all worldlings: thus he felt,
For there was soft remembrance, and sweet trust
In one fond breast, to which his own would melt,
And in its tenderer hour on that his bosom dwelt.

LIV

And he had learn'd to love,—I know not why,
For this in such as him seems strange of mood,—
The helpless looks of blooming infancy,
Even in its earliest nurture; what subdued,
To change like this, a mind so far imbued
With scorn of man, it little boots to know;
But thus it was; and though in solitude
Small power the nipp'd affections have to grow,
In him this glow'd when all beside had ceased to glow.

LV

And there was one soft breast, as hath been said,
Which unto his was bound by stronger ties
Than the church links withal; and, though unwed,
That love was pure, and, far above disguise,
Had stood the test of mortal enmities
Still undivided, and cemented more
By peril, dreaded most in female eyes;
But this was firm, and from a foreign shore
Well to that heart might his these absent greetings pour!

Childe Harold's Pilgrimage, III

1

The castled crag of Drachenfels
Frowns o'er the wide and winding Rhine,
Whose breast of waters broadly swells
Between the banks which bear the vine,
And hills all rich with blossom'd trees,   *500*
And fields which promise corn and wine,
And scatter'd cities crowning these,
Whose far white walls along them shine,
Have strew'd a scene, which I should see
With double joy wert *thou* with me.

2

And peasant girls, with deep blue eyes,
And hands which offer early flowers,
Walk smiling o'er this paradise;
Above, the frequent feudal towers
Through green leaves lift their walls of gray,   *510*
And many a rock which steeply lowers,
And noble arch in proud decay,
Look o'er this vale of vintage-bowers;
But one thing want these banks of Rhine,—
Thy gentle hand to clasp in mine!

3

I send the lilies given to me;
Though long before thy hand they touch,
I know that they must wither'd be,
But yet reject them not as such;
For I have cherish'd them as dear,   *520*
Because they yet may meet thine eye,
And guide thy soul to mine even here,
When thou behold'st them drooping nigh,
And know'st them gather'd by the Rhine,
And offer'd from my heart to thine!

4

The river nobly foams and flows,
The charm of this enchanted ground,
And all its thousand turns disclose
Some fresher beauty varying round:
The haughtiest breast its wish might bound   *530*
Through life to dwell delighted here;
Nor could on earth a spot be found
To nature and to me so dear,
Could thy dear eyes in following mine
Still sweeten more these banks of Rhine!

LVI

By Coblentz, on a rise of gentle ground,
There is a small and simple pyramid,
Crowning the summit of the verdant mound;
Beneath its base are heroes' ashes hid,
Our enemy's—but let not that forbid
Honour to Marceau! o'er whose early tomb
Tears, big tears, gush'd from the rough soldier's lid,
Lamenting and yet envying such a doom,
Falling for France, whose rights he battled to resume.

LVII

Brief, brave, and glorious was his young career,—
His mourners were two hosts, his friends and foes;
And fitly may the stranger lingering here
Pray for his gallant spirit's bright repose;
For he was Freedom's champion, one of those,
The few in number, who had not o'erstept
The charter to chastise which she bestows
On such as wield her weapons; he had kept
The whiteness of his soul, and thus men o'er him wept.

LVIII

Here Ehrenbreitstein, with her shatter'd wall
Black with the miner's blast, upon her height
Yet shows of what she was, when shell and ball
Rebounding idly on her strength did light:
A tower of victory! from whence the flight
Of baffled foes was watch'd along the plain:
But Peace destroy'd what War could never blight
And laid those proud roofs bare to Summer's rain—
On which the iron shower for years had pour'd in vain.

LIX

Adieu to thee, fair Rhine! How long delighted
The stranger fain would linger on his way!
Thine is a scene alike where souls united
Or lonely contemplation thus might stray;
And could the ceaseless vultures cease to prey
On self-condemning bosoms, it were here,
Where Nature, nor too sombre nor too gay,
Wild but not rude, awful yet not austere,
Is to the mellow Earth as Autumn to the year.

Childe Harold's Pilgrimage, III

LX

Adieu to thee again! a vain adieu!
There can be no farewell to scene like thine;
The mind is colour'd by thy every hue;
And if reluctantly the eyes resign
Their cherish'd gaze upon thee, lovely Rhine!
'Tis with the thankful glance of parting praise;
More mighty spots may rise—more glaring shine,
But none unite in one attaching maze
The brilliant, fair, and soft,—the glories of old days,   *580*

LXI

The negligently grand, the fruitful bloom
Of coming ripeness, the white city's sheen,
The rolling stream, the precipice's gloom,
The forest's growth, and Gothic walls between,
The wild rocks shaped as they had turrets been
In mockery of man's art; and these withal
A race of faces happy as the scene,
Whose fertile bounties here extend to all,
Still springing o'er thy banks, though Empires near them fall.

LXII

But these recede.   Above me are the Alps,   *590*
The palaces of Nature, whose vast walls
Have pinnacled in clouds their snowy scalps,
And throned Eternity in icy halls
Of cold sublimity, where forms and falls
The avalanche—the thunderbolt of snow!
All that expands the spirit, yet appals,
Gather around these summits, as to show
How Earth may pierce to Heaven, yet leave vain man below.

LXIII

But ere these matchless heights I dare to scan,
There is a spot should not be pass'd in vain,—   *600*
Morat! the proud, the patriot field! where man
May gaze on ghastly trophies of the slain,
Nor blush for those who conquer'd on that plain;
Here Burgundy bequeath'd his tombless host,
A bony heap, through ages to remain,
Themselves their monument;—the Stygian coast
Unsepulchred they roam'd, and shriek'd each wandering ghost.

LXIV

While Waterloo with Cannae's carnage vies,
Morat and Marathon twin names shall stand;
They were true Glory's stainless victories,
Won by the unambitious heart and hand
Of a proud, brotherly, and civic band,
All unbought champions in no princely cause
Of vice-entail'd Corruption; they no land
Doom'd to bewail the blasphemy of laws
Making kings' rights divine, by some Draconic clause.

LXV

By a lone wall a lonelier column rears
A gray and grief-worn aspect of old days;
'Tis the last remnant of the wreck of years,
And looks as with the wild bewilder'd gaze
Of one to stone converted by amaze,
Yet still with consciousness; and there it stands
Making a marvel that it not decays,
When the coeval pride of human hands,
Levell'd Aventicum, hath strew'd her subject lands.

LXVI

And there—oh! sweet and sacred be the name!—
Julia—the daughter, the devoted—gave
Her youth to Heaven; her heart, beneath a claim
Nearest to Heaven's, broke o'er a father's grave.
Justice is sworn 'gainst tears, and hers would crave
The life she lived in; but the judge was just,
And then she died on him she could not save.
Their tomb was simple, and without a bust,
And held within their urn one mind, one heart, one dust.

LXVII

But these are deeds which should not pass away,
And names that must not wither, though the earth
Forgets her empires with a just decay,
The enslavers and the enslaved, their death and birth;
The high, the mountain-majesty of worth
Should be, and shall, survivor of its woe,
And from its immortality look forth
In the sun's face, like yonder Alpine snow,
Imperishably pure beyond all things below.

Childe Harold's Pilgrimage, III

LXVIII

Lake Leman woos me with its crystal face,
The mirror where the stars and mountains view
The stillness of their aspect in each trace
Its clear depth yields of their far height and hue:
There is too much of man here, to look through
With a fit mind the might which I behold;
But soon in me shall Loneliness renew   650
Thoughts hid, but not less cherish'd than of old,
Ere mingling with the herd had penn'd me in their fold.

LXIX

To fly from, need not be to hate, mankind:
All are not fit with them to stir and toil,
Nor is it discontent to keep the mind
Deep in its fountain, lest it overboil
In the hot throng, where we become the spoil
Of our infection, till too late and long
We may deplore and struggle with the coil,
In wretched interchange of wrong for wrong   660
Midst a contentious world, striving where none are strong.

LXX

There, in a moment, we may plunge our years
In fatal penitence, and in the blight
Of our own soul turn all our blood to tears,
And colour things to come with hues of Night;
The race of life becomes a hopeless flight
To those that walk in darkness: on the sea,
The boldest steer but where their ports invite,
But there are wanderers o'er Eternity
Whose bark drives on and on, and anchor'd ne'er shall be.   670

LXXI

Is it not better, then, to be alone,
And love Earth only for its earthly sake?
By the blue rushing of the arrowy Rhone,
Or the pure bosom of its nursing lake,
Which feeds it as a mother who doth make
A fair but froward infant her own care,
Kissing its cries away as these awake;—
Is it not better thus our lives to wear,
Than join the crushing crowd, doom'd to inflict or bear?

Childe Harold's Pilgrimage, III

LXXII

I live not in myself, but I become
Portion of that around me; and to me
High mountains are a feeling, but the hum
Of human cities torture: I can see
Nothing to loathe in nature, save to be
A link reluctant in a fleshly chain,
Class'd among creatures, when the soul can flee,
And with the sky, the peak, the heaving plain
Of ocean, or the stars, mingle, and not in vain.

LXXIII

And thus I am absorb'd, and this is life:
I look upon the peopled desert past,
As on a place of agony and strife,
Where, for some sin, to sorrow I was cast,
To act and suffer, but remount at last
With a fresh pinion; which I feel to spring,
Though young, yet waxing vigorous, as the blast
Which it would cope with, on delighted wing,
Spurning the clay-cold bonds which round our being cling.

LXXIV

And when, at length, the mind shall be all free
From what it hates in this degraded form,
Reft of its carnal life, save what shall be
Existent happier in the fly and worm,—
When elements to elements conform,
And dust is as it should be, shall I not
Feel all I see, less dazzling, but more warm?
The bodiless thought? the Spirit of each spot?
Of which, even now, I share at times the immortal lot?

LXXV

Are not the mountains, waves, and skies, a part
Of me and of my soul, as I of them?
Is not the love of these deep in my heart
With a pure passion? should I not contemn
All objects, if compared with these? and stem
A tide of suffering, rather than forego
Such feelings for the hard and worldly phlegm
Of those whose eyes are only turn'd below,
Gazing upon the ground, with thoughts which dare not glow?

LXXVI

But this is not my theme; and I return
To that which is immediate, and require
Those who find contemplation in the urn,
To look on One, whose dust was once all fire,
A native of the land where I respire   *720*
The clear air for a while—a passing guest,
Where he became a being,—whose desire
Was to be glorious; 'twas a foolish quest,
The which to gain and keep, he sacrificed all rest.

LXXVII

Here the self-torturing sophist, wild Rousseau,
The apostle of affliction, he who threw
Enchantment over passion, and from woe
Wrung overwhelming eloquence, first drew
The breath which made him wretched; yet he knew
How to make madness beautiful, and cast   *730*
O'er erring deeds and thoughts a heavenly hue
Of words, like sunbeams, dazzling as they past
The eyes, which o'er them shed tears feelingly and fast.

LXXVIII

His love was passion's essence—as a tree
On fire by lightning; with ethereal flame
Kindled he was, and blasted; for to be
Thus, and enamour'd, were in him the same.
But his was not the love of living dame,
Nor of the dead who rise upon our dreams,
But of ideal beauty, which became   *740*
In him existence, and o'erflowing teems
Along his burning page, distemper'd though it seems.

LXXIX

This breathed itself to life in Julie, *this*
Invested her with all that's wild and sweet;
This hallow'd, too, the memorable kiss
Which every morn his fever'd lip would greet,
From hers, who but with friendship his would meet;
But to that gentle touch, through brain and breast
Flash'd the thrill'd spirit's love-devouring heat;
In that absorbing sigh perchance more blest   *750*
Than vulgar minds may be with all they seek possest.

Childe Harold's Pilgrimage, III

LXXX

His life was one long war with self-sought foes,
Or friends by him self-banish'd; for his mind
Had grown Suspicion's sanctuary, and chose,
For its own cruel sacrifice, the kind,
'Gainst whom he raged with fury strange and blind.
But he was phrensied,—wherefore, who may know?
Since cause might be which skill could never find;
But he was phrensied by disease or woe,
To that worst pitch of all, which wears a reasoning show.   760

LXXXI

For then he was inspired, and from him came,
As from the Pythian's mystic cave of yore,
Those oracles which set the world in flame,
Nor ceased to burn till kingdoms were no more:
Did he not this for France? which lay before
Bow'd to the inborn tyranny of years?
Broken and trembling to the yoke she bore,
Till by the voice of him and his compeers
Roused up to too much wrath, which follows o'ergrown fears?

LXXXII

They made themselves a fearful monument!   770
The wreck of old opinions—things which grew,
Breathed from the birth of time: the veil they rent,
And what behind it lay all earth shall view.
But good with ill they also overthrew,
Leaving but ruins, wherewith to rebuild
Upon the same foundation, and renew
Dungeons and thrones, which the same hour refill'd,
As heretofore, because ambition was self-will'd.

LXXXIII

But this will not endure, nor be endured!
Mankind have felt their strength, and made it felt.   780
They might have used it better, but, allured
By their new vigour, sternly have they dealt
On one another; pity ceased to melt
With her once natural charities. But they,
Who in oppression's darkness caved had dwelt,
They were not eagles, nourish'd with the day;
What marvel then, at times, if they mistook their prey?

LXXXIV

What deep wounds ever closed without a scar?
The heart's bleed longest, and but heal to wear
That which disfigures it; and they who war
With their own hopes, and have been vanquish'd, bear
Silence, but not submission: in his lair
Fix'd Passion holds his breath, until the hour
Which shall atone for years; none need despair:
It came, it cometh, and will come,—the power
To punish or forgive—in *one* we shall be slower.

LXXXV

Clear, placid Leman! thy contrasted lake,
With the wild world I dwelt in, is a thing
Which warns me, with its stillness, to forsake
Earth's troubled waters for a purer spring.
This quiet sail is as a noiseless wing
To waft me from distraction; once I loved
Torn ocean's roar, but thy soft murmuring
Sounds sweet as if a Sister's voice reproved,
That I with stern delights should e'er have been so moved.

LXXXVI

It is the hush of night, and all between
Thy margin and the mountains, dusk, yet clear,
Mellow'd and mingling, yet distinctly seen,
Save darken'd Jura, whose capt heights appear
Precipitously steep; and drawing near,
There breathes a living fragrance from the shore,
Of flowers yet fresh with childhood; on the ear
Drops the light drip of the suspended oar,
Or chirps the grasshopper one good-night carol more;

LXXXVII

He is an evening reveller, who makes
His life an infancy, and sings his fill;
At intervals, some bird from out the brakes
Starts into voice a moment, then is still.
There seems a floating whisper on the hill,
But that is fancy, for the starlight dews
All silently their tears of love instil,
Weeping themselves away, till they infuse
Deep into Nature's breast the spirit of her hues.

Childe Harold's Pilgrimage, III

LXXXVIII

Ye stars! which are the poetry of heaven
If in your bright leaves we would read the fate
Of men and empires,—'tis to be forgiven,
That in our aspirations to be great,
Our destinies o'erleap their mortal state,
And claim a kindred with you; for ye are
A beauty and a mystery, and create *830*
In us such love and reverence from afar,
That fortune, fame, power, life, have named themselves a star

LXXXIX

All heaven and earth are still—though not in sleep,
But breathless, as we grow when feeling most;
And silent, as we stand in thoughts too deep:—
All heaven and earth are still: From the high host
Of stars, to the lull'd lake and mountain-coast,
All is concenter'd in a life intense,
Where not a beam, nor air, nor leaf is lost,
But hath a part of being, and a sense *840*
Of that which is of all Creator and defence.

XC

Then stirs the feeling infinite, so felt
In solitude, where we are *least* alone;
A truth, which through our being then doth melt
And purifies from self: it is a tone,
The soul and source of music, which makes known
Eternal harmony, and sheds a charm,
Like to the fabled Cytherea's zone,
Binding all things with beauty;—'twould disarm
The spectre Death, had he substantial power to harm. *850*

XCI

Not vainly did the early Persian make
His altar the high places and the peak
Of earth-o'ergazing mountains, and thus take
A fit and unwall'd temple, there to seek
The Spirit in whose honour shrines are weak,
Uprear'd of human hands. Come, and compare
Columns and idol-dwellings, Goth or Greek,
With Nature's realms of worship, earth and air,
Nor fix on fond abodes to circumscribe thy pray'r!

XCII

Thy sky is changed!—and such a change!   Oh night,   860
And storm, and darkness, ye are wondrous strong,
Yet lovely in your strength, as is the light
Of a dark eye in woman!   Far along,
From peak to peak, the rattling crags among
Leaps the live thunder!   Not from one lone cloud,
But every mountain now hath found a tongue,
And Jura answers, through her misty shroud,
Back to the joyous Alps, who call to her aloud!

XCIII

And this is in the night:—Most glorious night!
Thou wert not sent for slumber! let me be   870
A sharer in thy fierce and far delight,—
A portion of the tempest and of thee!
How the lit lake shines, a phosphoric sea,
And the big rain comes dancing to the earth!
And now again 'tis black,—and now, the glee
Of the loud hills shakes with its mountain-mirth,
As if they did rejoice o'er a young earthquake's birth.

XCIV

Now, where the swift Rhone cleaves his way between
Heights which appear as lovers who have parted
In hate, whose mining depths so intervene,   880
That they can meet no more, though broken-hearted;
Though in their souls, which thus each other thwarted,
Love was the very root of the fond rage
Which blighted their life's bloom, and then departed:
Itself expired, but leaving them an age
Of years all winters,—war within themselves to wage.

XCV

Now, where the quick Rhone thus hath cleft his way,
The mightiest of the storms hath ta'en his stand:
For here, not one, but many, make their play,
And fling their thunder-bolts from hand to hand,   890
Flashing and cast around: of all the band,
The brightest through these parted hills hath fork'd
His lightnings,—as if he did understand,
That in such gaps as desolation work'd,
There the hot shaft should blast whatever therein lurk'd.

Childe Harold's Pilgrimage, III

XCVI

Sky, mountains, river, winds, lake, lightnings! ye!
With night, and clouds, and thunder, and a soul
To make these felt and feeling, well may be
Things that have made me watchful; the far roll
Of your departing voices, is the knoll
Of what in me is sleepless,—if I rest.
But where of ye, oh tempests! is the goal?
Are ye like those within the human breast?
Or do ye find, at length, like eagles, some high nest?

XCVII

Could I embody and unbosom now
That which is most within me,—could I wreak
My thoughts upon expression, and thus throw
Soul, heart, mind, passions, feelings, strong or weak,
All that I would have sought, and all I seek,
Bear, know, feel, and yet breathe—into *one* word,
And that one word were Lightning, I would speak;
But as it is, I live and die unheard,
With a most voiceless thought, sheathing it as a sword.

XCVIII

The morn is up again, the dewy morn,
With breath all incense, and with cheek all bloom,
Laughing the clouds away with playful scorn,
And living as if earth contain'd no tomb—
And glowing into day: we may resume
The march of our existence: and thus I,
Still on thy shores, fair Leman! may find room
And food for meditation, nor pass by
Much, that may give us pause, if ponder'd fittingly.

XCIX

Clarens! sweet Clarens, birthplace of deep Love,
Thine air is the young breath of passionate thought,
Thy trees take root in Love; the snows above
The very Glaciers have his colours caught,
And sunset into rose-hues sees them wrought
By rays which sleep there lovingly: the rocks,
The permanent crags, tell here of Love, who sought
In them a refuge from the worldly shocks,
Which stir and sting the soul with hope that woos, then mocks.

Childe Harold's Pilgrimage, III

C

Clarens! by heavenly feet thy paths are trod,—
Undying Love's, who here ascends a throne
To which the steps are mountains; where the god
Is a pervading life and light,—so shown
Not on those summits solely, nor alone
In the still cave and forest; o'er the flower
His eye is sparkling, and his breath hath blown,
His soft and summer breath, whose tender power
Passes the strength of storms in their most desolate hour.   940

CI

All things are here of *him*; from the black pines,
Which are his shade on high, and the loud roar
Of torrents, where he listeneth, to the vines
Which slope his green path downward to the shore,
Where the bow'd waters meet him, and adore,
Kissing his feet with murmurs; and the wood,
The covert of old trees, with trunks all hoar,
But light leaves, young as joy, stands where it stood,
Offering to him, and his, a populous solitude.

CII

A populous solitude of bees and birds,   950
And fairy-formed and many-colour'd things,
Who worship him with notes more sweet than words,
And innocently open their glad wings,
Fearless and full of life; the gush of springs,
And fall of lofty fountains, and the bend
Of stirring branches, and the bud which brings
The swiftest thought of beauty, here extend,
Mingling, and made by Love, unto one mighty end.

CIII

He who hath loved not, here would learn that lore,
And make his heart a spirit; he who knows   960
That tender mystery, will love the more,
For this is Love's recess, where vain men's woes,
And the world's waste, have driven him far from those,
For 'tis his nature to advance or die;
He stands not still, but or decays, or grows
Into a boundless blessing, which may vie
With the immortal lights, in its eternity!

CIV

'Twas not for fiction chose Rousseau this spot,
Peopling it with affections; but he found
It was the scene which passion must allot   *970*
To the mind's purified beings; 'twas the ground
Where early Love his Psyche's zone unbound,
And hallow'd it with loveliness: 'tis lone,
And wonderful, and deep, and hath a sound,
And sense, and sight of sweetness; here the Rhone
Hath spread himself a couch, the Alps have rear'd a throne.

CV

Lausanne! and Ferney! ye have been the abodes
Of names which unto you bequeathed a name;
Mortals, who sought and found, by dangerous roads
A path to perpetuity of fame: *980*
They were gigantic minds, and their steep aim
Was, Titan-like, on daring doubts to pile
Thoughts which should call down thunder, and the flame
Of Heaven, again assail'd, if Heaven the while
On man and man's research could deign do more than smile.

CVI

The one was fire and fickleness, a child,
Most mutable in wishes, but in mind,
A wit as various,—gay, grave, sage, or wild,—
Historian, bard, philosopher, combined;
He multiplied himself among mankind,   *990*
The Proteus of their talents: But his own
Breathed most in ridicule,—which, as the wind,
Blew where it listed, laying all things prone,—
Now to o'erthrow a fool, and now to shake a throne.

CVII

The other, deep and slow, exhausting thought,
And hiving wisdom with each studious year,
In meditation dwelt, with learning wrought,
And shaped his weapon with an edge severe,
Sapping a solemn creed with solemn sneer;
The lord of irony,—that master-spell,   *1000*
Which stung his foes to wrath, which grew from fear,
And doom'd him to the zealot's ready Hell,
Which answers to all doubts so eloquently well.

CVIII

Yet, peace be with their ashes,—for by them,
If merited, the penalty is paid;
It is not ours to judge,—far less condemn;
The hour must come when such things shall be made
Known unto all,—or hope and dread allay'd
By slumber, on one pillow,—in the dust,
Which, thus much we are sure, must lie decay'd;   *1010*
And when it shall revive, as is our trust,
'Twill be to be forgiven, or suffer what is just.

CIX

But let me quit man's works, again to read
His Maker's, spread around me, and suspend
This page, which from my reveries I feed,
Until it seems prolonging without end.
The clouds above me to the white Alps tend,
And I must pierce them, and survey whate'er
May be permitted, as my steps I bend
To their most great and growing region, where   *1020*
The earth to her embrace compels the powers of air.

CX

Italia! too, Italia! looking on thee,
Full flashes on the soul the light of ages,
Since the fierce Carthaginian almost won thee,
To the last halo of the chiefs and sages
Who glorify thy consecrated pages;
Thou wert the throne and grave of empires; still,
The fount at which the panting mind assuages
Her thirst of knowledge, quaffing there her fill,
Flows from the eternal source of Rome's imperial hill.   *1030*

CXI

Thus far have I proceeded in a theme
Renew'd with no kind auspices:—to feel
We are not what we have been, and to deem
We are not what we should be,—and to steel
The heart against itself; and to conceal,
With a proud caution, love, or hate, or aught—
Passion or feeling, purpose, grief, or zeal,—
Which is the tyrant spirit of our thought,
Is a stern task of soul:—No matter,—it is taught.

CXII

And for these words, thus woven into song,   *1040*
It may be that they are a harmless wile,—
The colouring of the scenes which fleet along,
Which I would seize, in passing, to beguile
My breast, or that of others, for a while.
Fame is the thirst of youth,—but I am not
So young as to regard men's frown or smile,
As loss or guerdon of a glorious lot;
I stood and stand alone,—remember'd or forgot.

CXIII

I have not loved the world, nor the world me;
I have not flatter'd its rank breath, nor bow'd   *1050*
To its idolatries a patient knee,—
Nor coin'd my cheek to smiles,—nor cried aloud
In worship of an echo; in the crowd
They could not deem me one of such; I stood
Among them, but not of them; in a shroud
Of thoughts which were not their thoughts, and still could,
Had I not filed my mind, which thus itself subdued.

CXIV

I have not loved the world, nor the world me,—
But let us part fair foes; I do believe,
Though I have found them not, that there may be   *1060*
Words which are things,—hopes which will not deceive,
And virtues which are merciful, or weave
Snares for the failing: I would also deem
O'er others' griefs that some sincerely grieve;
That two, or one, are almost what they seem,—
That goodness is no name, and happiness no dream.

CXV

My daughter! with thy name this song begun—
My daughter! with thy name thus much shall end—
I see thee not,—I hear thee not,—but none
Can be so wrapt in thee; thou art the friend   *1070*
To whom the shadows of far years extend:
Albeit my brow thou never should'st behold,
My voice shall with thy future visions blend
And reach into thy heart,—when mine is cold,—
A token and a tone, even from thy father's mould.

CXVI

To aid thy mind's development,—to watch
Thy dawn of little joys,—to sit and see
Almost thy very growth,—to view thee catch
Knowledge of objects,—wonders yet to thee!
To hold thee lightly on a gentle knee,   *1080*
And print on thy soft cheek a parent's kiss,—
This, it should seem, was not reserved for me;
Yet this was in my nature:—as it is,
I know not what is there, yet something like to this.

CXVII

Yet, though dull Hate as duty should be taught,
I know that thou wilt love me; though my name
Should be shut from thee, as a spell still fraught
With desolation,—and a broken claim:
Though the grave closed between us,—'twere the same,
I know that thou wilt love me; though to drain   *1090*
My blood from out thy being were an aim,
And an attainment,—all would be in vain,—
Still thou would'st love me, still that more than life retain.

CXVIII

The child of love,—though born in bitterness
And nurtured in convulsion. Of thy sire
These were the elements,—and thine no less.
As yet such are around thee,—but thy fire
Shall be more temper'd, and thy hope far higher.
Sweet be thy cradled slumbers! O'er the sea,
And from the mountains where I now respire,   *1100*
Fain would I waft such blessing upon thee,
As, with a sigh, I deem thou might'st have been to me!

Childe Harold's Pilgrimage, IV

CANTO THE FOURTH

*Visto ho Toscana, Lombardia, Romagna,
Quel Monte che divide, e quel che serra
Italia, e un mare e l' altro, che la bagna.*
ARIOSTO, Satira iii.

I

I STOOD in Venice, on the Bridge of Sighs;
A palace and a prison on each hand:
I saw from out the wave her structures rise
As from the stroke of the enchanter's wand:
A thousand years their cloudy wings expand
Around me, and a dying Glory smiles
O'er the far times, when many a subject land
Look'd to the winged Lion's marble piles,
Where Venice sate in state, throned on her hundred isles!

II

She looks a sea Cybele, fresh from ocean,   *10*
Rising with her tiara of proud towers
At airy distance, with majestic motion,
A ruler of the waters and their powers:
And such she was;—her daughters had their dowers
From spoils of nations, and the exhaustless East
Pour'd in her lap all gems in sparkling showers.
In purple was she robed, and of her feast
Monarchs partook, and deem'd their dignity increased.

III

In Venice Tasso's echoes are no more,
And silent rows the songless gondolier;   *20*
Her palaces are crumbling to the shore,
And music meets not always now the ear;
Those days are gone—but Beauty still is here.
States fall, arts fade—but Nature doth not die,
Nor yet forget how Venice once was dear,
The pleasant place of all festivity,
The revel of the earth, the masque of Italy!

IV

But unto us she hath a spell beyond
Her name in story, and her long array
Of mighty shadows, whose dim forms despond   *30*
Above the dogeless city's vanish'd sway;
Ours is a trophy which will not decay
With the Rialto; Shylock and the Moor,
And Pierre, can not be swept or worn away—
The keystones of the arch! though all were o'er,
For us repeopled were the solitary shore.

93

V

The beings of the mind are not of clay;
Essentially immortal, they create
And multiply in us a brighter ray
And more beloved existence: that which Fate   40
Prohibits to dull life, in this our state
Of mortal bondage, by these spirits supplied
First exiles, then replaces what we hate;
Watering the heart whose early flowers have died,
And with a fresher growth replenishing the void.

VI

Such is the refuge of our youth and age,
The first from Hope, the last from Vacancy;
And this warn feeling peoples many a page,
And, may be, that which grows beneath mine eye:
Yet there are things whose strong reality   50
Outshines our fairy-land; in shape and hues
More beautiful than our fantastic sky,
And the strange constellations which the Muse
O'er her wild universe is skilful to diffuse:

VII

I saw or dream'd of such,—but let them go,—
They came like truth, and disappear'd like dreams;
And whatsoe'er they were—are now but so:
I could replace them if I would; still teems
My mind with many a form which aptly seems
Such as I sought for, and at moments found;   60
Let these too go—for waking Reason deems
Such overweening phantasies unsound,
And other voices speak, and other sights surround.

VIII

I've taught me other tongues—and in strange eyes
Have made me not a stranger; to the mind
Which is itself, no changes bring surprise;
Nor is it harsh to make, nor hard to find
A country with—ay, or without mankind;
Yet was I born where men are proud to be,
Not without cause; and should I leave behind   70
The inviolate island of the sage and free,
And seek me out a home by a remoter sea,

Childe Harold's Pilgrimage, IV

IX

Perhaps I loved it well; and should I lay
My ashes in a soil which is not mine,
My spirit shall resume it—if we may
Unbodied choose a sanctuary.   I twine
My hopes of being remember'd in my line
With my land's language: if too fond and far
These aspirations in their scope incline,—
If my fame should be, as my fortunes are, *80*
Of hasty growth and blight, and dull Oblivion bar

X

My name from out the temple where the dead
Are honour'd by the nations—let it be—
And light the laurels on a loftier head!
And be the Spartan's epitaph on me—
'Sparta hath many a worthier son than he.'
Meantime I seek no sympathies, nor need;
The thorns which I have reap'd are of the tree
I planted,—they have torn me,—and I bleed:
I should have known what fruit would spring from such a seed. *90*

XI

The spouseless Adriatic mourns her lord;
And, annual marriage now no more renew'd,
The Bucentaur lies rotting unrestored,
Neglected garment of her widowhood!
St. Mark yet sees his lion where he stood,
Stand, but in mockery of his wither'd power,
Over the proud Place where an Emperor sued,
And monarchs gazed and envied in the hour
When Venice was a queen with an unequall'd dower.

XII

The Suabian sued, and now the Austrian reigns— *100*
An Emperor tramples where an Emperor knelt;
Kingdoms are shrunk to provinces, and chains
Clank over sceptred cities; nations melt
From power's high pinnacle, when they have felt
The sunshine for a while, and downward go
Like lauwine loosen'd from the mountain's belt;
Oh for one hour of blind old Dandolo!
Th' octogenarian chief, Byzantium's conquering foe.

XIII

Before St. Mark still glow his steeds of brass,
Their gilded collars glittering in the sun;
But is not Doria's menace come to pass?
Are they not *bridled*?—Venice, lost and won,
Her thirteen hundred years of freedom done,
Sinks, like a sea-weed, into whence she rose!
Better be whelm'd beneath the waves, and shun,
Even in destruction's depth, her foreign foes,
From whom submission wrings an infamous repose.

XIV

In youth she was all glory,—a new Tyre,—
Her very by-word sprung from victory,
The 'Planter of the Lion,' which through fire
And blood she bore o'er subject earth and sea;
Though making many slaves, herself still free,
And Europe's bulwark 'gainst the Ottomite;
Witness Troy's rival, Candia! Vouch it, ye
Immortal waves that saw Lepanto's fight!
For ye are names no time nor tyranny can blight.

XV

Statues of glass—all shiver'd—the long file
Of her dead Doges are declined to dust;
But where they dwelt, the vast and sumptuous pile
Bespeaks the pageant of their splendid trust;
Their sceptre broken, and their sword in rust,
Have yielded to the stranger: empty halls,
Thin streets, and foreign aspects, such as must
Too oft remind her who and what enthrals,
Have flung a desolate cloud o'er Venice' lovely walls.

XVI

When Athens' armies fell at Syracuse,
And fetter'd thousands bore the yoke of war,
Redemption rose up in the Attic Muse,
Her voice their only ransom from afar:
See! as they chant the tragic hymn, the car
Of the o'ermaster'd victor stops, the reins
Fall from his hands—his idle scimitar
Starts from its belt—he rends his captive's chains,
And bids him thank the bard for freedom and his strains.

Childe Harold's Pilgrimage, IV

XVII

Thus, Venice, if no stronger claim were thine,
Were all thy proud historic deeds forgot,
Thy choral memory of the Bard divine,
Thy love of Tasso, should have cut the knot
Which ties thee to thy tyrants; and thy lot
Is shameful to the nations,—most of all, *150*
Albion! to thee: the Ocean queen should not
Abandon Ocean's children; in the fall
Of Venice think of thine, despite thy watery wall.

XVIII

I loved her from my boyhood—she to me
Was as a fairy city of the heart,
Rising like water-columns from the sea,
Of joy the sojourn, and of wealth the mart;
And Otway, Radcliffe, Schiller, Shakespeare's art,
Had stamp'd her image in me, and even so,
Although I found her thus, we did not part, *160*
Perchance even dearer in her day of woe,
Than when she was a boast, a marvel, and a show.

XIX

I can repeople with the past—and of
The present there is still for eye and thought,
And meditation chasten'd down, enough;
And more, it may be, than I hoped or sought;
And of the happiest moments which were wrought
Within the web of my existence, some
From thee, fair Venice! have their colours caught:
There are some feelings Time cannot benumb, *170*
Nor Torture shake, or mine would now be cold and dumb.

XX

But from their nature will the tannen grow
Loftiest on loftiest and least shelter'd rocks,
Rooted in barrenness, where nought below
Of soil supports them 'gainst the Alpine shocks
Of eddying storms; yet springs the trunk, and mocks
The howling tempest, till its height and frame
Are worthy of the mountains from whose blocks
Of bleak, gray granite into life it came,
And grew a giant tree;—the mind may grow the same. *180*

XXI

Existence may be borne, and the deep root
Of life and sufferance make its firm abode
In bare and desolated bosoms: mute
The camel labours with the heaviest load,
And the wolf dies in silence,—not bestow'd
In vain should such example be; if they,
Things of ignoble or of savage mood,
Endure and shrink not, we of nobler clay
May temper it to bear,—it is but for a day.

XXII

All suffering doth destroy, or is destroy'd, 190
Even by the sufferer; and, in each event,
Ends:—Some, with hope replenish'd and rebuoy'd,
Return to whence they came—with like intent,
And weave their web again; some, bow'd and bent,
Wax gray and ghastly, withering ere their time,
And perish with the reed on which they leant;
Some seek devotion, toil, war, good or crime,
According as their souls were form'd to sink or climb.

XXIII

But ever and anon of griefs subdued
There comes a token like a scorpion's sting, 200
Scarce seen, but with fresh bitterness imbued
And slight withal may be the things which bring
Back on the heart the weight which it would fling
Aside for ever: it may be a sound—
A tone of music—summer's eve—or spring—
A flower—the wind—the ocean—which shall wound,
Striking the electric chain wherewith we are darkly bound;

XXIV

And how and why we know not, nor can trace
Home to its cloud this lightning of the mind,
But feel the shock renew'd, nor can efface 210
The blight and blackening which it leaves behind,
Which out of things familiar, undesign'd,
When least we deem of such, calls up to view
The spectres whom no exorcism can bind,
The cold—the changed—perchance the dead—anew,
The mourn'd, the loved, the lost—too many!—yet how few!

XXV

But my soul wanders; I demand it back
To meditate amongst decay, and stand
A ruin amidst ruins; there to track
Fall'n states and buried greatness, o'er a land *220*
Which *was* the mightiest in its old command,
And *is* the loveliest, and must ever be
The master-mould of Nature's heavenly hand,
Wherein were cast the heroic and the free,
The beautiful, the brave—the lords of earth and sea,

XXVI

The commonwealth of kings, the men of Rome!
And even since, and now, fair Italy!
Thou art the garden of the world, the home
Of all Art yields, and Nature can decree;
Even in thy desert, what is like to thee? *230*
Thy very weeds are beautiful, thy waste
More rich than other climes' fertility;
Thy wreck a glory, and thy ruin graced
With an immaculate charm which cannot be defaced.

XXVII

The moon is up, and yet it is not night—
Sunset divides the sky with her—a sea
Of glory streams along the Alpine height
Of blue Friuli's mountains; Heaven is free
From clouds, but of all colours seems to be
Melted to one vast Iris of the West, *240*
Where the Day joins the past Eternity;
While, on the other hand, meek Dian's crest
Floats through the azure air—an island of the blest!

XXVIII

A single star is at her side, and reigns
With her o'er half the lovely heaven; but still
Yon sunny sea heaves brightly, and remains
Roll'd o'er the peak of the far Rhaetian hill,
As Day and Night contending were, until
Nature reclaim'd her order:—gently flows
The deep-dyed Brenta, where their hues instil *250*
The odorous purple of a new-born rose,
Which streams upon her stream, and glass'd within it glows,

XXIX

Fill'd with the face of heaven, which, from afar,
Comes down upon the waters; all its hues,
From the rich sunset to the rising star,
Their magical variety diffuse:
And now they change; a paler shadow strews
Its mantle o'er the mountains; parting day
Dies like the dolphin, whom each pang imbues
With a new colour as it gasps away,   260
The last still loveliest, till—'tis gone—and all is gray.

XXX

There is a tomb in Arqua;—rear'd in air,
Pillar'd in their sarcophagus, repose
The bones of Laura's lover; here repair
Many familiar with his well-sung woes,
The pilgrims of his genius. He arose
To raise a language, and his land reclaim
From the dull yoke of her barbaric foes:
Watering the tree which bears his lady's name
With his melodious tears, he gave himself to fame.   270

XXXI

They keep his dust in Arqua, where he died;
The mountain-village where his latter days
Went down the vale of years; and 'tis their pride—
An honest pride—and let it be their praise,
To offer to the passing stranger's gaze
His mansion and his sepulchre; both plain
And venerably simple, such as raise
A feeling more accordant with his strain
Than if a pyramid form'd his monumental fane.

XXXII

And the soft quiet hamlet where he dwelt   280
Is one of that complexion which seems made
For those who their mortality have felt,
And sought a refuge from their hopes decay'd
In the deep umbrage of a green hill's shade,
Which shows a distant prospect far away
Of busy cities, now in vain display'd,
For they can lure no further; and the ray
Of a bright sun can make sufficient holiday,

XXXIII

Developing the mountains, leaves, and flowers,
And shining in the brawling brook, where-by,
Clear as its current, glide the sauntering hours
With a calm languor, which, though to the eye
Idlesse it seem, hath its morality.
If from society we learn to live,
'Tis solitude should teach us how to die;
It hath no flatterers; vanity can give
No hollow aid; alone—man with his God must strive:

XXXIV

Or, it may be, with demons, who impair
The strength of better thoughts, and seek their prey
In melancholy bosoms, such as were
Of moody texture from their earliest day,
And loved to dwell in darkness and dismay,
Deeming themselves predestined to a doom
Which is not of the pangs that pass away;
Making the sun like blood, the earth a tomb,
The tomb a hell, and hell itself a murkier gloom.

XXXV

Ferrara! in thy wide and grass-grown streets,
Whose symmetry was not for solitude,
There seems as 'twere a curse upon the seats
Of former sovereigns, and the antique brood
Of Este, which for many an age made good
Its strength within thy walls, and was of yore
Patron or tyrant, as the changing mood
Of petty power impell'd, of those who wore
The wreath which Dante's brow alone had worn before.

XXXVI

And Tasso is their glory and their shame.
Hark to his strain! and then survey his cell!
And see how dearly earn'd Torquato's fame,
And where Alfonso bade his poet dwell:
The miserable despot could not quell
The insulted mind he sought to quench, and blend
With the surrounding maniacs, in the hell
Where he had plunged it. Glory without end
Scatter'd the clouds away—and on that name attend

XXXVII

The tears and praises of all time; while thine
Would rot in its oblivion—in the sink
Of worthless dust, which from thy boasted line
Is shaken into nothing; but the link
Thou formest in his fortunes bids us think
Of thy poor malice, naming thee with scorn—
Alfonso! how thy ducal pageants shrink
From thee! if in another station born,
Scarce fit to be the slave of him thou mad'st to mourn:

XXXVIII

Thou! form'd to eat, and be despised, and die,
Even as the beasts that perish, save that thou
Hadst a more splendid trough and wider sty:
He! with a glory round his furrow'd brow,
Which emanated then, and dazzles now,
In face of all his foes, the Cruscan quire,
And Boileau, whose rash envy could allow
No strain which shamed his country's creaking lyre,
That whetstone of the teeth—monotony in wire!

XXXIX

Peace to Torquato's injured shade! 'twas his
In life and death to be the mark where Wrong
Aim'd with her poison'd arrows, but to miss.
Oh, victor unsurpass'd in modern song!
Each year brings forth its millions; but how long
The tide of generations shall roll on,
And not the whole combined and countless throng
Compose a mind like thine? though all in one
Condensed their scatter'd rays, they would not form a sun.

XL

Great as thou art, yet parallel'd by those,
Thy countrymen, before thee born to shine,
The Bards of Hell and Chivalry: first rose
The Tuscan father's comedy divine;
Then, not unequal to the Florentine,
The southern Scott, the minstrel who call'd forth
A new creation with his magic line,
And, like the Ariosto of the North,
Sang ladye-love and war, romance and knightly worth.

Childe Harold's Pilgrimage, IV

XLI

The lightning rent from Ariosto's bust
The iron crown of laurel's mimick'd leaves;
Nor was the ominous element unjust,
For the true laurel-wreath which Glory weaves
Is of the tree no bolt of thunder cleaves,
And the false semblance but disgraced his brow;
Yet still, if fondly Superstition grieves,
Know, that the lightning sanctifies below
Whate'er it strikes;—yon head is doubly sacred now.

XLII

Italia! oh Italia! thou who hast   *370*
The fatal gift of beauty, which became
A funeral dower of present woes and past,
On thy sweet brow is sorrow plough'd by shame,
And annals graved in characters of flame.
Oh, God! that thou wert in thy nakedness
Less lovely or more powerful, and couldst claim
Thy right, and awe the robbers back, who press
To shed thy blood, and drink the tears of thy distress;

XLIII

Then might'st thou more appal; or, less desired,
Be homely and be peaceful, undeplored   *380*
For thy destructive charms; then, still untired,
Would not be seen the armed torrents pour'd
Down the deep Alps; nor would the hostile horde
Of many-nation'd spoilers from the Po
Quaff blood and water; nor the stranger's sword
Be thy sad weapon of defence, and so,
Victor or vanquish'd, thou the slave of friend or foe.

XLIV

Wandering in youth, I traced the path of him,
The Roman friend of Rome's least-mortal mind,
The friend of Tully: as my bark did skim   *390*
The bright blue waters with a fanning wind,
Came Megara before me, and behind
Aegina lay, Piraeus on the right,
And Corinth on the left; I lay reclined
Along the prow, and saw all these unite
In ruin, even as he had seen the desolate sight;

XLV

For Time hath not rebuilt them, but uprear'd
Barbaric dwellings on their shatter'd site,
Which only make more mourn'd and more endear'd
The few last rays of their far-scatter'd light,   *400*
And the crush'd relics of their vanish'd might.
The Roman saw these tombs in his own age,
These sepulchres of cities, which excite
Sad wonder, and his yet surviving page
The moral lesson bears, drawn from such pilgrimage.

XLVI

That page is now before me, and on mine
His country's ruin added to the mass
Of perish'd states he mourn'd in their decline,
And I in desolation: all that *was*
Of then destruction *is*; and now, alas!   *410*
Rome—Rome imperial, bows her to the storm,
In the same dust and blackness, and we pass
The skeleton of her Titanic form,
Wrecks of another world, whose ashes still are warm.

XLVII

Yet, Italy! through every other land
Thy wrongs should ring, and shall, from side to side;
Mother of Arts! as once of arms; thy hand
Was then our guardian, and is still our guide;
Parent of our Religion! whom the wide
Nations have knelt to for the keys of heaven!   *420*
Europe, repentant of her parricide,
Shall yet redeem thee, and, all backward driven,
Roll the barbarian tide, and sue to be forgiven.

XLVIII

But Arno wins us to the fair white walls,
Where the Etrurian Athens claims and keeps
A softer feeling for her fairy halls.
Girt by her theatre of hills, she reaps
Her corn, and wine, and oil, and Plenty leaps
To laughing life, with her redundant horn.
Along the banks where smiling Arno sweeps   *430*
Was modern Luxury of Commerce born,
And buried Learning rose, redeem'd to a new morn.

Childe Harold's Pilgrimage, IV

XLIX

There, too, the Goddess loves in stone, and fills
The air around with beauty; we inhale
The ambrosial aspect, which, beheld, instils
Part of its immortality; the veil
Of heaven is half undrawn; within the pale
We stand, and in that form and face behold
What mind can make, when Nature's self would fail;
And to the fond idolaters of old   *440*
Envy the innate flash which such a soul could mould:

L

We gaze and turn away, and know not where,
Dazzled and drunk with beauty, till the heart
Reels with its fulness; there—for ever there—
Chain'd to the chariot of triumphal Art,
We stand as captives, and would not depart.
Away!—there need no words, nor terms precise,
The paltry jargon of the marble mart,
Where Pedantry gulls Folly—we have eyes?
Blood, pulse, and breast confirm the Dardan Shepherd's prize.   *450*

LI

Appear'dst thou not to Paris in this guise?
Or to more deeply blest Anchises? or,
In all thy perfect goddess-ship, when lies
Before thee thy own vanquish'd Lord of War?
And gazing in thy face as toward a star,
Laid on thy lap, his eyes to thee upturn,
Feeding on thy sweet cheek! while thy lips are
With lava kisses melting while they burn,
Shower'd on his eyelids, brow, and mouth, as from an urn!

LII

Glowing, and circumfused in speechless love,   *460*
Their full divinity inadequate
That feeling to express, or to improve,
The gods become as mortals, and man's fate
Has moments like their brightest; but the weight
Of earth recoils upon us;—let it go!
We can recall such visions, and create,
From what has been, or might be, things which grow
Into thy statue's form, and look like gods below.

Childe Harold's Pilgrimage, IV

LIII

I leave to learned fingers, and wise hands,
The artist and his ape, to teach and tell 470
How well his connoisseurship understands
The graceful bend, and the voluptuous swell:
Let these describe the undescribable:
I would not their vile breath should crisp the stream
Wherein that image shall for ever dwell;
The unruffled mirror of the loveliest dream
That ever left the sky on the deep soul to beam.

LIV

In Santa Croce's holy precincts lie
Ashes which make it holier, dust which is
Even in itself an immortality, 480
Though there were nothing save the past, and this,
The particle of those sublimities
Which have relapsed to chaos:—here repose
Angelo's, Alfieri's bones, and his,
The starry Galileo, with his woes;
Here Machiavelli's earth return'd to whence it rose.

LV

These are four minds, which, like the elements,
Might furnish forth creation:—Italy!
Time, which hath wrong'd thee with ten thousand rents
Of thine imperial garment, shall deny, 490
And hath denied, to every other sky,
Spirits which soar from ruin:—thy decay
Is still impregnate with divinity,
Which gilds it with revivifying ray;
Such as the great of yore, Canova is to-day.

LVI

But where repose the all Etruscan three—
Dante, and Petrarch, and, scarce less than they,
The Bard of Prose, creative spirit! he
Of the Hundred Tales of love—where did they lay
Their bones, distinguish'd from our common clay 500
In death as life? Are they resolved to dust,
And have their country's marbles nought to say?
Could not her quarries furnish forth one bust?
Did they not to her breast their filial earth intrust?

Childe Harold's Pilgrimage, IV

LVII

Ungrateful Florence! Dante sleeps afar,
Like Scipio, buried by the upbraiding shore;
The factions, in their worse than civil war,
Proscribed the bard whose name for evermore
Their children's children would in vain adore
With the remorse of ages; and the crown 510
Which Petrarch's laureate brow supremely wore,
Upon a far and foreign soil had grown,
His life, his fame, his grave, though rifled—not thine own.

LVIII

Boccaccio to his parent earth bequeath'd
His dust,—and lies it not her Great among,
With many a sweet and solemn requiem breathed
O'er him who form'd the Tuscan's siren tongue?
That music in itself, whose sounds are song,
The poetry of speech? No;—even his tomb
Uptorn, must bear the hyaena bigot's wrong, 520
No more amidst the meaner dead find room,
Nor claim a passing sigh, because it told for *whom*!

LIX

And Santa Croce wants their mighty dust;
Yet for this want more noted, as of yore
The Caesar's pageant, shorn of Brutus' bust,
Did but of Rome's best Son remind her more:
Happier Ravenna! on thy hoary shore,
Fortress of falling empire! honour'd sleeps
The immortal exile;—Arqua, too, her store
Of tuneful relics proudly claims and keeps, 530
While Florence vainly begs her banish'd dead and weeps.

LX

What is her pyramid of precious stones?
Of porphyry, jasper, agate, and all hues
Of gem and marble, to encrust the bones
Of merchant-dukes? the momentary dews
Which, sparkling to the twilight stars, infuse
Freshness in the green turf that wraps the dead,
Whose names are mausoleums of the Muse,
Are gently prest with far more reverent tread
Than ever paced the slab which paves the princely head. 540

Childe Harold's Pilgrimage, IV

LXI

There be more things to greet the heart and eyes
In Arno's dome of Art's most princely shrine,
Where Sculpture with her rainbow sister vies;
There be more marvels yet—but not for mine;
For I have been accustom'd to entwine
My thoughts with Nature rather in the fields,
Than Art in galleries: though a work divine
Calls for my spirit's homage, yet it yields
Less than it feels, because the weapon which it wields

LXII

Is of another temper, and I roam 550
By Thrasimene's lake, in the defiles
Fatal to Roman rashness, more at home;
For there the Carthaginian's warlike wiles
Come back before me, as his skill beguiles
The host between the mountains and the shore,
Where Courage falls in her despairing files,
And torrents, swoll'n to rivers with their gore,
Reek through the sultry plain, with legions scatter'd o'er.

LXIII

Like to a forest fell'd by mountain winds;
And such the storm of battle on this day, 560
And such the frenzy, whose convulsion blinds
To all save carnage, that, beneath the fray,
An earthquake reel'd unheededly away!
None felt stern Nature rocking at his feet,
And yawning forth a grave for those who lay
Upon their bucklers for a winding sheet;
Such is the absorbing hate when warring nations meet!

LXIV

The Earth to them was as a rolling bark
Which bore them to Eternity; they saw
The Ocean round, but had no time to mark 570
The motions of their vessel; Nature's law,
In them suspended, reck'd not of the awe
Which reigns when mountains tremble, and the birds
Plunge in the clouds for refuge and withdraw
From their down-toppling nests; and bellowing herds
Stumble o'er heaving plains, and man's dread hath no words,

Childe Harold's Pilgrimage, IV

LXV

Far other scene is Thrasimene now;
Her lake a sheet of silver, and her plain
Rent by no ravage save the gentle plough;
Her aged trees rise thick as once the slain   580
Lay where their roots are; but a brook hath ta'en—
A little rill of scanty stream and bed—
A name of blood from that day's sanguine rain;
And Sanguinetto tells ye where the dead
Made the earth wet, and turn'd the unwilling waters red.

LXVI

But thou, Clitumnus! in thy sweetest wave
Of the most living crystal that was e'er
The haunt of river nymph, to gaze and lave
Her limbs where nothing hid them, thou dost rear
Thy grassy banks whereon the milk-white steer   590
Grazes; the purest god of gentle waters!
And most serene of aspect, and most clear;
Surely that stream was unprofaned by slaughters—
A mirror and a bath for Beauty's youngest daughters!

LXVII

And on thy happy shore a Temple still,
Of small and delicate proportion, keeps,
Upon a mild declivity of hill
Its memory of thee; beneath it sweeps
Thy current's calmness; oft from out it leaps
The finny darter with the glittering scales,   600
Who dwells and revels in thy glassy deeps;
While, chance, some scatter'd water-lily sails
Down where the shallower wave still tells its bubbling tales.

LXVIII

Pass not unblest the Genius of the place!
If through the air a zephyr more serene
Win to the brow, 'tis his; and if ye trace
Along his margin a more eloquent green,
If on the heart the freshness of the scene
Sprinkle its coolness, and from the dry dust
Of weary life a moment lave it clean   610
With Nature's baptism,—'tis to him ye must
Pay orisons for this suspension of disgust.

LXIX

The roar of waters!—from the headlong height
Velino cleaves the wave-worn precipice;
The fall of waters! rapid as the light
The flashing mass foams shaking the abyss;
The hell of waters! where they howl and hiss,
And boil in endless torture; while the sweat
Of their great agony, wrung out from this
Their Phlegethon, curls round the rocks of jet   620
That gird the gulf around, in pitiless horror set,

LXX

And mounts in spray the skies, and thence again
Returns in an unceasing shower, which round,
With its unemptied cloud of gentle rain,
Is an eternal April to the ground,
Making it all one emerald:—how profound
The gulf! and how the giant element
From rock to rock leaps with delirious bound,
Crushing the cliffs, which, downward worn and rent
With his fierce footsteps, yield in chasms a fearful vent   630

LXXI

To the broad column which rolls on, and shows
More like the fountain of an infant sea
Torn from the womb of mountains by the throes
Of a new world, than only thus to be
Parent of rivers, which flow gushingly,
With many windings, through the vale:—Look back!
Lo! where it comes like an eternity,
As if to sweep down all things in its track,
Charming the eye with dread,—a matchless cataract,

LXXII

Horribly beautiful! but on the verge,   640
From side to side, beneath the glittering morn,
An Iris sits, amidst the infernal surge,
Like Hope upon a death-bed, and, unworn
Its steady dyes, while all around is torn
By the distracted waters, bears serene
Its brilliant hues with all their beams unshorn:
Resembling, 'mid the torture of the scene,
Love watching Madness with unalterable mien.

LXXIII

Once more upon the woody Apennine,
The infant Alps, which—had I not before
Gazed on their mightier parents, where the pine
Sits on more shaggy summits, and where roar
The thundering lauwine—might be worshipp'd more;
But I have seen the soaring Jungfrau rear
Her never-trodden snow, and seen the hoar
Glaciers of bleak Mont Blanc both far and near,
And in Chimari heard the thunder-hills of fear,

LXXIV

Th' Acroceraunian mountains of old name;
And on Parnassus seen the eagles fly
Like spirits of the spot, as 'twere for fame,
For still they soar'd unutterably high:
I 've look'd on Ida with a Trojan's eye;
Athos, Olympus, Aetna, Atlas, made
These hills seem things of lesser dignity,
All, save the lone Soracte's heights display'd
Not *now* in snow, which asks the lyric Roman's aid

LXXV

For our remembrance, and from out the plain
Heaves like a long-swept wave about to break,
And on the curl hangs pausing: not in vain
May he, who will, his recollections rake
And quote in classic raptures, and awake
The hills with Latian echoes; I abhorr'd
Too much, to conquer for the poet's sake,
The drill'd dull lesson, forced down word by word
In my repugnant youth, with pleasure to record

LXXVI

Aught that recalls the daily drug which turn'd
My sickening memory; and, though Time hath taught
My mind to meditate what then it learn'd,
Yet such the fix'd inveteracy wrought
By the impatience of my early thought,
That, with the freshness wearing out before
My mind could relish what it might have sought,
If free to choose, I cannot now restore
Its health; but what it then detested, still abhor.

LXXVII

Then farewell, Horace; whom I hated so,
Not for thy faults, but mine; it is a curse
To understand, not feel thy lyric flow.
To comprehend, but never love thy verse,
Although no deeper Moralist rehearse
Our little life, nor Bard prescribe his art, *690*
Nor livelier Satirist the conscience pierce,
Awakening without wounding the touch'd heart,
Yet fare thee well—upon Soracte's ridge we part.

LXXVIII

Oh Rome! my country! city of the soul!
The orphans of the heart must turn to thee,
Lone mother of dead empires! and control
In their shut breasts their petty misery.
What are our woes and sufferance? Come and see
The cypress, hear the owl, and plod your way
O'er steps of broken thrones and temples, Ye! *700*
Whose agonies are evils of a day—
A world is at our feet as fragile as our clay.

LXXIX

The Niobe of nations! there she stands,
Childless and crownless, in her voiceless woe;
An empty urn within her wither'd hands,
Whose holy dust was scatter'd long ago;
The Scipios' tomb contains no ashes now;
The very sepulchres lie tenantless
Of their heroic dwellers: dost thou flow,
Old Tiber! through a marble wilderness? *710*
Rise, with thy yellow waves, and mantle her distress.

LXXX

The Goth, the Christian, Time, War, Flood, and Fire,
Have dealt upon the seven-hill'd city's pride;
She saw her glories star by star expire,
And up the steep barbarian monarchs ride,
Where the car climb'd the capitol; far and wide
Temple and tower went down, nor left a site:—
Chaos of ruins! who shall trace the void,
O'er the dim fragments cast a lunar light,
And say, 'here was, or is,' where all is doubly night? *720*

Childe Harold's Pilgrimage, IV

LXXXI

The double night of ages, and of her,
Night's daughter, Ignorance, hath wrapt and wrap
All round us; we but feel our way to err:
The ocean hath his chart, the stars their map,
And Knowledge spreads them on her ample lap;
But Rome is as the desert, where we steer
Stumbling o'er recollections; now we clap
Our hands, and cry 'Eureka!' it is clear—
When but some false mirage of ruin rises near.

LXXXII

Alas! the lofty city! and alas! 730
The trebly hundred triumphs! and the day
When Brutus made the dagger's edge surpass
The conqueror's sword in bearing fame away!
Alas, for Tully's voice, and Virgil's lay,
And Livy's pictured page!—but these shall be
Her resurrection; all beside—decay.
Alas, for Earth, for never shall we see
That brightness in her eye she bore when Rome was free!

LXXXIII

Oh thou, whose chariot roll'd on Fortune's wheel,
Triumphant Sylla! Thou, who didst subdue 740
Thy country's foes ere thou wouldst pause to feel
The wrath of thy own wrongs, or reap the due
Of hoarded vengeance till thine eagles flew
O'er prostrate Asia;—thou, who with thy frown
Annihilated senates—Roman, too,
With all thy vices, for thou didst lay down
With an atoning smile a more than earthly crown—

LXXXIV

The dictatorial wreath,—couldst thou divine
To what would one day dwindle that which made
Thee more than mortal? and that so supine 750
By aught than Romans Rome should thus be laid?
She who was named Eternal, and array'd
Her warriors but to conquer—she who veil'd
Earth with her haughty shadow, and display'd,
Until the o'er-canopied horizon fail'd,
Her rushing wings—Oh! she who was Almighty hail'd!

113

LXXXV

Sylla was first of victors; but our own
The sagest of usurpers, Cromwell; he
Too swept off senates while he hew'd the throne
Down to a block—immortal rebel! See 760
What crimes it costs to be a moment free
And famous through all ages! but beneath
His fate the moral lurks of destiny;
His day of double victory and death
Beheld him win two realms, and, happier, yield his breath.

LXXXVI

The third of the same moon whose former course
Had all but crown'd him, on the selfsame day
Deposed him gently from his throne of force,
And laid him with the earth's preceding clay.
And show'd not Fortune thus how fame and sway, 770
And all we deem delightful, and consume
Our souls to compass through each arduous way,
Are in her eyes less happy than the tomb?
Were they but so in man's, how different were his doom!

LXXXVII

And thou, dread statue! yet existent in
The austerest form of naked majesty,
Thou who beheldest, 'mid the assassins' din,
At thy bathed base the bloody Caesar lie,
Folding his robe in dying dignity,
An offering to thine altar from the queen 780
Of gods and men, great Nemesis! did he die,
And thou, too, perish, Pompey? have ye been
Victors of countless kings, or puppets of a scene?

LXXXVIII

And thou, the thunder-stricken nurse of Rome!
She-wolf! whose brazen-imaged dugs impart
The milk of conquest yet within the dome
Where, as a monument of antique art,
Thou standest:—Mother of the mighty heart,
Which the great founder suck'd from thy wild teat,
Scorch'd by the Roman Jove's ethereal dart, 790
And thy limbs black with lightning—dost thou yet
Guard thine immortal cubs, nor thy fond charge forget?

LXXXIX

Thou dost;—but all thy foster-babes are dead—
The men of iron; and the world hath rear'd
Cities from out their sepulchres: men bled
In imitation of the things they fear'd,
And fought and conquer'd, and the same course steer'd,
At apish distance; but as yet none have,
Nor could, the same supremacy have near'd,
Save one vain man, who is not in the grave,
But, vanquish'd by himself, to his own slaves a slave—

XC

The fool of false dominion—and a kind
Of bastard Caesar, following him of old
With steps unequal; for the Roman's mind
Was modell'd in a less terrestrial mould,
With passions fiercer, yet a judgment cold,
And an immortal instinct which redeem'd
The frailties of a heart so soft, yet bold,
Alcides with the distaff now he seem'd
At Cleopatra's feet,—and now himself he beam'd,

XCI

And came—and saw—and conquer'd! But the man
Who would have tamed his eagles down to flee,
Like a train'd falcon, in the Gallic van,
Which he, in sooth, long led to victory,
With a deaf heart which never seem'd to be
A listener to itself, was strangely framed;
With but one weakest weakness—vanity,
Coquettish in ambition—still he aim'd—
At what? can he avouch—or answer what he claim'd?

XCII

And would be all or nothing—nor could wait
For the sure grave to level him; few years
Had fixed him with the Caesars in his fate,
On whom we tread: For *this* the conqueror rears
The arch of triumph! and for this the tears
And blood of earth flow on as they have flow'd,
An universal deluge, which appears
Without an ark for wretched man's abode,
And ebbs but to reflow!—Renew thy rainbow, God!

XCIII

What from this barren being do we reap?
Our senses narrow, and our reason frail, 830
Life short, and truth a gem which loves the deep,
And all things weigh'd in custom's falsest scale;
Opinion an omnipotence,—whose veil
Mantles the earth with darkness, until right
And wrong are accidents, and men grow pale
Lest their own judgments should become too bright,
And their free thoughts be crimes, and earth have too much light.

XCIV

And thus they plod in sluggish misery,
Rotting from sire to son, and age to age,
Proud of their trampled nature, and so die, 840
Bequeathing their hereditary rage
To the new race of inborn slaves, who wage
War for their chains, and rather than be free,
Bleed gladiator-like, and still engage
Within the same arena where they see
Their fellows fall before, like leaves of the same tree.

XCV

I speak not of men's creeds—they rest between
Man and his Maker—but of things allow'd,
Averr'd, and known,—and daily, hourly seen—
The yoke that is upon us doubly bow'd, 850
And the intent of tyranny avow'd,
The edict of Earth's rulers, who are grown
The apes of him who humbled once the proud,
And shook them from their slumbers on the throne;
Too glorious, were this all his mighty arm had done.

XCVI

Can tyrants but by tyrants conquer'd be,
And Freedom find no champion and no child
Such as Columbia saw arise when she
Sprung forth a Pallas, arm'd and undefiled?
Or must such minds be nourish'd in the wild, 860
Deep in the unpruned forest, 'midst the roar
Of cataracts, where nursing Nature smiled
On infant Washington? Has Earth no more
Such seeds within her breast, or Europe no such shore?

Childe Harold's Pilgrimage, IV

XCVII

But France got drunk with blood to vomit crime,
And fatal have her Saturnalia been
To Freedom's cause, in every age and clime;
Because the deadly days which we have seen,
And vile Ambition, that built up between
Man and his hopes an adamantine wall,   870
And the base pageant last upon the scene,
Are grown the pretext for the eternal thrall
Which nips life's tree, and dooms man's worst—his second fall.

XCVIII

Yet, Freedom! yet thy banner, torn, but flying,
Streams like the thunder-storm *against* the wind;
Thy trumpet voice, though broken now and dying,
The loudest still the tempest leaves behind;
Thy tree hath lost its blossoms, and the rind,
Chopp'd by the axe, looks rough and little worth,
But the sap lasts, and still the seed we find   880
Sown deep, even in the bosom of the North;
So shall a better spring less bitter fruit bring forth.

XCIX

There is a stern round tower of other days,
Firm as a fortress, with its fence of stone,
Such as an army's baffled strength delays,
Standing with half its battlements alone,
And with two thousand years of ivy grown,
The garland of eternity, where wave
The green leaves over all by time o'erthrown;—
What was this tower of strength? within its cave   890
What treasure lay so lock'd, so hid?—A woman's grave.

C

But who was she, the lady of the dead,
Tomb'd in a palace? Was she chaste and fair?
Worthy a king's—or more—a Roman's bed?
What race of chiefs and heroes did she bear?
What daughter of her beauties was the heir?
How lived—how loved—how died she? Was she not
So honour'd—and conspicuously there,
Where meaner relics must not dare to rot,
Placed to commemorate a more than mortal lot?   900

Childe Harold's Pilgrimage, IV

CI

Was she as those who love their lords, or they
Who love the lords of others? such have been
Even in the olden time, Rome's annals say.
Was she a matron of Cornelia's mien,
Or the light air of Egypt's graceful queen,
Profuse of joy—or 'gainst it did she war,
Inveterate in virtue?   Did she lean
To the soft side of the heart, or wisely bar
Love from amongst her griefs?—for such the affections are.

CII

Perchance she died in youth: it may be, bow'd
With foes far heavier than the ponderous tomb
That weigh'd upon her gentle dust, a cloud
Might gather o'er her beauty, and a gloom
In her dark eye, prophetic of the doom
Heaven gives its favourites—early death; yet shed
A sunset charm around her, and illume
With hectic light, the Hesperus of the dead,
Of her consuming cheek the autumnal leaf-like red.

CIII

Perchance she died in age—surviving all,
Charms, kindred, children—with the silver gray
On her long tresses, which might yet recall,
It may be, still a something of the day
When they were braided, and her proud array
And lovely form were envied, praised, and eyed
By Rome—but whither would Conjecture stray?
Thus much alone we know—Metella died,
The wealthiest Roman's wife: Behold his love or pride!

CIV

I know not why—but standing thus by thee
It seems as if I had thine inmate known,
Thou tomb! and other days come back on me
With recollected music, though the tone
Is changed and solemn, like the cloudy groan
Of dying thunder on the distant wind;
Yet could I seat me by this ivied stone
Till I had bodied forth the heated mind,
Forms from the floating wreck which Ruin leaves behind;

Childe Harold's Pilgrimage, IV

CV

And from the planks, far shatter'd o'er the rocks,
Built me a little bark of hope, once more
To battle with the ocean and the shocks
Of the loud breakers, and the ceaseless roar　　　　　　　　940
Which rushes on the solitary shore
Where all lies founder'd that was ever dear:
But could I gather from the wave-worn store
Enough for my rude boat, where should I steer?
There woos no home, nor hope, nor life, save what is here.

CVI

Then let the winds howl on! their harmony
Shall henceforth be my music, and the night
The sound shall temper with the owlets' cry,
As I now hear them, in the fading light
Dim o'er the bird of darkness' native site,　　　　　　　　950
Answering each other on the Palatine,
With their large eyes, all glistening gray and bright,
And sailing pinions.—Upon such a shrine
What are our petty griefs?—let me not number mine.

CVII

Cypress and ivy, weed and wallflower grown
Matted and mass'd together, hillocks heap'd
On what were chambers, arch crush'd, column strown
In fragments, choked-up vaults, and frescos steep'd
In subterranean damps, where the owl peep'd,
Deeming it midnight:—Temples, baths, or halls?　　　　　　960
Pronounce who can; for all that Learning reap'd
From her research hath been, that these are walls—
Behold the Imperial Mount! 'tis thus the mighty falls.

CVIII

There is the moral of all human tales;
'Tis but the same rehearsal of the past,
First Freedom, and then Glory—when that fails,
Wealth, vice, corruption,—barbarism at last.
And History, with all her volumes vast,
Hath, but *one* page,—'tis better written here,
Where gorgeous Tyranny hath thus amass'd　　　　　　　　970
All treasures, all delights, that eye or ear,
Heart, soul could seek, tongue ask—Away with words! draw near,

CIX

Admire, exult—despise—laugh, weep,—for here
There is such matter for all feeling:—Man!
Thou pendulum betwixt a smile and tear,
Ages and realms are crowded in this span,
This mountain, whose obliterated plan
The pyramid of empires pinnacled,
Of Glory's gewgaws shining in the van
Till the sun's rays with added flame were fill'd!
Where are its golden roofs! where those who dared to build?

CX

Tully was not so eloquent as thou,
Thou nameless column with the buried base!
What are the laurels of the Caesar's brow?
Crown me with ivy from his dwelling-place.
Whose arch or pillar meets me in the face,
Titus or Trajan's? No—'tis that of Time:
Triumph, arch, pillar, all he doth displace,
Scoffing; and apostolic statues climb
To crush the imperial urn, whose ashes slept sublime,

CXI

Buried in air, the deep blue sky of Rome,
And looking to the stars: they had contain'd
A spirit which with these would find a home,
The last of those who o'er the whole earth reign'd,
The Roman globe, for after none sustain'd,
But yielded back his conquests:—he was more
Than a mere Alexander, and, unstain'd
With household blood and wine, serenely wore
His sovereign virtues—still we Trajan's name adore.

CXII

Where is the rock of Triumph, the high place
Where Rome embraced her heroes? where the steep
Tarpeian? fittest goal of Treason's race,
The promontory whence the Traitor's Leap
Cured all ambition. Did the conquerors heap
Their spoils here? Yes; and in yon field below,
A thousand years of silenced factions sleep—
The Forum, where the immortal accents glow,
And still the eloquent air breathes—burns with Cicero!

CXIII

The field of freedom, faction, fame, and blood:
Here a proud people's passions were exhaled, *1010*
From the first hour of empire in the bud
To that when further worlds to conquer fail'd;
But long before had Freedom's face been veil'd,
And Anarchy assumed her attributes;
Till every lawless soldier who assail'd
Trod on the trembling senate's slavish mutes,
Or raised the venal voice of baser prostitutes.

CXIV

Then turn we to her latest tribune's name,
From her ten thousand tyrants turn to thee,
Redeemer of dark centuries of shame— *1020*
The friend of Petrarch—hope of Italy—
Rienzi! last of Romans! While the tree
Of freedom's wither'd trunk puts forth a leaf,
Even for thy tomb a garland let it be—
The forum's champion, and the people's chief—
Her new-born Numa thou—with reign, alas! too brief.

CXV

Egeria! sweet creation of some heart
Which found no mortal resting-place so fair
As thine ideal breast; whate'er thou art
Or wert,—a young Aurora of the air, *1030*
The nympholepsy of some fond despair;
Or, it might be, a beauty of the earth,
Who found a more than common votary there
Too much adoring; whatsoe'er thy birth,
Thou wert a beautiful thought, and softly bodied forth.

CXVI

The mosses of thy fountain still are sprinkled
With thine Elysian water-drops; the face
Of thy cave-guarded spring, with years unwrinkled,
Reflects the meek-eyed genius of the place,
Whose green, wild margin now no more erase *1040*
Art's works; nor must the delicate waters sleep,
Prison'd in marble, bubbling from the base
Of the cleft statue, with a gentle leap
The rill runs o'er, and round, fern, flowers, and ivy, creep,

CXVII

Fantastically tangled; the green hills
Are clothed with early blossoms, through the grass
The quick-eyed lizard rustles, and the bills
Of summer-birds sing welcome as ye pass;
Flowers fresh in hue, and many in their class,
Implore the pausing step, and with their dyes   *1050*
Dance in the soft breeze in a fairy mass;
The sweetness of the violet's deep blue eyes,
Kiss'd by the breath of heaven, seems colour'd by its skies.

CXVIII

Here didst thou dwell, in this enchanted cover,
Egeria! thy all heavenly bosom beating
For the far footsteps of thy mortal lover;
The purple Midnight veiled that mystic meeting
With her most starry canopy, and seating
Thyself by thine adorer, what befell?
This cave was surely shaped out for the greeting   *1060*
Of an enamoured Goddess, and the cell
Haunted by holy Love—the earliest oracle!

CXIX

And didst thou not, thy breast to his replying,
Blend a celestial with a human heart;
And Love, which dies as it was born, in sighing,
Share with immortal transports? could thine art
Make them indeed immortal, and impart
The purity of heaven to earthly joys,
Expel the venom and not blunt the dart—
The dull satiety which all destroys—   *1070*
And root from out the soul the deadly weed which cloys?

CXX

Alas! our young affections run to waste,
Or water but the desert; whence arise
But weeds of dark luxuriance, tares of haste,
Rank at the core, though tempting to the eyes,
Flowers whose wild odours breathe but agonies,
And trees whose gums are poison; such the plants
Which spring beneath her steps as Passion flies
O'er the world's wilderness, and vainly pants
For some celestial fruit forbidden to our wants.   *1080*

CXXI

Oh Love! no habitant of earth thou art—
An unseen seraph, we believe in thee,
A faith whose martyrs are the broken heart,
But never yet hath seen, nor e'er shall see
The naked eye, thy form, as it should be;
The mind hath made thee, as it peopled heaven,
Even with its own desiring phantasy,
And to a thought such shape and image given,
As haunts the unquench'd soul—parch'd—wearied—wrung and riven.

CXXII

Of its own beauty is the mind diseased, *1090*
And fevers into false creation:—where,
Where are the forms the sculptor's soul hath seized?
In him alone. Can Nature show so fair?
Where are the charms and virtues which we dare
Conceive in boyhood and pursue as men,
The unreach'd Paradise of our despair,
Which o'er-informs the pencil and the pen,
And overpowers the page where it would bloom again?

CXXIII

Who loves, raves—'tis youth's frenzy—but the cure
Is bitterer still; as charm by charm unwinds *1100*
Which robed our idols, and we see too sure
Nor worth nor beauty dwells from out the mind's
Ideal shape of such; yet still it binds
The fatal spell, and still it draws us on,
Reaping the whirlwind from the oft-sown winds;
The stubborn heart, its alchemy begun,
Seems ever near the prize—wealthiest when most undone.

CXXIV

We wither from our youth, we gasp away—
Sick—sick; unfound the boon—unslaked the thirst, *1110*
Though to the last, in verge of our decay,
Some phantom lures, such as we sought at first—
But all too late,—so are we doubly curst.
Love, fame, ambition, avarice—'tis the same,
Each idle—and all ill—and none the worst—
For all are meteors with a different name,
And Death the sable smoke where vanishes the flame.

CXXV

Few—none—find what they love or could have loved,
Though accident, blind contact, and the strong
Necessity of loving, have removed
Antipathies—but to recur, ere long,   *1120*
Envenom'd with irrevocable wrong;
And Circumstance, that unspiritual god
And miscreator, makes and helps along
Our coming evils with a crutch-like rod,
Whose touch turns Hope to dust,—the dust we all have trod.

CXXVI

Our life is a false nature—'tis not in
The harmony of things,—this hard decree,
This uneradicable taint of sin,
This boundless upas, this all-blasting tree,
Whose root is earth, whose leaves and branches be   *1130*
The skies which rain their plagues on men like dew—
Disease, death, bondage—all the woes we see—
And worse, the woes we see not—which throb through
The immedicable soul, with heart-aches ever new.

CXXVII

Yet let us ponder boldly—'tis a base
Abandonment of reason to resign
Our right of thought—our last and only place
Of refuge; this, at least, shall still be mine:
Though from our birth the faculty divine
Is chain'd and tortured—cabin'd, cribb'd, confined,   *1140*
And bred in darkness, lest the truth should shine
Too brightly on the unprepared mind,
The beam pours in, for time and skill will couch the blind.

CXXVIII

Arches on arches! as it were that Rome,
Collecting the chief trophies of her line,
Would build up all her triumphs in one dome,
Her Coliseum stands; the moonbeams shine
As 'twere its natural torches, for divine
Should be the light which streams here, to illume
This long-explored but still exhaustless mine   *1150*
Of contemplation; and the azure gloom
Of an Italian night, where the deep skies assume

Childe Harold's Pilgrimage, IV

CXXIX

Hues which have words, and speak to ye of heaven,
Floats o'er this vast and wondrous monument,
And shadows forth its glory.   There is given
Unto the things of earth, which Time hath bent,
A spirit's feeling, and where he hath leant
His hand, but broke his scythe, there is a power
And magic in the ruin'd battlement,
For which the palace of the present hour   *1160*
Must yield its pomp, and wait till ages are its dower.

CXXX

Oh Time! the beautifier of the dead,
Adorner of the ruin, comforter
And only healer when the heart hath bled—
Time! the corrector where our judgments err,
The test of truth, love,—sole philosopher,
For all beside are sophists, from thy thrift,
Which never loses though it doth defer—
Time, the avenger! unto thee I lift
My hands, and eyes, and heart, and crave of thee a gift: *1170*

CXXXI

Amidst this wreck, where thou hast made a shrine
And temple more divinely desolate,
Among thy mightier offerings here are mine,
Ruins of years—though few, yet full of fate:—
If thou hast ever seen me too elate,
Hear me not; but if calmly I have borne
Good, and reserved my pride against the hate
Which shall not whelm me, let me not have worn
This iron in my soul in vain—shall *they* not mourn?

CXXXII

And thou, who never yet of human wrong   *1180*
Left the unbalanced scale, great Nemesis!
Here, where the ancient paid thee homage long—
Thou, who didst call the Furies from the abyss,
And round Orestes bade them howl and hiss
For that unnatural retribution—just,
Had it but been from hands less near—in this
Thy former realm, I call thee from the dust!
Dost thou not hear my heart?—Awake! thou shalt, and must.

CXXXIII

It is not that I may not have incurr'd
For my ancestral faults or mine the wound
I bleed withal, and, had it been conferr'd
With a just weapon, it had flow'd unbound;
But now my blood shall not sink in the ground;
To thee I do devote it—*thou* shalt take
The vengeance, which shall yet be sought and found,
Which if *I* have not taken for the sake——
But let that pass—I sleep, but thou shalt yet awake.

CXXXIV

And if my voice break forth, 'tis not that now
I shrink from what is suffer'd: let him speak
Who hath beheld decline upon my brow,
Or seen my mind's convulsion leave it weak;
But in this page a record will I seek.
Not in the air shall these my words disperse,
Though I be ashes; a far hour shall wreak
The deep prophetic fulness of this verse,
And pile on human heads the mountain of my curse!

CXXXV

That curse shall be Forgiveness.—Have I not—
Hear me, my mother Earth! behold it, Heaven!—
Have I not had to wrestle with my lot?
Have I not suffer'd things to be forgiven?
Have I not had my brain sear'd, my heart riven,
Hopes sapp'd, name blighted, Life's life lied away?
And only not to desperation driven,
Because not altogether of such clay
As rots into the souls of those whom I survey.

CXXXVI

From mighty wrongs to petty perfidy
Have I not seen what human things could do?
From the loud roar of foaming calumny
To the small whisper of the as paltry few,
And subtler venom of the reptile crew,
The Janus glance of whose significant eye,
Learning to lie with silence, would *seem* true,
And without utterance, save the shrug or sigh,
Deal round to happy fools its speechless obloquy.

Childe Harold's Pilgrimage, IV

CXXXVII

But I have lived, and have not lived in vain:
My mind may lose its force, my blood its fire,
And my frame perish even in conquering pain;
But there is that within me which shall tire
Torture and Time, and breathe when I expire;
Something unearthly, which they deem not of,   *1230*
Like the remember'd tone of a mute lyre,
Shall on their soften'd spirits sink, and move
In hearts all rocky now the late remorse of love.

CXXXVIII

The seal is set.—Now welcome, thou dread power!
Nameless, yet thus omnipotent, which here
Walk'st in the shadow of the midnight hour
With a deep awe, yet all distinct from fear;
Thy haunts are ever where the dead walls rear
Their ivy mantles, and the solemn scene
Derives from thee a sense so deep and clear   *1240*
That we become a part of what has been,
And grow unto the spot, all-seeing but unseen.

CXXXIX

And here the buzz of eager nations ran,
In murmur'd pity, or loud-roar'd applause,
As man was slaughter'd by his fellow man.
And wherefore slaughter'd? wherefore, but because
Such were the bloody Circus' genial laws,
And the imperial pleasure.—Wherefore not?
What matters where we fall to fill the maws
Of worms—on battle-plains or listed spot?   *1250*
Both are but theatres where the chief actors rot.

CXL

I see before me the Gladiator lie:
He leans upon his hand—his manly brow
Consents to death, but conquers agony,
And his droop'd head sinks gradually low—
And through his side the last drops, ebbing slow
From the red gash, fall heavy, one by one,
Like the first of a thunder-shower; and now
The arena swims around him—he is gone,
Ere ceased the inhuman shout which hail'd the wretch   *1260*
    who won.

CXLI

He heard it, but he heeded not—his eyes
Were with his heart, and that was far away:
He reck'd not of the life he lost nor prize,
But where his rude hut by the Danube lay,
There were his young barbarians all at play,
There was their Dacian mother—he, their sire,
Butcher'd to make a Roman holiday—
All this rush'd with his blood—Shall he expire
And unavenged?—Arise! ye Goths, and glut your ire!

CXLII

But here, where Murder breathed her bloody steam; 1270
And here, where buzzing nations choked the ways,
And roar'd or murmur'd like a mountain stream
Dashing or winding as its torrent strays;
Here, where the Roman millions' blame or praise
Was death or life, the playthings of a crowd,
My voice sounds much—and fall the stars' faint rays
On the arena void—seats crush'd—walls bow'd—
And galleries, where my steps seem echoes strangely loud.

CXLIII

A ruin—yet what ruin! from its mass
Walls, palaces, half-cities, have been rear'd; 1280
Yet oft the enormous skeleton ye pass,
And marvel where the spoil could have appear'd.
Hath it indeed been plunder'd, or but clear'd?
Alas! developed, opens the decay,
When the colossal fabric's form is near'd:
It will not bear the brightness of the day,
Which streams too much on all years, man, have reft away.

CXLIV

But when the rising moon begins to climb
Its topmost arch, and gently pauses there;
When the stars twinkle through the loops of time, 1290
And the low night-breeze waves along the air,
The garland forest, which the gray walls wear,
Like laurels on the bald first Caesar's head;
When the light shines serene but doth not glare,
Then in this magic circle raise the dead:
Heroes have trod this spot—'tis on their dust ye tread.

Childe Harold's Pilgrimage, IV

CXLV

'While stands the Coliseum, Rome shall stand;
When falls the Coliseum, Rome shall fall;
And when Rome falls—the World.'   From our own land
Thus spake the pilgrims o'er this mighty wall   *1300*
In Saxon times, which we are wont to call
Ancient; and these three mortal things are still
On their foundations, and unalter'd all;
Rome and her Ruin past Redemption's skill,
The World, the same wide den—of thieves, or what ye will.

CXLVI

Simple, erect, severe, austere, sublime—
Shrine of all saints and temple of all gods,
From Jove to Jesus—spared and blest by time;
Looking tranquillity, while falls or nods
Arch, empire, each thing round thee, and man plods   *1310*
His way through thorns to ashes—glorious dome!
Shalt thou not last?   Time's scythe and tyrants' rods
Shiver upon thee—sanctuary and home
Of art and piety—Pantheon!—pride of Rome!

CXLVII

Relic of nobler days, and noblest arts!
Despoil'd yet perfect, with thy circle spreads
A holiness appealing to all hearts—
To art a model; and to him who treads
Rome for the sake of ages, Glory shecs
Her light through thy sole aperture; to those   *1320*
Who worship, here are altars for their beads;
And they who feel for genius may repose
Their eyes on honour'd forms, whose busts around them close.

CXLVIII

There is a dungeon, in whose dim drear light
What do I gaze on?   Nothing: Look again!
Two forms are slowly shadow'd on my sight—
Two insulated phantoms of the brain:
It is not so; I see them full and plain—
An old man, and a female young and fair,
Fresh as a nursing mother, in whose vein   *1330*
The blood is nectar:—but what doth she there,
With her unmantled neck, and bosom white and bare?

CXLIX

Full swells the deep pure fountain of young life,
Where *on* the heart and *from* the heart we took
Our first and sweetest nurture, when the wife,
Blest into mother, in the innocent look,
Or even the piping cry of lips that brook
No pain and small suspense, a joy perceives
Man knows not, when from out its cradled nook
She sees her little bud put forth its leaves—   *1340*
What may the fruit be yet?—I know not—Cain was Eve's.

CL

But here youth offers to old age the food,
The milk of his own gift:—it is her sire
To whom she renders back the debt of blood
Born with her birth. No; he shall not expire
While in those warm and lovely veins the fire
Of health and holy feeling can provide
Great Nature's Nile, whose deep stream rises higher
Than Egypt's river:—from that gentle side
Drink, drink and live, old man! Heaven's realm holds no *1350*
    such tide.

CLI

The starry fable of the milky way
Has not thy story's purity; it is
A constellation of a sweeter ray,
And sacred Nature triumphs more in this
Reverse of her decree, than in the abyss
Where sparkle distant worlds:—Oh, holiest nurse!
No drop of that clear stream its way shall miss
To thy sire's heart, replenishing its source
With life, as our freed souls rejoin the universe.

CLII

Turn to the Mole which Hadrian rear'd on high,   *1360*
Imperial mimic of old Egypt's piles,
Colossal copyist of deformity,
Whose travell'd phantasy from the far Nile's
Enormous model, doom'd the artist's toils
To build for giants, and for his vain earth,
His shrunken ashes, raise this dome: How smiles
The gazer's eye with philosophic mirth,
To view the huge design which sprung from such a birth!

Childe Harold's Pilgrimage, IV

CLIII

But lo! the dome—the vast and wondrous dome,
To which Diana's marvel was a cell—   *1370*
Christ's mighty shrine above his martyr's tomb!
I have beheld the Ephesian's miracle—
Its columns strew the wilderness, and dwell
The hyaena and the jackal in their shade;
I have beheld Sophia's bright roofs swell
Their glittering mass i' the sun, and have survey'd
Its sanctuary the while the usurping Moslem pray'd;

CLIV

But thou, of temples old, or altars new,
Standest alone—with nothing like to thee—
Worthiest of God, the holy and the true,   *1380*
Since Zion's desolation, when that He
Forsook his former city, what could be,
Of earthly structures, in his honour piled,
Of a sublimer aspect? Majesty,
Power, Glory, Strength, and Beauty, all are aisled
In this eternal ark of worship undefiled.

CLV

Enter; its grandeur overwhelms thee not;
And why? it is not lessen'd; but thy mind,
Expanded by the genius of the spot,
Has grown colossal, and can only find   *1390*
A fit abode wherein appear enshrined
Thy hopes of immortality; and thou
Shalt one day, if found worthy, so defined,
See thy God face to face, as thou dost now
His Holy of Holies, nor be blasted by his brow.

CLVI

Thou movest—but increasing with the advance,
Like climbing some great Alp, which still doth rise,
Deceived by its gigantic elegance;
Vastness which grows—but grows to harmonize—
All musical in its immensities;   *1400*
Rich marbles—richer painting—shrines where flame
The lamps of gold—and haughty dome which vies
In air with Earth's chief structures, though their frame
Sits on the firm-set ground—and this the clouds must claim.

CLVII

Thou seest not all; but piecemeal thou must break,
To separate contemplation, the great whole;
And as the ocean many bays will make,
That ask the eye—so here condense thy soul
To more immediate objects, and control
Thy thoughts until thy mind hath got by heart   *1410*
Its eloquent proportions, and unroll
In mighty graduations, part by part,
The glory which at once upon thee did not dart,

CLVIII

Not by its fault—but thine: Our outward sense
Is but of gradual grasp—and as it is
That what we have of feeling most intense
Outstrips our faint expression; even so this
Outshining and o'erwhelming edifice
Fools our fond gaze, and greatest of the great
Defies at first our nature's littleness,   *1420*
Till, growing with its growth, we thus dilate
Our spirits to the size of that they contemplate.

CLIX

Then pause, and be enlighten'd; there is more
In such a survey than the sating gaze
Of wonder pleased, or awe which would adore
The worship of the place, or the mere praise
Of art and its great masters, who could raise
What former time, nor skill, nor thought could plan;
The fountain of sublimity displays
Its depth, and thence may draw the mind of man   *1430*
Its golden sands, and learn what great conceptions can.

CLX

Or, turning to the Vatican, go see
Laocoön's torture dignifying pain—
A father's love and mortal's agony
With an immortal's patience blending:—Vain
The struggle; vain, against the coiling strain
And gripe, and deepening of the dragon's grasp,
The old man's clench: the long envenom'd chain
Rivets the living links,—the enormous asp
Enforces pang on pang, and stifles gasp on gasp.   *1440*

Childe Harold's Pilgrimage, IV

CLXI

Or view the Lord of the unerring bow,
The God of life, and poesy, and light—
The Sun in human limbs array'd, and brow
All radiant from his triumph in the fight;
The shaft hath just been shot—the arrow bright
With an immortal's vengeance; in his eye
And nostril beautiful disdain, and might
And majesty, flash their full lightnings by,
Developing in that one glance the Deity.

CLXII

But in his delicate form—a dream of Love,   *1450*
Shaped by some solitary nymph, whose breast
Long'd for a deathless lover from above,
And madden'd in that vision—are exprest
All that ideal beauty ever bless'd
The mind with in its most unearthly mood,
When each conception was a heavenly guest—
A ray of immortality—and stood,
Starlike, around, until they gather'd to a god!

CLXIII

And if it be Prometheus stole from Heaven
The fire which we endure, it was repaid   *1460*
By him to whom the energy was given
Which this poetic marble hath array'd
With an eternal glory—which, if made
By human hands, is not of human thought;
And Time himself hath hallow'd it, nor laid
One ringlet in the dust—nor hath it caught
A tinge of years, but breathes the flame with which 'twas wrought.

CLXIV

But where is he, the Pilgrim of my song,
The being who upheld it through the past?
Methinks he cometh late and tarries long.   *1470*
He is no more—these breathings are his last;
His wanderings done, his visions ebbing fast,
And he himself as nothing:—if he was
Aught but a phantasy, and could be class'd
With forms which live and suffer—let that pass—
His shadow fades away into Destruction's mass,

CLXV

Which gathers shadow, substance, life, and all
That we inherit in its mortal shroud,
And spreads the dim and universal pall
Through which all things grow phantoms; and the cloud *1480*
Between us sinks and all which ever glow'd,
Till Glory's self is twilight, and displays
A melancholy halo scarce allow'd
To hover on the verge of darkness; rays
Sadder than saddest night, for they distract the gaze,

CLXVI

And send us prying into the abyss,
To gather what we shall be when the frame
Shall be resolved to something less than this
Its wretched essence; and to dream of fame,
And wipe the dust from off the idle name *1490*
We never more shall hear,—but never more,
Oh, happier thought! can we be made the same:
It is enough in sooth that *once* we bore
These fardels of the heart—the heart whose sweat was gore.

CLXVII

Hark! forth from the abyss a voice proceeds,
A long low distant murmur of dread sound,
Such as arises when a nation bleeds
With some deep and immedicable wound;
Through storm and darkness yawns the rending ground,
The gulf is thick with phantoms, but the chief *1500*
Seems royal still, though with her head discrown'd,
And pale, but lovely, with maternal grief
She clasps a babe, to whom her breast yields no relief.

CLXVIII

Scion of chiefs and monarchs, where art thou?
Fond hope of many nations, art thou dead?
Could not the grave forget thee, and lay low
Some less majestic, less beloved head?
In the sad midnight, while thy heart still bled,
The mother of a moment, o'er thy boy,
Death hush'd that pang for ever: with thee fled *1510*
The present happiness and promised joy
Which fill'd the imperial isles so full it seem'd to cloy.

Childe Harold's Pilgrimage, IV

CLXIX

Peasants bring forth in safety.—Can it be,
Oh thou that wert so happy, so adored!
Those who weep not for kings shall weep for thee,
And Freedom's heart, grown heavy, cease to hoard
Her many griefs for ONE; for she had pour'd
Her orisons for thee, and o'er thy head
Beheld her Iris.—Thou, too, lonely lord,
And desolate consort—vainly wert thou wed! *1520*
The husband of a year! the father of the dead!

CLXX

Of sackcloth was thy wedding garment made;
Thy bridal's fruit is ashes: in the dust
The fair-hair'd Daughter of the Isles is laid,
The love of millions! How we did intrust
Futurity to her! and, though it must
Darken above our bones, yet fondly deem'd
Our children should obey her child, and bless'd
Her and her hoped-for seed, whose promise seem'd
Like stars to shepherds' eyes:—'twas but a meteor beam'd. *1530*

CLXXI

Woe unto us, not her; for she sleeps well:
The fickle reek of popular breath, the tongue
Of hollow counsel, the false oracle,
Which from the birth of monarchy hath rung
Its knell in princely ears, till the o'erstrung
Nations have arm'd in madness, the strange fate
Which tumbles mightiest sovereigns, and hath flung
Against their blind omnipotence a weight
Within the opposing scale, which crushes soon or late,—

CLXXII

These might have been her destiny; but no, *1540*
Our hearts deny it: and so young, so fair,
Good without effort, great without a foe;
But now a bride and mother—and now *there*!
How many ties did that stern moment tear!
From thy Sire's to his humblest subject's breast
Is link'd the electric chain of that despair,
Whose shock was as an earthquake's, and opprest
The land which loved thee so that none could love thee best.

CLXXIII

Lo, Nemi! navell'd in the woody hills
So far, that the uprooting wind which tears
The oak from his foundation, and which spills
The ocean o'er its boundary, and bears
Its foam against the skies, reluctant spares
The oval mirror of thy glassy lake;
And, calm as cherish'd hate, its surface wears
A deep cold settled aspect nought can shake,
All coil'd into itself and round, as sleeps the snake.

CLXXIV

And near, Albano's scarce divided waves
Shine from a sister valley;—and afar
The Tiber winds, and the broad ocean laves
The Latian coast where sprang the Epic war,
'Arms and the Man,' whose reascending star
Rose o'er an empire:—but beneath thy right
Tully reposed from Rome;—and where yon bar
Of girdling mountains intercepts the sight
The Sabine farm was till'd, the weary bard's delight.

CLXXV

But I forget.—My Pilgrim's shrine is won,
And he and I must part,—so let it be,—
His task and mine alike are nearly done;
Yet once more let us look upon the sea;
The midland ocean breaks on him and me,
And from the Alban Mount we now behold
Our friend of youth, that ocean, which when we
Beheld it last by Calpe's rock unfold
Those waves, we follow'd on till the dark Euxine roll'd

CLXXVI

Upon the blue Symplegades: long years—
Long, though not very many, since have done
Their work on both; some suffering and some tears
Have left us nearly where we had begun:
Yet not in vain our mortal race hath run,
We have had our reward—and it is here;
That we can yet feel gladden'd by the sun,
And reap from earth, sea, joy almost as dear
As if there were no man to trouble what is clear.

Childe Harold's Pilgrimage, IV

CLXXVII

Oh! that the Desert were my dwelling-place,
With one fair Spirit for my minister,
That I might all forget the human race,
And, hating no one, love but only her!
Ye Elements!—in whose ennobling stir
I feel myself exalted—Can ye not   *1590*
Accord me such a being? Do I err
In deeming such inhabit many a spot?
Though with them to converse can rarely be our lot.

CLXXVIII

There is a pleasure in the pathless woods,
There is a rapture on the lonely shore,
There is society, where none intrudes,
By the deep Sea, and music in its roar:
I love not Man the less, but Nature more,
From these our interviews, in which I steal
From all I may be, or have been before,   *1600*
To mingle with the Universe, and feel
What I can ne'er express, yet cannot all conceal.

CLXXIX

Roll on, thou deep and dark blue Ocean—roll!
Ten thousand fleets sweep over thee in vain;
Man marks the earth with ruin—his control
Stops with the shore;—upon the watery plain
The wrecks are all thy deed, nor doth remain
A shadow of man's ravage, save his own,
When, for a moment, like a drop of rain,
He sinks into thy depths with bubbling groan,   *1610*
Without a grave, unknell'd, uncoffin'd, and unknown.

CLXXX

His steps are not upon thy paths,—thy fields
Are not a spoil for him,—thou dost arise
And shake him from thee; the vile strength he wields
For earth's destruction thou dost all despise,
Spurning him from thy bosom to the skies,
And send'st him, shivering in thy playful spray
And howling, to his Gods, where haply lies
His petty hope in some near port or bay,
And dashest him again to earth:—there let him lay.   *1620*

CLXXXI

The armaments which thunder-strike the walls
Of rock-built cities, bidding nations quake,
And monarchs tremble in their capitals,
The oak leviathans, whose huge ribs make
Their clay creator the vain title take
Of lord of thee, and arbiter of war;
These are thy toys, and, as the snowy flake,
They melt into thy yeast of waves, which mar
Alike the Armada's pride, or spoils of Trafalgar.

CLXXXII

Thy shores are empires, changed in all save thee— *1630*
Assyria, Greece, Rome, Carthage, what are they?
Thy waters washed them power while they were free,
And many a tyrant since; their shores obey
The stranger, slave, or savage; their decay
Has dried up realms to deserts:—not so thou,
Unchangeable save to thy wild waves' play—
Time writes no wrinkle on thine azure brow—
Such as creation's dawn beheld, thou rollest now.

CLXXXIII

Thou glorious mirror, where the Almighty's form
Glasses itself in tempests; in all time, *1640*
Calm or convulsed—in breeze, or gale, or storm,
Icing the pole, or in the torrid clime
Dark-heaving;—boundless, endless, and sublime—
The image of Eternity—the throne
Of the Invisible; even from out thy slime
The monsters of the deep are made; each zone
Obeys thee; thou goest forth, dread, fathomless, alone.

CLXXXIV

And I have loved thee, Ocean! and my joy
Of youthful sports was on thy breast to be
Borne, like thy bubbles, onward: from a boy *1650*
I wanton'd with thy breakers—they to me
Were a delight; and if the freshening sea
Made them a terror—'twas a pleasing fear,
For I was as it were a child of thee,
And trusted to thy billows far and near,
And laid my hand upon thy mane—as I do here.

CLXXXV

My task is done—my song hath ceased—my theme
Has died into an echo; it is fit
The spell should break of this protracted dream,
The torch shall be extinguish'd which hath lit   *1660*
My midnight lamp—and what is writ, is writ,—
Would it were worthier! but I am not now
That which I have been—and my visions flit
Less palpably before me—and the glow
Which in my spirit dwelt is fluttering, faint, and low.

CLXXXVI

Farewell! a word that must be, and hath been—
A sound which makes us linger;—yet—farewell!
Ye! who have traced the Pilgrim to the scene
Which is his last, if in your memories dwell
A thought which once was his, if on ye swell   *1670*
A single recollection, not in vain
He wore his sandal-shoon, and scallop-shell;
Farewell! with *him* alone may rest the pain,
If such there were—with *you*, the moral of his strain!

THE GIAOUR

A FRAGMENT OF A TURKISH TALE

One fatal remembrance—one sorrow that throws
Its bleak shade alike o'er our joys and our woes—
To which Life nothing darker nor brighter can bring,
For which joy hath no balm—and affliction no sting.
                                        MOORE.

ADVERTISEMENT

The tale which these disjointed fragments present is founded upon circumstances now less common in the East than formerly; either because the ladies are more circumspect than in the 'olden time,' or because the Christians have better fortune, or less enterprise. The story, when entire, contained the adventures of a female slave, who was thrown, in the Mussulman manner, into the sea for infidelity, and avenged by a young Venetian, her lover, at the time the Seven Islands were possessed by the Republic of Venice, and soon after the Arnauts were beaten back from the Morea, which they had ravaged for some time subsequent to the Russian invasion. The desertion of the Mainotes, on being refused the plunder of Misitra, led to the abandonment of that enterprise, and to the desolation of the Morea, during which the cruelty exercised on all sides was unparalleled even in the annals of the faithful.

THE GIAOUR

No breath of air to break the wave
That rolls below the Athenian's grave,
That tomb which, gleaming o'er the cliff
First greets the homeward-veering skiff,
High o'er the land he saved in vain:
When shall such hero live again?

*   *   *   *   *

Fair clime! where every season smiles
Benignant o'er those blessed isles,
Which, seen from far Colonna's height
Make glad the heart that hails the sight,　　　　　　　*10*
And lend to loneliness delight.
There mildly dimpling, Ocean's cheek
Reflects the tints of many a peak
Caught by the laughing tides that lave
These Edens of the eastern wave:
And if at times a transient breeze
Break the blue crystal of the seas,
Or sweep one blossom from the trees,
How welcome is each gentle air
That wakes and wafts the odours there!　　　　　　　*20*
For there—the Rose o'er crag or vale,
Sultana of the Nightingale,
The maid for whom his melody,
His thousand songs are heard on high,
Blooms blushing to her lover's tale:
His queen, the garden queen, his Rose,
Unbent by winds, unchill'd by snows,
Far from the winters of the west,
By every breeze and season blest,
Returns the sweets by nature given　　　　　　　*30*
In softest incense back to heaven;
And grateful yields that smiling sky
Her fairest hue and fragrant sigh.
And many a summer flower is there,
And many a shade that love might share,
And many a grotto, meant for rest,
That holds the pirate for a guest;
Whose bark in sheltering cove below
Lurks for the passing peaceful prow,
Till the gay mariner's guitar　　　　　　　*40*
Is heard, and seen the evening star;
Then stealing with the muffled oar

The Giaour

Far shaded by the rocky shore,
Rush the night-prowlers on the prey,
And turn to groans his roundelay.
Strange—that where Nature loved to trace
As if for Gods, a dwelling place,
And every charm and grace hath mix'd
Within the paradise she fix'd,
There man, enamour'd of distress,   50
Should mar it into wilderness,
And trample, brute-like, o'er each flower
That tasks not one laborious hour;
Nor claims the culture of his hand
To bloom along the fairy land,
But springs as to preclude his care,
And sweetly woos him—but to spare!
Strange—that where all is peace beside,
There passion riots in her pride,
And lust and rapine wildly reign   60
To darken o'er the fair domain.
It is as though the fiends prevail'd
Against the seraphs they assail'd,
And, fix'd on heavenly thrones, should dwell
The free inheritors of hell;
So soft the scene, so form'd for joy,
So curst the tyrants that destroy!
He who hath bent him o'er the dead
Ere the first day of death is fled,
The first dark day of nothingness,   70
The last of danger and distress,
(Before Decay's effacing fingers
Have swept the lines where beauty lingers,)
And mark'd the mild angelic air,
The rapture of repose that's there,
The fix'd yet tender traits that streak
The languor of the placid cheek,
And—but for that sad shrouded eye,
That fires not, wins not, weeps not, now,
And but for that chill, changeless brow,   80
Where cold Obstruction's apathy
Appals the gazing mourner's heart,
As if to him it could impart
The doom he dreads, yet dwells upon;
Yes, but for these and these alone,
Some moments, ay, one treacherous hour,
He still might doubt the tyrant's power;
So fair, so calm, so softly seal'd,

The Giaour

The first, last look by death reveal'd!
Such is the aspect of this shore;
'Tis Greece, but living Greece no more!
So coldly sweet, so deadly fair,
We start, for soul is wanting there.
Hers is the loveliness in death,
That parts not quite with parting breath;
But beauty with that fearful bloom,
That hue which haunts it to the tomb,
Expression's last receding ray,
A gilded halo hovering round decay,
The farewell beam of Feeling past away!
Spark of that flame, perchance of heavenly birth,
Which gleams, but warms no more its cherish'd earth!

Clime of the unforgotten brave!
Whose land from plain to mountain-cave
Was Freedom's home or Glory's grave!
Shrine of the mighty! can it be,
That this is all remains of thee?
Approach, thou craven crouching slave:
Say, is not this Thermopylae?
These waters blue that round you lave,
Oh servile offspring of the free—
Pronounce what sea, what shore is this?
The gulf, the rock of Salamis!
These scenes, their story not unknown,
Arise, and make again your own;
Snatch from the ashes of your sires
The embers of their former fires;
And he who in the strife expires
Will add to theirs a name of fear
That Tyranny shall quake to hear,
And leave his sons a hope, a fame,
They too will rather die than shame:
For Freedom's battle once begun,
Bequeath'd by bleeding Sire to Son,
Though baffled oft is ever won.
Bear witness, Greece, thy living page,
Attest it many a deathless age!
While kings, in dusty darkness hid,
Have left a nameless pyramid,
Thy heroes, though the general doom
Hath swept the column from their tomb,
A mightier monument command,
The mountains of their native land!

The Giaour

There points thy Muse to stranger's eye
The graves of those that cannot die!
'Twere long to tell, and sad to trace,
Each step from splendour to disgrace;
Enough—no foreign foe could quell
Thy soul, till from itself it fell;
Yes! Self-abasement paved the way   140
To villain-bonds and despot sway.

What can he tell who treads thy shore?
No legend of thine olden time,
No theme on which the muse might soar
High as thine own in days of yore,
When man was worthy of thy clime.
The hearts within thy valleys bred,
The fiery souls that might have led
Thy sons to deeds sublime,
Now crawl from cradle to the grave,   150
Slaves—nay the bondsmen of a slave,
And callous, save to crime;
Stain'd with each evil that pollutes
Mankind, where least above the brutes;
Without even savage virtue blest,
Without one free or valiant breast,
Still to the neighbouring ports they waft
Proverbial wiles, and ancient craft;
In this the subtle Greek is found,
For this, and this alone, renown'd.   160
In vain might Liberty invoke
The spirit to its bondage broke,
Or raise the neck that courts the yoke:
No more her sorrows I bewail,
Yet this will be a mournful tale,
And they who listen may believe,
Who heard it first had cause to grieve.

* * * * *

Far, dark, along the blue sea glancing,
The shadows of the rocks advancing
Start on the fisher's eye like boat   170
Of island-pirate or Mainote;
And fearful for his light caique,
He shuns the near but doubtful creek:
Though worn and weary with his toil,
And cumber'd with his scaly spoil,
Slowly, yet strongly, plies the oar,
Till Port Leone's safer shore

The Giaour

Receives him by the lovely light
That best becomes an Eastern night.

* * * * *

Who thundering comes on blackest steed,   *180*
With slacken'd bit and hoof of speed?
Beneath the clattering iron's sound
The cavern'd echoes wake around
In lash for lash, and bound for bound;
The foam that streaks the courser's side
Seems gather'd from the ocean-tide:
Though weary waves are sunk to rest,
There's none within his rider's breast;
And though to-morrow's tempest lower,
'Tis calmer than thy heart, young Giaour!   *190*
I know thee not, I loathe thy race,
But in thy lineaments I trace
What time shall strengthen, not efface:
Though young and pale, that sallow front
Is scathed by fiery passion's brunt;
Though bent on earth thine evil eye,
As meteor-like thou glidest by,
Right well I view and deem thee one
Whom Othman's sons should slay or shun.
On—on he hasten'd, and he drew   *200*
My gaze of wonder as he flew:
Though like a demon of the night
He pass'd, and vanish'd from my sight,
His aspect and his air impress'd
A troubled memory on my breast,
And long upon my startled ear
Rung his dark courser's hoofs of fear.
He spurs his steed; he nears the steep,
That, jutting, shadows o'er the deep;
He winds around; he hurries by;   *210*
The rock relieves him from mine eye;
For well I ween unwelcome he
Whose glance is fix'd on those that flee;
And not a star but shines too bright
On him who takes such timeless flight.
He wound along; but ere he pass'd
One glance he snatch'd, as if his last,
A moment check'd his wheeling steed,
A moment breathed him from his speed,
A moment on his stirrup stood—   *220*
Why looks he o'er the olive wood?
The crescent glimmers on the hill,

The Giaour

The Mosque's high lamps are quivering still:
Though too remote for sound to wake
In echoes of the far tophaike,
The flashes of each joyous peal
Are seen to prove the Moslem's zeal,
To-night, set Rhamazani's sun;
To-night, the Bairam feast 's begun;
To-night—but who and what art thou   230
Of foreign garb and fearful brow?
And what are these to thine or thee,
That thou should'st either pause or flee?

He stood—some dread was on his face,
Soon Hatred settled in its place:
It rose not with the reddening flush
Of transient Anger's hasty blush,
But pale as marble o'er the tomb,
Whose ghastly whiteness aids its gloom.
His brow was bent, his eye was glazed;   240
He raised his arm, and fiercely raised
And sternly shook his hand on high,
As doubting to return or fly:
Impatient of his flight delay'd,
Here loud his raven charger neigh'd—
Down glanced that hand, and grasp'd his blade;
That sound had burst his waking dream,
As Slumber starts at owlet's scream.
The spur hath lanced his courser's sides;
Away, away, for life he rides: 250
Swift as the hurl'd on high jerreed
Springs to the touch his startled steed;
The rock is doubled, and the shore
Shakes with the clattering tramp no more;
The crag is won, no more is seen
His Christian crest and haughty mien.
'Twas but an instant he restrain'd
That fiery barb so sternly rein'd;
'Twas but a moment that he stood,
Then sped as if by death pursued: 260
But in that instant o'er his soul
Winters of Memory seemed to roll,
And gather in that drop of time
A life of pain, an age of crime.
O'er him who loves, or hates, or fears
Such moment pours the grief of years:
What felt *he* then, at once opprest

The Giaour

By all that most distracts the breast?
That pause, which ponder'd o'er his fate,
Oh, who its dreary length shall date! 270
Though in Time's record nearly nought,
It was Eternity to Thought!
For infinite as boundless space
The thought that Conscience must embrace,
Which in itself can comprehend
Woe without name, or hope, or end.

The hour is past, the Giaour is gone;
And did he fly or fall alone?
Woe to that hour he came or went!
The curse for Hassan's sin was sent 280
To turn a palace to a tomb;
He came, he went, like the Simoom,
That harbinger of fate and gloom,
Beneath whose widely-wasting breath
The very cypress droops to death—
Dark tree, still sad when others' grief is fled,
The only constant mourner o'er the dead!

The steed is vanish'd from the stall;
No serf is seen in Hassan's hall;
The lonely Spider's thin gray pall 290
Waves slowly widening o'er the wall;
The Bat builds in his Haram bower
And in the fortress of his power
The Owl usurps the beacon-tower;
The wild-dog howls o'er the fountain's brim,
With baffled thirst, and famine, grim;
For the stream has shrunk from its marble bed,
Where the weeds and the desolate dust are spread.
'Twas sweet of yore to see it play
And chase the sultriness of day, 300
As springing high the silver dew
In whirls fantastically flew,
And flung luxurious coolness round
The air, and verdure o'er the ground.
'Twas sweet, when cloudless stars were bright,
To view the wave of watery light,
And hear its melody by night.
And oft had Hassan's Childhood play'd
Around the verge of that cascade;
And oft upon his mother's breast 310
That sound had harmonized his rest;

The Giaour

And oft had Hassan's Youth along
Its bank been soothed by Beauty's song;
And softer seem'd each melting tone
Of Music mingled with its own.
But ne'er shall Hassan's Age repose
Along the brink at Twilight's close:
The stream that fill'd that font is fled—
The blood that warm'd his heart is shed!
And here no more shall human voice   320
Be heard to rage, regret, rejoice.
The last sad note that swell'd the gale
Was woman's wildest funeral wail:
That quench'd in silence, all is still,
But the lattice that flaps when the wind is shrill:
Though raves the gust, and floods the rain,
No hand shall close its clasp again.
On desert sands 'twere joy to scan
The rudest steps of fellow man,
So here the very voice of Grief   330
Might wake an Echo like relief—
At least 'twould say, 'All are not gone;
There lingers Life, though but in one'—
For many a gilded chamber 's there,
Which Solitude might well forbear;
Within that dome as yet Decay
Hath slowly work'd her cankering way—
But gloom is gather'd o'er the gate,
Nor there the Fakir's self will wait;
Nor there will wandering Dervise stay,   340
For bounty cheers not his delay;
Nor there will weary stranger halt
To bless the sacred 'bread and salt.'
Alike must Wealth and Poverty
Pass heedless and unheeded by,
For Courtesy and Pity died
With Hassan on the mountain side.
His roof, that refuge unto men,
Is Desolation's hungry den.
The guest flies the hall, and the vassal from labour   350
Since his turban was cleft by the infidel's sabre!

*   *   *   *   *

I hear the sound of coming feet,
But not a voice mine ear to greet;
More near—each turban I can scan,
And silver-sheathed ataghan;

The Giaour

The foremost of the band is seen
An Emir by his garb of green:
'Ho! who art thou?'—'This low salam
Replies of Moslem faith I am.'—
'The burthen ye so gently bear   360
Seems one that claims your utmost care,
And, doubtless, holds some precious freight,
My humble bark would gladly wait.'

'Thou speakest sooth: thy skiff unmoor,
And waft us from the silent shore;
Nay, leave the sail still furl'd, and ply
The nearest oar that's scatter'd by,
And midway to those rocks where sleep
The channel'd waters dark and deep.
Rest from your task—so—bravely done,   370
Our course has been right swiftly run;
Yet 'tis the longest voyage, I trow,
That one of— * * *
 * * * * *'
Sullen it plunged, and slowly sank,
The calm wave rippled to the bank;
I watch'd it as it sank, methought
Some motion from the current caught
Bestirr'd it more,—'twas but the beam
That checker'd o'er the living stream:
I gazed, till vanishing from view   380
Like lessening pebble it withdrew;
Still less and less, a speck of white
That gemm'd the tide, then mock'd the sight;
And all its hidden secrets sleep,
Known but to Genii of the deep,
Which, trembling in their coral caves,
They dare not whisper to the waves.

 * * * * *

As rising on its purple wing
The insect-queen of eastern spring,
O'er emerald meadows of Kashmeer   390
Invites the young pursuer near,
And leads him on from flower to flower
A weary chase and wasted hour,
Then leaves him, as it soars on high,
With panting heart and tearful eye:
So Beauty lures the full-grown child,
With hue as bright, and wing as wild;
A chase of idle hopes and fears,

The Giaour

Begun in folly, closed in tears.
If won, to equal ills betray'd,   *400*
Woe waits the insect and the maid;
A life of pain, the loss of peace,
From infant's play, and man's caprice:
The lovely toy so fiercely sought
Hath lost its charm by being caught,
For every touch that woo'd its stay
Hath brush'd its brightest hues away,
Till charm, and hue, and beauty gone,
'Tis left to fly or fall alone.
With wounded wing, or bleeding breast,   *410*
Ah! where shall either victim rest?
Can this with faded pinion soar
From rose to tulip as before?
Or Beauty, blighted in an hour,
Find joy within her broken bower?
No: gayer insects fluttering by
Ne'er droop the wing o'er those that die,
And lovelier things have mercy shown
To every failing but their own,
And every woe a tear can claim   *420*
Except an erring sister's shame.

*   *   *   *   *

The Mind, that broods o'er guilty woes,
Is like the Scorpion girt by fire,
In circle narrowing as it glows,
The flames around their captive close,
Till inly search'd by thousand throes,
And maddening in her ire,
One sad and sole relief she knows,
The sting she nourish'd for her foes,
Whose venom never yet was vain,   *430*
Gives but one pang, and cures all pain,
And darts into her desperate brain;
So do the dark in soul expire,
Or live like Scorpion girt by fire;
So writhes the mind Remorse hath riven,
Unfit for earth, undoom'd for heaven,
Darkness above, despair beneath,
Around it flame, within it death!

*   *   *   *   *

Black Hassan from the Haram flies,
Nor bends on woman's form his eyes;   *440*
The unwonted chase each hour employs,
Yet shares he not the hunter's joys.

The Giaour

Not thus was Hassan wont to fly
When Leila dwelt in his Serai.
Doth Leila there no longer dwell?
That tale can only Hassan tell:
Strange rumours in our city say
Upon that eve she fled away
When Rhamazan's last sun was set,
And flashing from each minaret *450*
Millions of lamps proclaim'd the feast
Of Bairam through the boundless East.
'Twas then she went as to the bath,
Which Hassan vainly search'd in wrath;
For she was flown her master's rage
In likeness of a Georgian page,
And far beyond the Moslem's power
Had wrong'd him with the faithless Giaour.
Somewhat of this had Hassan deem'd;
But still so fond, so fair she seem'd, *460*
Too well he trusted to the slave
Whose treachery deserved a grave:
And on that eve had gone to mosque,
And thence to feast in his kiosk.
Such is the tale his Nubians tell,
Who did not watch their charge too well;
But others say, that on that night,
By pale Phingari's trembling light,
The Giaour upon his jet-black steed
Was seen, but seen alone to speed *470*
With bloody spur along the shore,
Nor maid nor page behind him bore.

* * * * *

Her eye's dark charm 'twere vain to tell,
But gaze on that of the Gazelle,
It will assist thy fancy well;
As large, as languishingly dark,
But Soul beam'd forth in every spark
That darted from beneath the lid,
Bright as the jewel of Giamschid.
Yea, *Soul,* and should our prophet say *480*
That form was nought but breathing clay,
By Alla! I would answer nay;
Though on Al-Sirat's arch I stood,
Which totters o'er the fiery flood,
With Paradise within my view,
And all his Houris beckoning through.
Oh! who young Leila's glance could read

The Giaour

And keep that portion of his creed,
Which saith that woman is but dust,
A soulless toy for tyrants's lust?   490
On her might Muftis gaze, and own
That through her eye the Immortal shone;
On her fair cheek's unfading hue
The young pomegranate's blossoms strew
Their bloom in blushes ever new;
Her hair in hyacinthine flow,
When left to roll its folds below,
As midst her handmaids in the hall
She stood superior to them all,
Hath swept the marble where her feet   500
Gleam'd whiter than the mountain sleet
Ere from the cloud that gave it birth
It fell, and caught one stain of earth.
The cygnet nobly walks the water;
So moved on earth Circassia's daughter,
The loveliest bird of Franguestan!
As rears her crest the ruffled Swan,
And spurns the wave with wings of pride,
When pass the steps of stranger man
Along the banks that bound her tide;   510
Thus rose fair Leila's whiter neck:—
Thus arm'd with beauty would she check
Intrusion's glance, till Folly's gaze
Shrunk from the charms it meant to praise.
Thus high and graceful was her gait;
Her heart as tender to her mate;
Her mate—stern Hassan, who was he?
Alas! that name was not for thee!

   *   *   *   *   *

Stern Hassan hath a journey ta'en!
With twenty vassals in his train,   520
Each arm'd, as best becomes a man,
With arquebuss and ataghan;
The chief before, as deck'd for war,
Bears in his belt the scimitar
Stain'd with the best of Arnaut blood,
When in the pass the rebels stood,
And few return'd to tell the tale
Of what befell in Parne's vale.
The pistols which his girdle bore
Were those that once a pasha wore,   530
Which still, though gemm'd and boss'd with gold,
Even robbers tremble to behold.

The Giaour

'Tis said he goes to woo a bride
More true than her who left his side;
The faithless slave that broke her bower,
And, worse than faithless, for a Giaour!

* * * *

The sun's last rays are on the hill,
And sparkle in the fountain rill,
Whose welcome waters, cool and clear,
Draw blessings from the mountaineer: 540
Here may the loitering merchant Greek
Find that repose 'twere vain to seek
In cities lodged too near his lord,
And trembling for his secret hoard—
Here may he rest where none can see,
In crowds a slave, in deserts free;
And with forbidden wine may stain
The bowl a Moslem must not drain.

* * * * *

The foremost Tartar 's in the gap,
Conspicuous by his yellow cap;   550
The rest in lengthening line the while
Wind slowly through the long defile:
Above, the mountain rears a peak,
Where vultures whet the thirsty beak,
And theirs may be a feast to-night,
Shall tempt them down ere morrow's light;
Beneath, a river's wintry stream
Has shrunk before the summer beam,
And left a channel bleak and bare,
Save shrubs that spring to perish there: 560
Each side the midway path there lay
Small broken crags of granite gray,
By time, or mountain lightning, riven
From summits clad in mists of heaven;
For where is he that hath beheld
The peak of Liakura unveil'd?

* * * * *

They reach the grove of pine at last:
'Bismillah! now the peril 's past;
For yonder view the opening plain,
And there we 'll prick our steeds amain:'   570
The Chiaus spake, and as he said,
A bullet whistled o'er his head;
The foremost Tartar bites the ground!
Scarce had they time to check the rein,
Swift from their steeds the riders bound;

The Giaour

But three shall never mount again:
Unseen the foes that gave the wound,
The dying asked revenge in vain.
With steel unsheath'd, and carbine bent,
Some o'er their courser's harness leant,   *580*
Half shelter'd by the steed;
Some fly behind the nearest rock,
And there await the coming shock,
Nor tamely stand to bleed
Beneath the shaft of foes unseen,
Who dare not quit their craggy screen.
Stern Hassan only from his horse
Disdains to light, and keeps his course,
Till fiery flashes in the van
Proclaim too sure the robber-clan   *590*
Have well secured the only way
Could now avail the promised prey;
Then curl'd his very beard with ire,
And glared his eye with fiercer fire:
'Though far and near the bullets hiss,
I 've 'scaped a bloodier hour than this.'
And now the foe their covert quit,
And call his vassals to submit;
But Hassan's frown and furious word
Are dreaded more than hostile sword,   *600*
Nor of his little band a man
Resign'd carbine or ataghan,
Nor raised the craven cry, Amaun!
In fuller sight, more near and near,
The lately ambush'd foes appear,
And, issuing from the grove, advance
Some who on battle-charger prance.
Who leads them on with foreign brand,
Far flashing in his red right hand?
''Tis he! 'tis he! I know him now;   *610*
I know him by his pallid brow;
I know him by the evil eye
That aids his envious treachery;
I know him by his jet-black barb:
Though now array'd in Arnaut garb,
Apostate from his own vile faith,
It shall not save him from the death:
'Tis he! well met in any hour,
Lost Leila's love, accursed Giaour!'

The Giaour

As rolls the river into ocean, 620
In sable torrent wildly streaming;
As the sea-tide's opposing motion,
In azure column proudly gleaming,
Beats back the current many a rood,
In curling foam and mingling flood,
While eddying whirl, and breaking wave,
Roused by the blast of winter, rave;
Through sparkling spray, in thundering clash,
The lightnings of the waters flash
In awful whiteness o'er the shore, 630
That shines and shakes beneath the roar;
Thus—as the stream and ocean greet,
With waves that madden as they meet—
Thus join the bands, whom mutual wrong,
And fate, and fury, drive along.
The bickering sabres' shivering jar;
And pealing wide or ringing near
Its echoes on the throbbing ear,
The deathshot hissing from afar;
The shock, the shout, the groan of war, 640
Reverberate along that vale,
More suited to the shepherd's tale:
Though few the numbers—theirs the strife,
That neither spares nor speaks for life!
Ah! fondly youthful hearts can press,
To seize and share the dear caress:
But Love itself could never pant
For all that Beauty sighs to grant,
With half the fervour Hate bestows
Upon the last embrace of foes, 650
When grappling in the fight they fold
Those arms that ne'er shall lose their hold:
Friends meet to part; Love laughs at faith;
True foes, once met, are join'd till death!

* * * * *

With sabre shiver'd to the hilt,
Yet dripping with the blood he spilt;
Yet strain'd within the sever'd hand
Which quivers round that faithless brand;
His turban far behind him roll'd,
And cleft in twain its firmest fold; 660
His flowing robe by falchion torn,
And crimson as those clouds of morn
That, streak'd with dusky red, portend
The day shall have a stormy end;

The Giaour

A stain on every bush that bore
A fragment of his palampore,
His breast with wounds unnumber'd riven,
His back to earth, his face to heaven,
Fall'n Hassan lies—his unclosed eye
Yet lowering on his enemy,   670
As if the hour that seal'd his fate
Surviving left his quenchless hate;
And o'er him bends that foe with brow
As dark as his that bled below.—

    *   *   *   *   *

'Yes, Leila sleeps beneath the wave,
But his shall be a redder grave;
Her spirit pointed well the steel
Which taught that felon heart to feel.
He call'd the Prophet, but his power
Was vain against the vengeful Giaour: 680
He call'd on Alla—but the word
Arose unheeded or unheard.
Thou Paynim fool! could Leila's prayer
Be pass'd, and thine accorded there?
I watch'd my time, I leagued with these,
The traitor in his turn to seize;
My wrath is wreak'd, the deed is done,
And now I go—but go alone.'

    *   *   *   *   *
    *   *   *   *   *

The browsing camels' bells are tinkling:
His Mother look'd from her lattice high,   690
She saw the dews of eve besprinkling
The pasture green beneath her eye,
She saw the planets faintly twinkling:
''Tis twilight—sure his train is nigh.'
She could not rest in the garden-bower,
But gazed through the grate of his steepest tower:
'Why comes he not? his steeds are fleet,
Nor shrink they from the summer heat;
Why sends not the Bridegroom his promised gift:
Is his heart more cold, or his barb less swift?   700
Oh, false reproach! yon Tartar now
Has gain'd our nearest mountain's brow,
And warily the steep descends,
And now within the valley bends;
And he bears the gift at his saddle bow—
How could I deem his courser slow?
Right well my largess shall repay
His welcome speed, and weary way.'

The Giaour

The Tartar lighted at the gate,
But scarce upheld his fainting weight: 710
His swarthy visage spake distress,
But this might be from weariness;
His garb with sanguine spots was dyed,
But these might be from his courser's side;
He drew the token from his vest—
Angel of Death! 'tis Hassan's cloven crest!
His calpac rent—his caftan red—
'Lady, a fearful bride thy Son hath wed:
Me, not from mercy, did they spare,
But this empurpled pledge to bear.   720
Peace to the brave! whose blood is spilt;
Woe to the Giaour! for his guilt.'

*   *   *   *   *

A turban carved in coarsest stone,
A pillar with rank weeds o'ergrown,
Whereon can now be scarcely read
The Koran verse that mourns the dead,
Point out the spot where Hassan fell
A victim in that lonely dell.
There sleeps as true an Osmanlie
As e'er at Mecca bent the knee;   730
As ever scorn'd forbidden wine,
Or pray'd with face towards the shrine,
In orisons resumed anew
At solemn sound of 'Alla Hu!'
Yet died he by a stranger's hand,
And stranger in his native land;
Yet died he as in arms he stood,
And unavenged, at least in blood.
But him the maids of Paradise
Impatient to their halls invite,   740
And the dark Heaven of Houris' eyes
On him shall glance for ever bright;
They come—their kerchiefs green they wave,
And welcome with a kiss the brave!
Who falls in battle 'gainst a Giaour
Is worthiest an immortal bower.

*   *   *   *   *

But thou, false Infidel! shalt writhe
Beneath avenging Monkir's scythe;
And from its torment 'scape alone
To wander round lost Eblis' throne;   750
And fire unquench'd, unquenchable,

The Giaour

Around, within, thy heart shall dwell!
Nor ear can hear nor tongue can tell
The tortures of that inward hell!
But first, on earth as vampire sent,
Thy corse shall from its tomb be rent:
Then ghastly haunt thy native place,
And suck the blood of all thy race;
There from thy daughter, sister, wife,
At midnight drain the stream of life; 760
Yet loathe the banquet which perforce
Must feed thy livid living corse:
Thy victims ere they yet expire
Shall know the demon for their sire,
As cursing thee, thou cursing them,
The flowers are wither'd on the stem.
But one that for thy crime must fall,
The youngest, most beloved of all,
Shall bless thee with a *father's* name—
That word shall wrap thy heart in flame! 770
Yet must thou end thy task, and mark
Her cheek's last tinge, her eye's last spark,
And the last glassy glance must view
Which freezes o'er its lifeless blue;
Then with unhallow'd hand shall tear
The tresses of her yellow hair,
Of which in life a lock when shorn
Affection's fondest pledge was worn,
But now is borne away by thee,
Memorial of thine agony! 780
Wet with thine own best blood shall drip
Thy gnashing tooth and haggard lip;
Then stalking to thy sullen grave,
Go—and with Gouls and Afrits rave;
Till these in horror shrink away
From spectre more accursed than they!

* * * *

'How name ye yon lone Caloyer?
His features I have scanned before
In mine own land: 'tis many a year,
Since, dashing by the lonely shore, 790
I saw him urge as fleet a steed
As ever served a horseman's need.
But once I saw that face, yet then
It was so mark'd with inward pain,
I could not pass it by again;
It breathes the same dark spirit now,
As death were stamp'd upon his brow.

The Giaour

"'Tis twice three years at summer tide
Since first among our freres he came;
And here it soothes him to abide   800
For some dark deed he will not name.
But never at our vesper prayer,
Nor e'er before confession chair
Kneels he, nor recks he when arise
Incense or anthem to the skies,
But broods within his cell alone,
His faith and race alike unknown.
The sea from Paynim land he crost,
And here ascended from the coast;
Yet seems he not of Othman race,   810
But only Christian in his face:
I 'd judge him some stray renegade,
Repentant of the change he made,
Save that he shuns our holy shrine,
Nor tastes the sacred bread and wine.
Great largess to these walls he brought,
And thus our abbot's favour bought;
But were I prior, not a day
Should brook such stranger's further stay,
Or pent within our penance cell   820
Should doom him there for aye to dwell.
Much in his visions mutters he
Of maiden whelm'd beneath the sea;
Of sabres clashing, foemen flying,
Wrongs avenged, and Moslem dying.
On cliff he hath been known to stand,
And rave as to some bloody hand
Fresh sever'd from its parent limb,
Invisible to all but him,
Which beckons onward to his grave,   830
And lures to leap into the wave.'

  * * * * *
  * * * * *

Dark and unearthly is the scowl
That glares beneath his dusky cowl:
The flash of that dilating eye
Reveals too much of times gone by;
Though varying, indistinct its hue
Oft will his glance the gazer rue,
For in it lurks that nameless spell,
Which speaks, itself unspeakable,
A spirit yet unquell'd and high,   840
That claims and keeps ascendency;

The Giaour

And like the bird whose pinions quake,
But cannot fly the gazing snake,
Will others quail beneath his look,
Nor 'scape the glance they scarce can brook.
From him the half-affrighted Friar
When met alone would fain retire,
As if that eye and bitter smile
Transferr'd to others fear and guile:
Not oft to smile descendeth he, 850
And when he doth 'tis sad to see
That he but mocks at Misery.
How that pale lip will curl and quiver!
Then fix once more as if for ever;
As if his sorrow or disdain
Forbade him e'er to smile again.
Well were it so—such ghastly mirth
From joyaunce ne'er derived its birth.
But sadder still it were to trace
What once were feelings in that face: 860
Time hath not yet the features fix'd,
But brighter traits with evil mix'd;
And there are hues not always faded,
Which speak a mind not all degraded
Even by the crimes through which it waded:
The common crowd but see the gloom
Of wayward deeds, and fitting doom;
The close observer can espy
A noble soul, and lineage high:
Alas! though both bestow'd in vain, 870
Which Grief could change, and Guilt could stain,
It was no vulgar tenement
To which such lofty gifts were lent,
And still with little less than dread
On such the sight is riveted.
The roofless cot, decay'd and rent,
Will scarce delay the passer by;
The tower by war or tempest bent,
While yet may frown one battlement,
Demands and daunts the stranger's eye; 880
Each ivied arch, and pillar lone,
Pleads haughtily for glories gone!

'His floating robe around him folding,
Slow sweeps he through the column'd aisle;
With dread beheld, with gloom beholding
The rites that sanctify the pile.

The Giaour

But when the anthem shakes the choir,
And kneel the monks, his steps retire;
By yonder lone and wavering torch
His aspect glares within the porch;   890
There will he pause till all is done—
And hear the prayer, but utter none.
See—by the half-illumined wall
His hood fly back, his dark hair fall,
That pale brow wildly wreathing round,
As if the Gorgon there had bound
The sablest of the serpent-braid
That o'er her fearful forehead stray'd:
For he declines the convent oath,
And leaves those locks unhallow'd growth,   900
But wears our garb in all beside;
And, not from piety but pride,
Gives wealth to walls that never heard
Of his one holy vow nor word.
Lo!—mark ye, as the harmony
Peals louder praises to the sky,
That livid cheek, that stony air
Of mix'd defiance and despair!
Saint Francis, keep him from the shrine!
Else may we dread the wrath divine   910
Made manifest by awful sign.
If ever evil angel bore
The form of mortal, such he wore:
By all my hope of sins forgiven,
Such looks are not of earth nor heaven!'

To love the softest hearts are prone,
But such can ne'er be all his own;
Too timid in his woes to share,
Too meek to meet, or brave despair;
And sterner hearts alone may feel   920
The wound that time can never heal.
The rugged metal of the mine
Must burn before its surface shine,
But plunged within the furnace-flame,
It bends and melts—though still the same;
Then temper'd to thy want, or will,
'Twill serve thee to defend or kill;
A breast-plate for thine hour of need,
Or blade to bid thy foeman bleed;
But if a dagger's form it bear,   930
Let those who shape its edge, beware!

The Giaour

Thus passion's fire, and woman's art,
Can turn and tame the sterner heart;
From these its form and tone are ta'en,
And what they make it, must remain,
But break—before it bend again.

* * * * *
* * * * *

If solitude succeed to grief,
Release from pain is slight relief;
The vacant bosom's wilderness
Might thank the pang that made it less.   940
We loathe what none are left to share:
Even bliss—'twere woe alone to bear;
The heart once left thus desolate
Must fly at last for ease—to hate.
It is as if the dead could feel
The icy worm around them steal,
And shudder, as the reptiles creep
To revel o'er their rotting sleep,
Without the power to scare away
The cold consumers of their clay!   950
It is as if the desert-bird,
Whose beak unlocks her bosom's stream
To still her famish'd nestlings' scream,
Nor mourns a life to them transferr'd,
Should rend her rash devoted breast,
And find them flown her empty nest.
The keenest pangs the wretched find
Are rapture to the dreary void,
The leafless desert of the mind,
The waste of feelings unemploy'd.   960
Who would be doom'd to gaze upon
A sky without a cloud or sun?
Less hideous far the tempest's roar
Than ne'er to brave the billows more—
Thrown, when the war of winds is o'er,
A lonely wreck on fortune's shore,
'Mid sullen calm, and silent bay,
Unseen to drop by dull decay;—
Better to sink beneath the shock
Than moulder piecemeal on the rock!   970

* * * * *

'Father! thy days have pass'd in peace,
'Mid counted beads, and countless prayer;
To bid the sins of others cease,

The Giaour

Thyself without a crime or care,
Save transient ills that all must bear,
Has been thy lot from youth to age;
And thou wilt bless thee from the rage
Of passions fierce and uncontroll'd,
Such as thy penitents unfold,
Whose secret sins and sorrows rest   *980*
Within thy pure and pitying breast.
My days, though few, have pass'd below
In much of joy, but more of woe;
Yet still in hours of love or strife,
I've 'scaped the weariness of life:
Now leagued with friends, now girt by foes,
I loathed the languor of repose.
Now nothing left to love or hate,
No more with hope or pride elate,
I'd rather be the thing that crawls   *990*
Most noxious o'er a dungeon's walls,
Than pass my dull, unvarying days,
Condemn'd to meditate and gaze.
Yet, lurks a wish within my breast
For rest—but not to feel 'tis rest.
Soon shall my fate that wish fulfil;
And I shall sleep without the dream
Of what I was, and would be still,
Dark as to thee my deeds may seem:
My memory now is but the tomb   *1000*
Of joys long dead; my hope, their doom:
Though better to have died with those
Than bear a life of lingering woes.
My spirit shrunk not to sustain
The searching throes of ceaseless pain;
Nor sought the self-accorded grave
Of ancient fool and modern knave:
Yet death I have not fear'd to meet;
And in the field it had been sweet,
Had danger woo'd me on to move   *1010*
The slave of glory, not of love.
I've braved it—not for honour's boast;
I smile at laurels won or lost;
To such let others carve their way,
For high renown, or hireling pay:
But place again before my eyes
Aught that I deem a worthy prize,
The maid I love, the man I hate;
And I will hunt the steps of fate,

The Giaour

To save or slay, as these require,   *1020*
Through rending steel, and rolling fire:
Nor needst thou doubt this speech from one
Who would but do—what he *hath* done.
Death is but what the haughty brave,
The weak must bear, the wretch must crave;
Then let Life go to him who gave:
I have not quail'd to danger's brow
When high and happy—need I *now*?

*   *   *   *   *

'I loved her, Friar! nay, adored—
But these are words that all can use—   *1030*
I proved it more in deed than word;
There's blood upon that dinted sword,
A stain its steel can never lose:
'Twas shed for her, who died for me,
It warmed the heart of one abhorr'd:
Nay, start not—no—nor bend thy knee,
Nor midst my sins such act record;
Thou wilt absolve me from the deed,
For he was hostile to thy creed!
The very name of Nazarene   *1040*
Was wormwood to his Paynim spleen.
Ungrateful fool! since but for brands
Well wielded in some hardy hands,
And wounds by Galileans given,
The surest pass to Turkish heaven,
For him his Houris still might wait
Impatient at the Prophet's gate.
I loved her—love will find its way
Through paths where wolves would fear to prey;
And if it dares enough, 'twere hard   *1050*
If passion met not some reward—
No matter how, or where, or why,
I did not vainly seek, nor sigh:
Yet sometimes, with remorse, in vain
I wish she had not loved again.
She died—I dare not tell thee how;
But look—'tis written on my brow!
There read of Cain the curse and crime,
In characters unworn by time:
Still, ere thou dost condemn me, pause;   *1060*
Not mine the act, though I the cause.
Yet did he but what I had done
Had she been false to more than one.
Faithless to him, he gave the blow;

The Giaour

But true to me, I laid him low:
Howe'er deserved her doom might be,
Her treachery was truth to me:
To me she gave her heart, that all
Which tyranny can ne'er enthrall;
And I, alas! too late to save!   *1070*
Yet all I then could give, I gave,
'Twas some relief, our foe a grave.
His death sits lightly; but her fate
Has made me—what thou well may'st hate.
His doom was seal'd—he knew it well,
Warn'd by the voice of stern Taheer,
Deep in whose darkly boding ear
The deathshot peal'd of murder near,
As filed the troop to where they fell!
He died too in the battle broil,   *1080*
A time that heeds nor pain nor toil;
One cry to Mahomet for aid,
One prayer to Alla all he made:
He knew and cross'd me in the fray—
I gazed upon him where he lay,
And watch'd his spirit ebb away:
Though pierced like pard by hunters' steel,
He felt not half that now I feel.
I search'd, but vainly search'd, to find
The workings of a wounded mind;   *1090*
Each feature of that sullen corse
Betray'd his rage, but no remorse.
Oh, what had Vengeance given to trace
Despair upon his dying face!
The late repentance of that hour,
When Penitence hath lost her power
To tear one terror from the grave,
And will not soothe, and cannot save.

*   *   *   *   *

'The cold in clime are cold in blood,
Their love can scarce deserve the name: *1100*
But mine was like the lava flood
That boils in Aetna's breast of flame.
I cannot prate in puling strain
Of ladye-love, and beauty's chain:
If changing cheek, and scorching vein,
Lips taught to writhe, but not complain,
If bursting heart, and madd'ning brain,
And daring deed, and vengeful steel,
And all that I have felt, and feel,

The Giaour

Betoken love—that love was mine,   *1110*
And shown by many a bitter sign.
'Tis true, I could not whine nor sigh,
I knew but to obtain or die.
I die—but first I have possess'd,
And come what may, I *have been* blest.
Shall I the doom I sought upbraid?
No—reft of all, yet undismay'd
But for the thought of Leila slain,
Give me the pleasure with the pain,
So would I live and love again.   *1120*
I grieve, but not, my holy guide!
For him who dies, but her who died:
She sleeps beneath the wandering wave—
Ah! had she but an earthly grave,
This breaking heart and throbbing head
Should seek and share her narrow bed.
She was a form of life and light,
That, seen, became a part of sight;
And rose, where'er I turn'd mine eye,
The Morning-star of Memory!   *1130*

'Yes, Love indeed is light from heaven;
A spark of that immortal fire
With angels shared, by Alla given,
To lift from earth our low desire.
Devotion wafts the mind above,
But Heaven itself descends in love;
A feeling from the Godhead caught,
To wean from self each sordid thought;
A Ray of him who form'd the whole;
A Glory circling round the soul!   *1140*
I grant *my* love imperfect, all
That mortals by the name miscall;
Then deem it evil, what thou wilt;
But say, oh say, *hers* was not guilt!
She was my life's unerring light:
That quench'd, what beam shall break my night?
Oh! would it shone to lead me still,
Although to death or deadliest ill!
Why marvel ye, if they who lose
This present joy, this future hope,   *1150*
No more with sorrow meekly cope;
In phrensy then their fate accuse:
In madness do those fearful deeds
That seem to add but guilt to woe?
Alas! the breast that inly bleeds

The Giaour

Hath nought to dread from outward blow:
Who falls from all he knows of bliss,
Cares little into what abyss.
Fierce as the gloomy vulture's now
To thee, old man, my deeds appear: *1160*
I read abhorrence on thy brow,
And this too was I born to bear!
'Tis true, that, like that bird of prey,
With havoc have I mark'd my way:
But this was taught me by the dove,
To die—and know no second love.
This lesson yet hath man to learn,
Taught by the thing he dares to spurn:
The bird that sings within the brake,
The swan that swims upon the lake,   *1170*
One mate, and one alone, will take.
And let the fool still prone to range,
And sneer on all who cannot change,
Partake his jest with boasting boys;
I envy not his varied joys,
But deem such feeble, heartless man,
Less than yon solitary swan;
Far, far beneath the shallow maid
He left believing and betray'd.
Such shame at least was never mine—   *1180*
Leila! each thought was only thine!
My good, my guilt, my weal, my woe,
My hope on high—my all below.
Earth holds no other like to thee,
Or, if it doth, in vain for me:
For worlds I dare not view the dame
Resembling thee, yet not the same.
The very crimes that mar my youth,
This bed of death—attest my truth!
'Tis all too late—thou wert, thou art   *1190*
The cherish'd madness of my heart!

'And she was lost—and yet I breathed,
But not the breath of human life:
A serpent round my heart was wreathed,
And stung my every thought to strife.
Alike all time, abhorr'd all place,
Shuddering I shrunk from Nature's face,
Where every hue that charm'd before
The blackness of my bosom wore.
The rest thou dost already know,   *1200*
And all my sins, and half my woe.

The Giaour

But talk no more of penitence;
Thou see'st I soon shall part from hence:
And if thy holy tale were true,
The deed that's done canst *thou* undo?
Think me not thankless—but this grief
Looks not to priesthood for relief.
My soul's estate in secret guess:
But wouldst thou pity more, say less.
When thou canst bid my Leila live,   1210
Then will I sue thee to forgive;
Then plead my cause in that high place
Where purchased masses proffer grace.
Go, when the hunter's hand hath wrung
From forest-cave her shrieking young,
And calm the lonely lioness:
But soothe not—mock not *my* distress!

'In earlier days, and calmer hours,
When heart with heart delights to blend,
Where bloom my native valley's bowers
I had—Ah! have I now?—a friend!   1220
To him this pledge I charge thee send,
Memorial of a youthful vow;
I would remind him of my end:
Though souls absorb'd like mine allow
Brief thought to distant friendship's claim,
Yet dear to him my blighted name.
'Tis strange—he prophesied my doom,
And I have smiled—I then could smile—
When Prudence would his voice assume,   1230
And warn—I reck'd not what—the while:
But now remembrance whispers o'er
Those accents scarcely mark'd before.
Say—that his bodings came to pass,
And he will start to hear their truth,
And wish his words had not been sooth:
Tell him, unheeding as I was,
Through many a busy bitter scene
Of all our golden youth had been,
In pain, my faltering tongue had tried   1240
To bless his memory ere I died;
But Heaven in wrath would turn away,
If Guilt should for the guiltless pray.
I do not ask him not to blame,
Too gentle he to wound my name;
And what have I to do with fame?
I do not ask him not to mourn,

The Giaour

Such cold request might sound like scorn;
And what than friendship's manly tear
May better grace a brother's bier? *1250*
But bear this ring, his own of old,
And tell him—what thou dost behold!
The wither'd frame, the ruin'd mind,
The wrack by passion left behind,
A shrivelled scroll, a scatter'd leaf,
Sear'd by the autumn blast of grief!

  * * * * *

'Tell me no more of fancy's gleam,
No, father, no, 'twas not a dream;
Alas! the dreamer first must sleep,
I only watch'd, and wish'd to weep; *1260*
But could not, for my burning brow
Throbb'd to the very brain as now:
I wish'd but for a single tear,
As something welcome, new, and dear:
I wish'd it then, I wish it still;
Despair is stronger than my will.
Waste not thine orison, despair
Is mightier than thy pious prayer:
I would not, if I might, be blest;
I want no paradise, but rest. *1270*
'Twas then, I tell thee, father! then
I saw her; yes, she lived again;
And shining in her white symar,
As through yon pale gray cloud the star
Which now I gaze on, as on her,
Who look'd and looks far lovelier;
Dimly I view its trembling spark;
To-morrow's night shall be more dark;
And I, before its rays appear,
That lifeless thing the living fear. *1280*
I wander, father! for my soul
Is fleeting towards the final goal.
I saw her, friar! and I rose
Forgetful of our former woes;
And rushing from my couch, I dart,
And clasp her to my desperate heart;
I clasp—what is it that I clasp?
No breathing form within my grasp,
No heart that beats reply to mine,
Yet, Leila! yet the form is thine! *1290*
And art thou, dearest, changed so much,
As meet my eye, yet mock my touch?

The Giaour

Ah! were thy beauties e'er so cold,
I care not; so my arms enfold
The all they ever wish'd to hold.
Alas! around a shadow prest
They shrink upon my lonely breast;
Yet still 'tis there! In silence stands,
And beckons with beseeching hands!
With braided hair, and bright-black eye— *1300*
I knew 'twas false—she could not die!
But he is dead! within the dell
I saw him buried where he fell;
He comes not, for he cannot break
From earth; why then art thou awake?
They told me wild waves roll'd above
The face I view, the form I love;
They told me—'twas a hideous tale!
I'd tell it, but my tongue would fail:
If true, and from thine ocean-cave *1310*
Thou com'st to claim a calmer grave,
Oh! pass thy dewy fingers o'er
This brow that then will burn no more;
Or place them on my hopeless heart:
But, shape or shade! whate'er thou art,
In mercy ne'er again depart!
Or farther with thee bear my soul
Than winds can waft or waters roll!

*   *   *   *   *

'Such is my name, and such my tale.
Confessor! to thy secret ear *1320*
I breathe the sorrows I bewail,
And thank thee for the generous tear
This glazing eye could never shed.
Then lay me with the humblest dead,
And, save the cross above my head,
Be neither name nor emblem spread,
By prying stranger to be read,
Or stay the passing pilgrim's tread.'

He pass'd—nor of his name and race
Hath left a token or a trace, *1330*
Save what the father must not say
Who shrived him on his dying day:
This broken tale was all we knew
Of her he loved, or him he slew.

THE PRISONER OF CHILLON

I

My hair is grey, but not with years,
   Nor grew it white,
   In a single night,
As men's have grown from sudden fears:
My limbs are bow'd, though not with toil,
But rusted with a vile repose,
For they have been a dungeon's spoil,
And mine has been the fate of those
To whom the goodly earth and air
Are bann'd, and barr'd—forbidden fare;   *10*
But this was for my father's faith
I suffer'd chains and courted death;
That father perish'd at the stake
For tenets he would not forsake;
And for the same his lineal race
In darkness found a dwelling-place;
We were seven—who now are one,
Six in youth and one in age,
Finish'd as they had begun,
Proud of Persecution's rage;   *20*
One in fire, and two in field,
Their belief with blood have seal'd:
Dying as their father died,
For the God their foes denied;—
Three were in a dungeon cast,
Of whom this wreck is left the last.

II

There are seven pillars of Gothic mould,
In Chillon's dungeons deep and old,
There are seven columns massy and grey,
Dim with a dull imprison'd ray,   *30*
A sunbeam which hath lost its way,
And through the crevice and the cleft
Of the thick wall is fallen and left:
Creeping o'er the floor so damp,
Like a marsh's meteor lamp:
And in each pillar there is a ring,
And in each ring there is a chain;
That iron is a cankering thing,
For in these limbs its teeth remain,

With marks that will not wear away,   40
Till I have done with this new day,
Which now is painful to these eyes,
Which have not seen the sun so rise
For years—I cannot count them o'er,
I lost their long and heavy score
When my last brother droop'd and died,
And I lay living by his side.

III

They chained us each to a column stone,
And we were three—yet, each alone;
We could not move a single pace,   50
We could not see each other's face,
But with that pale and livid light
That made us strangers in our sight:
And thus together—yet apart,
Fetter'd in hand, but join'd in heart,
'Twas still some solace, in the dearth
Of the pure elements of earth,
To hearken to each other's speech,
And each turn comforter to each
With some new hope or legend old,   60
Or song heroically bold;
But even these at length grew cold.
Our voices took a dreary tone,
An echo of the dungeon stone,
A grating sound—not full and free
As they of yore were wont to be;
It might be fancy—but to me
They never sounded like our own.

IV

I was the eldest of the three,
And to uphold and cheer the rest   70
I ought to do—and did my best—
And each did well in his degree.
The youngest, whom my father loved,
Because our mother's brow was given
To him—with eyes as blue as heaven,
For him my soul was sorely moved:
And truly might it be distress'd
To see such bird in such a nest;
For he was beautiful as day—
(When day was beautiful to me   80
As to young eagles being free)—

The Prisoner of Chillon

A polar day, which will not see
A sunset till its summer's gone,
Its sleepless summer of long light,
The snow-clad offspring of the sun:
And thus he was as pure and bright,
And in his natural spirit gay,
With tears for nought but others' ills,
And then they flow'd like mountain rills,
Unless he could assuage the woe   *90*
Which he abhorr'd to view below.

V

The other was as pure of mind,
But form'd to combat with his kind;
Strong in his frame, and of a mood
Which 'gainst the world in war had stood,
And perished in the foremost rank
With joy:—but not in chains to pine:
His spirit wither'd with their clank.
I saw it silently decline—
And so perchance in sooth did mine: *100*
But yet I forced it on to cheer
Those relics of a home so dear.
He was a hunter of the hills,
Had follow'd there the deer and wolf;
To him this dungeon was a gulf,
And fetter'd feet the worst of ills.

VI

Lake Leman lies by Chillon's walls:
A thousand feet in depth below
Its massy waters meet and flow;
Thus much the fathom-line was sent   *110*
From Chillon's snow-white battlement,
Which round about the wave inthrals:
A double dungeon wall and wave
Have made—and like a living grave.
Below the surface of the lake
The dark vault lies wherein we lay,
We heard it ripple night and day;
Sounding o'er our heads it knocked;
And I have felt the winter's spray
Wash through the bars when winds were high   *120*
And wanton in the happy sky;
And then the very rock hath rock'd
And I have felt it shake, unshock'd,
Because I could have smiled to see
The death that would have set me free.

The Prisoner of Chillon

VII

I said my nearer brother pined,
I said his mighty heart declined,
He loathed and put away his food;
It was not that 'twas coarse and rude,
For we were used to hunters' fare,   130
And for the like had little care:
The milk drawn from the mountain goat
Was changed for water from the moat,
Our bread was such as captives' tears
Have moisten'd many a thousand years,
Since man first pent his fellow men
Like brutes within an iron den;
But what were these to us or him?
These wasted not his heart or limb:
My brother's soul was of that mould   140
Which in a palace had grown cold,
Had his free breathing been denied
The range of the steep mountain's side;
But why delay the truth?—he died.
I saw, and could not hold his head,
Nor reach his dying hand—nor—dead,—
Though hard I strove, but strove in vain,
To rend and gnash my bonds in twain.
He died—and they unlock'd his chain,
And scoop'd for him a shallow grave   150
Even from the cold earth of our cave.
I begg'd them, as a boon, to lay
His corse in dust whereon the day
Might shine—it was a foolish thought,
But then within my brain it wrought,
That even in death his freeborn breast
In such a dungeon could not rest.
I might have spared my idle prayer—
They coldly laugh'd—and laid him there:
The flat and turfless earth above   160
The being we so much did love;
His empty chain above it leant,
Such murder's fitting monument!

VIII

But he, the favourite and the flower,
Most cherish'd since his natal hour,
His mother's image in fair face,
The infant love of all his race,
His martyr'd father's dearest thought,

The Prisoner of Chillon

My latest care, for whom I sought
To hoard my life, that his might be 170
Less wretched now, and one day free;
He, too, who yet had held untired
A spirit natural or inspired—
He, too, was struck, and day by day
Was wither'd on the stalk away.
Oh, God! it is a fearful thing
To see the human soul take wing
In any shape, in any mood:—
I've seen it rushing forth in blood,
I've seen it on the breaking ocean 180
Strive with a swoln convulsive motion,
I've seen the sick and ghastly bed
Of Sin delirious with its dread;
But these were horrors—this was woe
Unmix'd with such—but sure and slow:
He faded, and so calm and meek,
So softly worn, so sweetly weak,
So tearless, yet so tender—kind,
And grieved for those he left behind;·
With all the while a cheek whose bloom 190
Was as a mockery of the tomb,
Whose tints as gently sunk away
As a departing rainbow's ray—
An eye of most transparent light,
That almost made the dungeon bright,
And not a word of murmur—not
A groan o'er his untimely lot,—
A little talk of better days,
A little hope my own to raise,
For I was sunk in silence—lost 200
In this last loss, of all the most;
And then the sighs he would suppress
Of fainting nature's feebleness,
More slowly drawn, grew less and less:
I listen'd, but I could not hear—
I call'd, for I was wild with fear;
I knew 'twas hopeless, but my dread
Would not be thus admonished;
I call'd, and thought I heard a sound—
I burst my chain with one strong bound, 210
And rush'd to him:—I found him not,
I only stirr'd in this black spot,
I only lived—*I* only drew
The accursed breath of dungeon-dew;
The last—the sole—the dearest link

The Prisoner of Chillon

Between me and the eternal brink,
Which bound me to my failing race,
Was broken in this fatal place.
One on the earth, and one beneath—
My brothers—both had ceased to breathe: 220
I took that hand which lay so still,
Alas! my own was full as chill;
I had not strength to stir, or strive,
But felt that I was still alive—
A frantic feeling, when we know
That what we love shall ne'er be so.
    I know not why
    I could not die,
I had no earthly hope—but faith,
And that forbade a selfish death.   230

IX

What next befell me then and there
I know not well—I never knew—
First came the loss of light, and air,
And then of darkness too:
I had no thought, no feeling—none—
Among the stones I stood a stone,
And was, scarce conscious what I wist,
As shrubless crags within the mist;
For all was blank, and bleak, and grey,
It was not night—it was not day,   240
It was not even the dungeon light,
So hateful to my heavy sight.
But vacancy absorbing space,
And fixedness—without a place;
There were no stars—no earth—no time—
No check—no change—no good—no crime—
But silence, and a stirless breath
Which neither was of life nor death;
A sea of stagnant idleness,
Blind, boundless, mute, and motionless!   250

X

A light broke in upon my brain,—
It was the carol of a bird;
It ceased, and then it came again,
The sweetest song ear ever heard,
And mine was thankful till my eyes
Ran over with the glad surprise,
And they that moment could not see

The Prisoner of Chillon

I was the mate of misery;
But then by dull degrees came back
My senses to their wonted track,   *260*
I saw the dungeon walls and floor
Close slowly round me as before,
I saw the glimmer of the sun
Creeping as it before had done,
But through the crevice where it came
The bird was perch'd, as fond and tame,
And tamer than upon the tree;
A lovely bird, with azure wings,
And song that said a thousand things,
And seem'd to say them all for me!   *270*
I never saw its like before,
I ne'er shall see its likeness more:
It seem'd like me to want a mate,
But was not half so desolate,
And it was come to love me when
None lived to love me so again,
And cheering from my dungeon's brink,
Had brought me back to feel and think.
I know not if it late were free,
Or broke its cage to perch on mine,   *280*
But knowing well captivity,
Sweet bird! I could not wish for thine!
Or if it were, in winged guise,
A visitant from Paradise;
For—Heaven forgive that thought! the while
Which made me both to weep and smile;
I sometimes deem'd that it might be
My brother's soul come down to me;
But then at last away it flew,
And then 'twas mortal—well I knew,   *290*
For he would never thus have flown,
And left me twice so doubly lone,—
Lone—as the corse within its shroud,
Lone—as a solitary cloud.
A single cloud on a sunny day,
While all the rest of heaven is clear,
A frown upon the atmosphere,
That hath no business to appear
When skies are blue, and earth is gay.

XI

A kind of change came in my fate,   *300*
My keepers grew compassionate;
I know not what had made them so,

The Prisoner of Chillon

They were inured to sights of woe,
But so it was:—my broken chain
With links unfasten'd did remain,
And it was liberty to stride
Along my cell from side to side,
And up and down, and then athwart,
And tread it over every part;
And round the pillars one by one,   *310*
Returning where my walk begun,
Avoiding only, as I trod,
My brothers' graves without a sod;
For if I thought with heedless tread
My step profaned their lowly bed,
My breath came gaspingly and thick,
And my crush'd heart fell blind and sick.

XII

I made a footing in the wall,
It was not therefrom to escape,
For I had buried one and all   *320*
Who loved me in a human shape;
And the whole earth would henceforth be
A wider prison unto me;
No child—no sire—no kin had I,
No partner in my misery;
I thought of this, and I was glad,
For thought of them had made me mad;
But I was curious to ascend
To my barr'd windows, and to bend
Once more, upon the mountains high,   *330*
The quiet of a loving eye.

XIII

I saw them—and they were the same,
They were not changed like me in frame;
I saw their thousand years of snow
On high—their wide long lake below,
And the blue Rhône in fullest flow;
I heard the torrents leap and gush
O'er channell'd rock and broken bush;
I saw the white-wall'd distant town,
And whiter sails go skimming down;   *340*
And then there was a little isle,
Which in my very face did smile,
The only one in view;
A small green isle, it seem'd no more,
Scarce broader than my dungeon floor,
But in it there were three tall trees,

The Prisoner of Chillon

And o'er it blew the mountain breeze,
And by it there were waters flowing,
And on it there were young flowers growing,
Of gentle breath and hue. 350
The fish swam by the castle wall,
And they seem'd joyous each and all;
The eagle rode the rising blast,
Methought he never flew so fast
As then to me he seem'd to fly,
And then new tears came in my eye,
And I felt troubled—and would fain
I had not left my recent chain;
And when I did descend again,
The darkness of my dim abode 360
Fell on me as a heavy load;
It was as is a new-dug grave,
Closing o'er one we sought to save,—
And yet my glance, too much oppress'd,
Had almost need of such a rest.

XIV

It might be months, or years, or days,
I kept no count—I took no note,
I had no hope my eyes to raise,
And clear them of their dreary mote;
At last men came to set me free, 370
I ask'd not why, and reck'd not where.
It was at length the same to me,
Fetter'd or fetterless to be,
I learn'd to love despair.
And thus when they appear'd at last,
And all my bonds aside were cast,
These heavy walls to me had grown
A hermitage—and all my own!
And half I felt as they were come
To tear me from a second home: 380
With spiders I had friendship made,
And watch'd them in their sullen trade,
Had seen the mice by moonlight play,
And why should I feel less than they?
We were all inmates of one place,
And I, the monarch of each race,
Had power to kill—yet, strange to tell!
In quiet we had learn'd to dwell—
My very chains and I grew friends,
So much a long communion tends 390
To make us what we are:—even I
Regain'd my freedom with a sigh.

181

MAZEPPA

I

'Twas after dread Pultowa's day,
When fortune left the royal Swede,
Around a slaughter'd army lay,
No more to combat and to bleed.
The power and glory of the war,
Faithless as their vain votaries, men,
Had pass'd to the triumphant Czar,
And Moscow's walls were safe again,
Until a day more dark and drear,
And a more memorable year,
Should give to slaughter and to shame
A mightier host and haughtier name;
A greater wreck, a deeper fall,
A shock to one—a thunderbolt to all.

II

Such was the hazard of the die;
The wounded Charles was taught to fly
By day and night through field and flood,
Stain'd with his own and subjects' blood;
For thousands fell that flight to aid:
And not a voice was heard t' upbraid
Ambition in his humbled hour,
When truth had nought to dread from power.
His horse was slain, and Gieta gave
His own—and died the Russians' slave.
This too sinks after many a league
Of well-sustain'd, but vain fatigue;
And in the depth of forests darkling,
The watch-fires in the distance sparkling—
The beacons of surrounding foes—
A king must lay his limbs at length.
Are these the laurels and repose
For which the nations strain their strength?
They laid him by a savage tree,
In outworn nature's agony;
His wounds were stiff—his limbs were stark—
The heavy hour was chill and dark;
The fever in his blood forbade
A transient slumber's fitful aid:

Mazeppa

And thus it was; but yet through all,
Kinglike the monarch bore his fall,   *40*
And made, in this extreme of ill,
His pangs the vassals of his will:
All silent and subdued were they,
As once the nations round him lay.

III

A band of chiefs!—alas! how few,
Since but the fleeting of a day
Had thinn'd it: but this wreck was true
And chivalrous: upon the clay
Each sate him down, all sad and mute,
Beside his monarch and his steed,   *50*
For danger levels man and brute,
And all are fellows in their need.
Among the rest, Mazeppa made
His pillow in an old oak's shade—
Himself as rough, and scarce less old,
The Ukraine's Hetman, calm and bold;
But first, outspent with his long course,
The Cossack prince rubb'd down his horse,
And made for him a leafy bed,
And smooth'd his fetlocks and his mane,   *60*
And slack'd his girth, and stripp'd his rein,
And joy'd to see how well he fed·
For until now he had the dread
His wearied courser might refuse
To browse beneath the midnight dews:
But he was hardy as his lord,
And little cared for bed and board;
But spirited and docile too;
Whate'er was to be done, would do.
Shaggy and swift, and strong of limb,   *70*
All Tartar-like he carried him;
Obey'd his voice, and came to call,
And knew him in the midst of all:
Though thousands were around,—and Night,
Without a star, pursued her flight,—
That steed from sunset until dawn
His chief would follow like a fawn.

IV

This done, Mazeppa spread his cloak,
And laid his lance beneath his oak,
Felt if his arms in order good   *80*

Mazeppa

The long day's march had well withstood—
If still the powder fill'd the pan,
And flints unloosen'd kept their lock—
His sabre's hilt and scabbard felt,
And whether they had chafed his belt—
And next the venerable man,
From out his havresack and can,
Prepared and spread his slender stock;
And to the monarch and his men
The whole or portion offer'd then   90
With far less of inquietude
Than courtiers at a banquet would.
And Charles of this his slender share
With smiles partook a moment there,
To force of cheer a greater show,
And seem above both wounds and woe;—
And then he said—'Of all our band,
Though firm of heart and strong of hand,
In skirmish, march, or forage, none
Can less have said or more have done   100
Than thee, Mazeppa! On the earth
So fit a pair had never birth,
Since Alexander's days till now,
As thy Bucephalus and thou:
All Scythia's fame to thine should yield
For pricking on o'er flood and field.'
Mazeppa answer'd—'Ill betide
The school wherein I learn'd to ride!'
Quoth Charles—'Old Hetman, wherefore so,
Since thou hast learn'd the art so well?'   110
Mazeppa said—''Twere long to tell;
And we have many a league to go,
With every now and then a blow,
And ten to one at least the foe,
Before our steeds may graze at ease,
Beyond the swift Borysthenes:
And, sire, your limbs have need of rest,
And I will be the sentinel
Of this your troop.'—'But I request,'
Said Sweden's monarch, 'thou wilt tell   120
This tale of thine, and I may reap
Perchance, from this the boon of sleep;
For at this moment from my eyes
The hope of present slumber flies.'

Mazeppa

'Well, sire, with such a hope I'll track
My seventy years of memory back:
I think 'twas in my twentieth spring,—
Ay, 'twas,—when Casimir was king—
John Casimir,—I was his page
Six summers, in my earlier age: *130*
A learned monarch, faith! was he,
And most unlike your majesty:
He made no wars, and did not gain
New realms to lose them back again;
And (save debates in Warsaw's diet)
He reign'd in most unseemly quiet;
Not that he had no cares to vex;
He loved the muses and the sex;
And sometimes these so froward are,
They made him wish himself at war;   *140*
But soon his wrath being o'er, he took
Another mistress, or new book:
And then he gave prodigious fêtes—
All Warsaw gather'd round his gates
To gaze upon his splendid court,
And dames, and chiefs, of princely port:
He was the Polish Solomon,
So sung his poets, all but one,
Who, being unpension'd, made a satire,
And boasted that he could not flatter.   *150*
It was a court of jousts and mimes,
Where every courtier tried at rhymes;
Even I for once produced some verses,
And sign'd my odes 'Despairing Thyrsis.'
There was a certain Palatine,
A count of far and high descent,
Rich as a salt or silver mine;
And he was proud, ye may divine,
As if from heaven he had been sent:
He had such wealth in blood and ore   *160*
As few could match beneath the throne;
And he would gaze upon his store,
And o'er his pedigree would pore,
Until by some confusion led,
Which almost look'd like want of head,
He thought their merits were his own.
His wife was not of his opinion—
His junior she by thirty years—
Grew daily tired of his dominion;
And, after wishes, hopes, and fears,   *170*
To virtue a few farewell tears,

Mazeppa

A restless dream or two, some glances
At Warsaw's youth, some songs, and dances,
Awaited but the usual chances,
Those happy accidents which render
The coldest dames so very tender,
To deck her Count with titles given
'Tis said, as passports into heaven;
But, strange to say, they rarely boast
Of these, who have deserved them most.   *180*

v

'I was a goodly stripling then;
At seventy years I so may say,
That there were few, or boys or men,
Who, in my dawning time of day,
Of vassal or of knight's degree,
Could vie in vanities with me;
For I had strength, youth, gaiety,
A port, not like to this ye see,
But smooth, as all is rugged now;
For time, and care, and war, have plough'd   *190*
My very soul from out my brow;
And thus I should be disavow'd
By all my kind and kin, could they
Compare my day and yesterday;
This change was wrought, too, long ere age
Had ta'en my features for his page:
With years, ye know, have not declined
My strength, my courage, or my mind,
Or at this hour I should not be
Telling old tales beneath a tree,   *200*
With starless skies my canopy.
But let me on: Theresa's form—
Methinks it glides before me now,
Between me and yon chestnut's bough,
The memory is so quick and warm;
And yet I find no words to tell
The shape of her I loved so well.
She had the Asiatic eye,
Such as our Turkish neighbourhood,
Hath mingled with our Polish blood,   *210*
Dark as above us is the sky;
But through it stole a tender light,
Like the first moonrise of midnight;
Large, dark, and swimming in the stream,
Which seem'd to melt to its own beam;
All love, half languor, and half fire,

Like saints that at the stake expire,
And lift their raptured looks on high,
As though it were a joy to die.
A brow like a midsummer lake,   *220*
Transparent with the sun therein,
When waves no murmur dare to make,
And heaven beholds her face within.
A cheek and lip—but why proceed?
I loved her then—I love her still;
And such as I am, love indeed
In fierce extremes—in good and ill.
But still we love even in our rage,
And haunted to our very age
With the vain shadow of the past,   *230*
As is Mazeppa to the last.

VI

'We met—we gazed—I saw, and sigh'd,
She did not speak, and yet replied;
There are ten thousand tones and signs
We hear and see, but none defines—
Involuntary sparks of thought,
Which strike from out the heart o'erwrought,
And form a strange intelligence,
Alike mysterious and intense,
Which link the burning chain that binds,   *240*
Without their will, young hearts and minds;
Conveying, as the electric wire,
We know not how, the absorbing fire.—
I saw, and sigh'd—in silence wept,
And still reluctant distance kept.
Until I was made known to her,
And we might then and there confer
Without suspicion—then, even then,
I long'd, and was resolved to speak;
But on my lips they died again,   *250*
The accents tremulous and weak,
Until one hour.—There is a game,
A frivolous and foolish play,
Wherewith we while away the day;
It is—I have forgot the name—
And we to this, it seems, were set,
By some strange chance, which I forget:
I reck'd not if I won or lost,
It was enough for me to be
So near to hear, and oh! to see   *260*
The being whom I loved the most!

I watch'd her as a sentinel,
(May ours this dark night watch as well!)
Until I saw, and thus it was,
That she was pensive, nor perceived
Her occupation, nor was grieved
Nor glad to lose or gain; but still
Play'd on for hours, as if her will
Yet bound her to the place, though not
That hers might be the winning lot.   270
Then through my brain the thought did pass
Even as a flash of lightning there,
That there was something in her air
Which would not doom me to despair;
And on the thought my words broke forth,
All incoherent as they were—
Their eloquence was little worth,
But yet she listen'd—'tis enough—
Who listens once will listen twice;
Her heart, be sure, is not of ice,   280
And one refusal no rebuff.

VII

'I loved, and was beloved again—
They tell me, Sire, you never knew
Those gentle frailties; if 'tis true,
I shorten all my joy or pain;
To you 'twould seem absurd as vain;
But all men are not born to reign,
Or o'er their passions, or as you
Thus o'er themselves and nations too.
I am—or rather *was*—a prince,   290
A chief of thousands, and could lead
Them on where each would foremost bleed;
But could not o'er myself evince
The like control.—But to resume:
I loved, and was beloved again;
In sooth, it is a happy doom,
But yet where happiest ends in pain.—
We met in secret, and the hour
Which led me to that lady's bower
Was fiery Expectation's dower.   300
My days and nights were nothing—all
Except that hour which doth recall
In the long lapse from youth to age
No other like itself—I'd give
The Ukraine back again to live

Mazeppa

It o'er once more—and be a page,
The happy page, who was the lord
Of one soft heart, and his own sword,
And had no other gem nor wealth
Save nature's gift of youth and health.—   *310*
We met in secret—doubly sweet,
Some say, they find it so to meet;
I know not that—I would have given
My life but to have call'd her mine
In the full view of earth and heaven;
For I did oft and long repine
That we could only meet by stealth.

VIII

'For lovers there are many eyes,
And such there were on us;—the devil
On such occasions should be civil—   *320*
The devil!—I'm loth to do him wrong,
It might be some untoward saint,
Who would not be at rest too long,
But to his pious bile gave vent—
But one fair night, some lurking spies
Surprised and seized us both.
The Count was something more than wroth—
I was unarm'd; but if in steel,
All cap-à-pie from head to heel,
What 'gainst their numbers could I do?—   *330*
'Twas near his castle, far away
From city or from succour near,
And almost on the break of day;
I did not think to see another,
My moments seem'd reduced to few;
And with one prayer to Mary Mother,
And, it may be, a saint or two,
As I resigned me to my fate,
They led me to the castle gate:
Theresa's doom I never knew,   *340*
Our lot was henceforth separate.—
An angry man, ye may opine,
Was he, the proud Count Palatine;
And he had reason good to be,
But he was most enraged lest such
An accident should chance to touch
Upon his future pedigree;
Nor less amazed, that such a blot
His noble 'scutcheon should have got,
While he was highest of his line;   *350*

Mazeppa

Because unto himself he seem'd
The first of men, nor less he deem'd
In others' eyes, and most in mine.
'Sdeath! with a *page*—perchance a king
Had reconciled him to the thing;
But with a stripling of a page—
I felt, but cannot paint his rage.

IX

'"Bring forth the horse!"—the horse was brought;
In truth, he was a noble steed,
A Tartar of the Ukraine breed,
Who looked as though the speed of thought
Were in his limbs; but he was wild,
Wild as the wild deer, and untaught.
With spur and bridle undefiled—
'Twas but a day he had been caught;
And snorting, with erected mane,
And struggling fiercely, but in vain,
In the full foam of wrath and dread
To me the desert-born was led:
They bound me on, that menial throng,
Upon his back with many a thong;
Then loosed him with a sudden lash—
Away!—away!—and on we dash!—
Torrents less rapid and less rash.

X

'Away!—away!—My breath was gone—
I saw not where he hurried on:
'Twas scarcely yet the break of day,
And on he foam'd—away!—away!—
The last of human sounds which rose,
As I was darted from my foes,
Was the wild shout of savage laughter,
Which on the wind came roaring after
A moment from that rabble rout:
With sudden wrath I wrench'd my head,
And snapp'd the cord, which to the mane
Had bound my neck in lieu of rein,
And, writhing half my form about,
Howl'd back my curse; but 'midst the tread,
The thunder of my courser's speed,
Perchance they did not hear nor heed:
It vexes me—for I would fain

Mazeppa

Have paid their insult back again.
I paid it well in after days:
There is not of that castle gate,
Its drawbridge and portcullis' weight,
Stone, bar, moat, bridge, or barrier left;
Nor of its fields a blade of grass,
Save what grows on a ridge of wall,
Where stood the hearth-stone of the hall;
And many a time ye there might pass,   *400*
Nor dream that e'er that fortress was.
I saw its turrets in a blaze,
Their crackling battlements all cleft,
And the hot lead pour down like rain
From off the scorch'd and blackening roof,
Whose thickness was not vengeance-proof.
They little thought that day of pain,
When launch'd, as on the lightning's flash,
They bade me to destruction dash,
That one day I should come again,   *410*
With twice five thousand horse, to thank
The Count for his uncourteous ride.
They play'd me then a bitter prank,
When, with the wild horse for my guide,
They bound me to his foaming flank:
At length I play'd them one as frank—
For time at last sets all things even—
And if we do but watch the hour,
There never yet was human power
Which could evade, if unforgiven,   *420*
The patient search and vigil long
Of him who treasures up a wrong.

XI

'Away, away, my steed and I,
Upon the pinions of the wind,
All human dwellings left behind;
We sped like meteors through the sky,
When with its crackling sound the night
Is chequer'd with the northern light:
Town—village—none were on our track,
But a wild plain of far extent,   *430*
And bounded by a forest black;
And, save the scarce seen battlement
On distant heights of some strong hold,
Against the Tartars built of old,

Mazeppa

No trace of man. The year before
A Turkish army had march'd o'er;
And where the Spahi's hoof hath trod,
The verdure flies the bloody sod:—
The sky was dull, and dim, and gray,
And a low breeze crept moaning by—   440
I could have answer'd with a sigh—
But fast we fled, away, away—
And I could neither sigh nor pray;
And my cold sweat-drops fell like rain
Upon the courser's bristling mane;
But, snorting still with rage and fear,
He flew upon his far career:
At times I almost thought, indeed,
He must have slacken'd in his speed;
But no—my bound and slender frame   450
Was nothing to his angry might,
And merely like a spur became:
Each motion which I made to free
My swoln limbs from their agony
Increased his fury and affright:
I tried my voice,—'twas faint and low,
But yet he swerved as from a blow;
And, starting to each accent, sprang
As from a sudden trumpet's clang:
Meantime my cords were wet with gore,   460
Which, oozing through my limbs, ran o'er;
And in my tongue the thirst became
A something fierier far than flame.

XII

'We near'd the wild wood—'twas so wide,
I saw no bounds on either side;
'Twas studded with old sturdy trees,
That bent not to the roughest breeze
Which howls down from Siberia's waste,
And strips the forest in its haste,—
But these were few and far between,   470
Set thick with shrubs more young and green,
Luxuriant with their annual leaves,
Ere strown by those autumnal eves
That nip the forest's foliage dead,
Discolour'd with a lifeless red,
Which stands thereon like stiffen'd gore
Upon the slain when battle's o'er,
And some long winter's night hath shed
Its frost o'er every tombless head,

Mazeppa

So cold and stark the raven's beak   480
May peck unpierced each frozen cheek:
'Twas a wild waste of underwood,
And here and there a chestnut stood,
The strong oak, and the hardy pine;
But far apart—and well it were,
Or else a different lot were mine—
The boughs gave way, and did not tear
My limbs; and I found strength to bear
My wounds, already scarr'd with cold—
My bonds forbade to loose my hold.   490
We rustled through the leaves like wind,
Left shrubs, and trees, and wolves behind;
By night I heard them on the track,
Their troop came hard upon our back,
With their long gallop, which can tire
The hound's deep hate, and hunter's fire:
Where'er we flew they follow'd on,
Nor left us with the morning sun;
Behind I saw them, scarce a rood,
At day-break winding through the wood,   500
And through the night had heard their feet
Their stealing, rustling step repeat.
Oh! how I wish'd for spear or sword,
At least to die amidst the horde,
And perish—if it must be so—
At bay, destroying many a foe.
When first my courser's race begun,
I wish'd the goal already won;
But now I doubted strength and speed.
Vain doubt! his swift and savage breed   510
Had nerved him like the mountain-roe;
Nor faster falls the blinding snow
Which whelms the peasant near the door
Whose threshold he shall cross no more,
Bewilder'd with the dazzling blast,
Than through the forest-paths he past—
Untired, untamed, and worse than wild;
All furious as a favour'd child
Balk'd of its wish; or fiercer still—
A woman piqued—who has her will.   520

XIII

'The wood was past; 'twas more than noon,
But chill the air, although in June;
Or it might be my veins ran cold—
Prolong'd endurance tames the bold;

Mazeppa

And I was then not what I seem,
But headlong as a wintry stream,
And wore my feelings out before
I well could count their causes o'er:
And what with fury, fear, and wrath,
The tortures which beset my path,   530
Cold, hunger, sorrow, shame, distress,
Thus bound in nature's nakedness;
Sprung from a race whose rising blood
When stirr'd beyond its calmer mood,
And trodden hard upon, is like
The rattle-snake's, in act to strike,
What marvel if this worn-out trunk
Beneath its woes a moment sunk?
The earth gave way, the skies roll'd round,
I seem'd to sink upon the ground;   540
But err'd, for I was fastly bound.
My heart turn'd sick, my brain grew sore,
And throbb'd awhile, then beat no more:
The skies spun like a mighty wheel;
I saw the trees like drunkards reel,
And a slight flash sprang o'er my eyes,
Which saw no farther: he who dies
Can die no more than then I died.
O'ertortur'd by that ghastly ride,
I felt the blackness come and go.   550
And strove to wake; but could not make
My senses climb up from below:
I felt as on a plank at sea,
When all the waves that dash o'er thee,
At the same time upheave and whelm,
And hurl thee towards a desert realm.
My undulating life was as
The fancied lights that flitting pass
Our shut eyes in deep midnight, when
Fever begins upon the brain: 560
But soon it pass'd, with little pain,
But a confusion worse than such:
I own that I should deem it much,
Dying, to feel the same again;
And yet I do suppose we must
Feel far more ere we turn to dust:
No matter; I have bared my brow
Full in Death's face—before—and now.

XIV

'My thoughts came back; where was I?   Cold,
And numb, and giddy: pulse by pulse   570

Mazeppa

Life reassumed its lingering hold,
And throb by throb: till grown a pang
Which for a moment would convulse,
My blood reflow'd, though thick and chill;
My ear with uncouth noises rang,
My heart began once more to thrill;
My sight return'd, though dim; alas!
And thicken'd, as it were, with glass.
Methought the dash of waves was nigh;
There was a gleam too of the sky,   580
Studded with stars;—it is no dream;
The wild horse swims the wilder stream!
The bright broad river's gushing tide
Sweeps, winding onward, far and wide,
And we are half-way, struggling o'er
To yon unknown and silent shore.
The waters broke my hollow trance,
And with a temporary strength
My stiffen'd limbs were rebaptized.
My courser's broad breast proudly braves,   590
And dashes off the ascending waves,
And onward we advance!
We reach the slippery shore at length,
A haven I but little prized,
For all behind was dark and drear,
And all before was night and fear.
How many hours of night or day
In those suspended pangs I lay,
I could not tell; I scarcely knew
If this were human breath I drew.   600

XV

'With glossy skin, and dripping mane,
And reeling limbs, and reeking flank,
The wild steed's sinewy nerves still strain
Up the repelling bank.
We gain the top: a boundless plain
Spreads through the shadow of the night
And onward, onward, onward, seems,
Like precipices in our dreams,
To stretch beyond the sight;
And here and there a speck of white,   610
Or scatter'd spot of dusky green,
In masses broke into the light,
As rose the moon upon my right.
But nought distinctly seen
In the dim waste would indicate

Mazeppa

The omen of a cottage gate;
No twinkling taper from afar
Stood like a hospitable star;
Not even an ignis-fatuus rose
To make him merry with my woes: 620
That very cheat had cheer'd me then!
Although detected, welcome still,
Reminding me, through every ill,
Of the abodes of men.

XVI

'Onward we went—but slack and slow;
His savage force at length o'erspent,
The drooping courser, faint and low,
All feebly foaming went.
A sickly infant had had power
To guide him forward in that hour;   630
But useless all to me.
His new-born tameness nought avail'd,
My limbs were bound; my force had fail'd,
Perchance, had they been free.
With feeble effort still I tried
To rend the bonds so starkly tied—
But still it was in vain;
My limbs were only wrung the more,
And soon the idle strife gave o'er,
Which but prolong'd their pain: 640
The dizzy race seem'd almost done,
Although no goal was nearly won:
Some streaks announced the coming sun—
How slow, alas! he came!
Methought that mist of dawning gray
Would never dapple into day;
How heavily it roll'd away—
Before the eastern flame
Rose crimson, and deposed the stars,
And call'd the radiance from their cars,   650
And fill'd the earth, from his deep throne,
With lonely lustre, all his own.

XVII

'Up rose the sun; the mists were curl'd
Back from the solitary world
Which lay around—behind—before;
What booted it to traverse o'er
Plain, forest, river? Man nor brute,
Nor dint of hoof, nor print of foot,

Mazeppa

Lay in the wild luxuriant soil;
No sign of travel—none of toil;   *660*
The very air was mute;
And not an insect's shrill small horn,
Nor matin bird's new voice was borne
From herb nor thicket.   Many a werst,
Panting as if his heart would burst,
The weary brute still stagger'd on;
And still we were—or seem'd—alone:
At length, while reeling on our way,
Methought I heard a courser neigh,
From out yon tuft of blackening firs.   *670*
Is it the wind those branches stirs?
No, no! from out the forest prance
A trampling troop; I see them come!
In one vast squadron they advance!
I strove to cry—my lips were dumb.
The steeds rush on in plunging pride;
But where are they the reins to guide?
A thousand horse—and none to ride!
With flowing tail, and flying mane,
With nostrils—never stretch'd by pain,   *680*
Mouths bloodless to the bit or rein,
And feet that iron never shod,
And flanks unscarr'd by spur or rod,
A thousand horse, the wild, the free,
Like waves that follow o'er the sea,
Came thickly thundering on,
As if our faint approach to meet;
The sight re-nerved my courser's feet,
A moment staggering, feebly fleet,
A moment, with a faint low neigh,   *690*
He answer'd, and then fell;
With gasps and glazing eyes he lay,
And reeking limbs immoveable,
His first and last career is done!
On came the troop—they saw him stoop.
They saw me strangely bound along
His back with many a bloody thong:
They stop—they start—they snuff the air,
Gallop a moment here and there,
Approach, retire, wheel round and round,   *700*
Then plunging back with sudden bound,
Headed by one black mighty steed,
Who seem'd the patriarch of his breed,
Without a single speck or hair
Of white upon his shaggy hide:

Mazeppa

They snort—they foam—neigh—swerve aside,
And backward to the forest fly,
By instinct, from a human eye.—
They left me there to my despair,
Link'd to the dead and stiffening wretch,   *710*
Whose lifeless limbs beneath me stretch,
Relieved from that unwonted weight,
From whence I could not extricate
Nor him nor me—and there we lay
The dying on the dead!
I little deem'd another day
Would see my houseless, helpless head.
'And there from morn till twilight bound,
I felt the heavy hours toil round,
With just enough of life to see   *720*
My last of suns go down on me,
In hopeless certainty of mind,
That makes us feel at length resign'd
To that which our foreboding years
Presents the worst and last of fears
Inevitable—even a boon,
Nor more unkind for coming soon;
Yet shunn'd and dreaded with such care,
As if it only were a snare
That prudence might escape: *730*
At times both wish'd for and implored,
At times sought with self-pointed sword,
Yet still a dark and hideous close
To even intolerable woes,
And welcome in no shape.
And, strange to say, the sons of pleasure,
They who have revell'd beyond measure
In beauty, wassail, wine, and treasure,
Die calm, or calmer, oft than he
Whose heritage was misery: *740*
For he who hath in turn run through
All that was beautiful and new,
Hath nought to hope, and nought to leave;
And, save the future, (which is view'd
Not quite as men are base or good,
But as their nerves may be endued,)
With nought perhaps to grieve:—
The wretch still hopes his woes must end,
And Death, whom he should deem his friend,
Appears, to his distemper'd eyes,   *750*
Arrived to rob him of his prize,
The tree of his new Paradise.

Mazeppa

To-morrow would have given him all,
Repaid his pangs, repair'd his fall;
To-morrow would have been the first
Of days no more deplored or curst,
But bright, and long, and beckoning years,
Seen dazzling through the mist of tears,
Guerdon of many a painful hour;
To-morrow would have given him power   760
To rule, to shine, to smite, to save—
And must it dawn upon his grave?

XVIII

'The sun was sinking—still I lay
Chain'd to the chill and stiffening steed,
I thought to mingle there our clay;
And my dim eyes of death had need.
No hope arose of being freed:
I cast my last looks up the sky,
And there between me and the sun
I saw the expecting raven fly,   770
Who scarce would wait till both should die,
Ere his repast begun;
He flew, and perch'd, then flew once more,
And each time nearer than before;
I saw his wing through twilight flit,
And once so near me he alit
I could have smote, but lack'd the strength;
But the slight motion of my hand,
And feeble scratching of the sand
The exerted throat's faint struggling noise,   780
Which scarcely could be call'd a voice,
Together scared him off at length.—
I know no more—my latest dream
Is something of a lovely star
Which fix'd my dull eyes from afar,
And went and came with wandering beam,
And of the cold, dull, swimming, dense
Sensation of recurring sense,
And then subsiding back to death,
And then again a little breath,   790
A little thrill, a short suspense,
An icy sickness curdling o'er
My heart, and sparks that cross'd my brain—
A gasp, a throb, a start of pain,
A sigh, and nothing more.

XIX

'I woke—Where was I?—Do I see
A human face look down on me?
And doth a roof above me close?
Do these limbs on a couch repose?
Is this a chamber where I lie?
And is it mortal yon bright eye,
That watches me with gentle glance?
I closed my own again once more.
As doubtful that the former trance
Could not as yet be o'er.
A slender girl, long-hair'd, and tall,
Sate watching by the cottage wall;
The sparkle of her eye I caught
Even with my first return of thought
For ever and anon she threw
A prying, pitying glance on me
With her black eyes so wild and free;
I gazed, and gazed, until I knew
No vision it could be,—
But that I lived, and was released
From adding to the vulture's feast:
And when the Cossack maid beheld
My heavy eyes at length unseal'd,
She smiled—and I essay'd to speak,
But fail'd—and she approach'd, and made
With lip and finger signs that said,
I must not strive as yet to break
The silence, till my strength should be
Enough to leave my accents free;
And then her hand on mine she laid,
And smooth'd the pillow for my head,
And stole along on tiptoe tread,
And gently oped the door, and spake
In whispers—ne'er was voice so sweet!
Even music follow'd her light feet;
But those she call'd were not awake,
And she went forth; but, ere she pass'd,
Another look on me she cast,
Another sign she made, to say,
That I had nought to fear, that all
Were near, at my command or call,
And she would not delay
Her due return:—while she was gone,
Methought I felt too much alone.

XX

'She came with mother and with sire—   840
What need of more?—I will not tire
With long recital of the rest,
Since I became the Cossack's guest.
They found me senseless on the plain—
They bore me to the nearest hut—
They brought me into life again—
Me—one day o'er their realm to reign!
Thus the vain fool who strove to glut
His rage, refining on my pain,
Sent me forth to the wilderness,   850
Bound, naked, bleeding, and alone,
To pass the desert to a throne,—
What mortal his own doom may guess?—
Let none despond, let none despair!
To-morrow the Borysthenes
May see our coursers graze at ease
Upon his Turkish bank,—and never
Had I such welcome for a river
As I shall yield when safely there.
Comrades, good night!'—The Hetman threw   860
His length beneath the oak-tree shade,
With leafy couch already made,
A bed nor comfortless nor new
To him, who took his rest whene'er
The hour arrived, no matter where:
His eyes the hastening slumbers steep
And if ye marvel Charles forgot
To thank his tale, *he* wonder'd not,—
The king had been an hour asleep.

SHE WALKS IN BEAUTY

I

She walks in beauty, like the night
Of cloudless climes and starry skies;
And all that's best of dark and bright
Meet in her aspect and her eyes:
Thus mellow'd to that tender light
Which heaven to gaudy day denies.

II

One shade the more, one ray the less,
Had half impair'd the nameless grace
Which waves in every raven tress,
Or softly lightens o'er her face;
Where thoughts serenely sweet express
How pure, how dear their dwelling-place.

III

And on that cheek, and o'er that brow,
So soft, so calm, yet eloquent,
The smiles that win, the tints that glow,
But tell of days in goodness spent,
A mind at peace with all below,
A heart whose love is innocent!

OH! SNATCH'D AWAY IN BEAUTY'S BLOOM

I

Oh! snatch'd away in beauty's bloom,
On thee shall press no ponderous tomb;
But on thy turf shall roses rear
Their leaves, the earliest of the year;
And the wild cypress wave in tender gloom:

II

And oft by yon blue gushing stream
Shall Sorrow lean her drooping head,
And feed deep thought with many a dream,
And lingering pause and lightly tread;
Fond wretch! as if her step disturb'd the dead!

The Destruction of Sennacherib

III

Away! we know that tears are vain,
That death nor heeds nor hears distress:
Will this unteach us to complain?
Or make one mourner weep the less?
And thou—who tell'st me to forget,
Thy looks are wan, thine eyes are wet.

THE DESTRUCTION OF SENNACHERIB

I

The Assyrian came down like the wolf on the fold,
And his cohorts were gleaming in purple and gold;
And the sheen of their spears was like stars on the sea,
When the blue wave rolls nightly on deep Galilee.

II

Like the leaves of the forest when Summer is green,
That host with their banners at sunset were seen:
Like the leaves of the forest when Autumn hath blown,
That host on the morrow lay wither'd and strown.

III

For the Angel of Death spread his wings on the blast,
And breathed in the face of the foe as he pass'd;   *10*
And the eyes of the sleepers wax'd deadly and chill,
And their hearts but once heaved, and for ever grew still!

IV

And there lay the steed with his nostril all wide,
But through it there roll'd not the breath of his pride:
And the foam of his gasping lay white on the turf,
And cold as the spray of the rock-beating surf.

V

And there lay the rider distorted and pale,
With the dew on his brow, and the rust on his mail;
And the tents were all silent, the banners alone,
The lances unlifted, the trumpet unblown.

VI

And the widows of Ashur are loud in their wail,
And the idols are broke in the temple of Baal;
And the might of the Gentile, unsmote by the sword,
Hath melted like snow in the glance of the Lord!

STANZAS FOR MUSIC

THERE be none of Beauty's daughters
With a magic like thee;
And like music on the waters
Is thy sweet voice to me:
When, as if its sound were causing
The charmed ocean's pausing,
The waves lie still and gleaming,
And the lull'd winds seem dreaming.

And the midnight moon is weaving
Her bright chain o'er the deep;
Whose breast is gently heaving,
As an infant's asleep:
So the spirit bows before thee,
To listen and adore thee;
With a full but soft emotion,
Like the swell of Summer's ocean.

WHEN WE TWO PARTED

When we two parted
In silence and tears,
Half broken-hearted
To sever for years,
Pale grew thy cheek and cold,
Colder thy kiss;
Truly that hour foretold
Sorrow to this.

The dew of the morning
Sunk chill on my brow—　　　　　　　　*10*
It felt like the warning
Of what I feel now.
Thy vows are all broken,
And light is thy fame;
I hear thy name spoken,
And share in its shame.

They name thee before me,
A knell to mine ear;
A shudder comes o'er me—
Why wert thou so dear?　　　　　　　　*20*
They know not I knew thee,
Who knew thee too well:—
Long, long shall I rue thee,
Too deeply to tell.

In secret we met—
In silence I grieve,
That thy heart could forget,
Thy spirit deceive.
If I should meet thee
After long years,　　　　　　　　　　　*30*
How should I greet thee?—
With silence and tears.

DARKNESS

I HAD a dream which was not all a dream.
The bright sun was extinguish'd, and the stars
Did wander darkling in the eternal space,
Rayless, and pathless, and the icy earth
Swung blind and blackening in the moonless air;
Morn came and went—and came, and brought no day,
And men forgot their passions in the dread
Of this their desolation; and all hearts
Were chill'd into a selfish prayer for light:
And they did live by watchfires—and the thrones,   *10*
The palaces of crowned kings—the huts,
The habitations of all things which dwell,
Were burnt for beacons; cities were consumed,
And men were gather'd round their blazing homes
To look once more into each other's face;
Happy were those who dwelt within the eye
Of the volcanos, and their mountain-torch:
A fearful hope was all the world contain'd;
Forests were set on fire—but hour by hour
They fell and faded—and the crackling trunks   *20*
Extinguish'd with a crash—and all was black.
The brows of men by the despairing light
Wore an unearthly aspect, as by fits
The flashes fell upon them; some lay down
And hid their eyes and wept; and some did rest
Their chins upon their clenched hands, and smiled;
And others hurried to and fro, and fed
Their funeral piles with fuel and look'd up
With mad disquietude on the dull sky,
The pall of a past world; and then again   *30*
With curses cast them down upon the dust,
And gnash'd their teeth and howl'd: the wild birds shriek'd,
And, terrified, did flutter on the ground,
And flap their useless wings; the wildest brutes
Came tame and tremulous; and vipers crawl'd
And twined themselves among the multitude,
Hissing, but stingless—they were slain for food:
And War, which for a moment was no more,
Did glut himself again;—a meal was bought
With blood, and each sate sullenly apart   *40*
Gorging himself in gloom: no love was left;
All earth was but one thought—and that was death,

Darkness

Immediate and inglorious; and the pang
Of famine fed upon all entrails—men
Died, and their bones were tombless as their flesh;
The meagre by the meagre were devour'd,
Even dogs assail'd their masters, all save one,
And he was faithful to a corse, and kept
The birds and beasts and famish'd men at bay,
Till hunger clung them, or the dropping dead   50
Lured their lank jaws; himself sought out no food,
But with a piteous and perpetual moan,
And a quick desolate cry, licking the hand
Which answer'd not with a caress—he died.
The crowd was famish'd by degrees; but two
Of an enormous city did survive,
And they were enemies: they met beside
The dying embers of an altar-place
Where had been heap'd a mass of holy things
For an unholy usage; they raked up,   60
And shivering scraped with their cold skeleton hands
The feeble ashes, and their feeble breath
Blew for a little life, and made a flame
Which was a mockery; then they lifted up
Their eyes as it grew lighter and beheld
Each other's aspects—saw, and shriek'd, and died—
Even of their mutual hideousness they died,
Unknowing who he was upon whose brow
Famine had written Fiend. The world was void,
The populous and the powerful was a lump,   70
Seasonless, herbless, treeless, manless, lifeless—
A lump of death—a chaos of hard clay,
The rivers, lakes, and ocean all stood still,
And nothing stirr'd within their silent depths;
Ships sailorless lay rotting on the sea,
And their masts fell down piecemeal; as they dropp'd
They slept on the abyss without a surge—
The waves were dead; the tides were in their grave,
The Moon, their mistress, had expired before;
The winds were wither'd in the stagnant air,   80
And the clouds perish'd; Darkness had no need
Of aid from them—She was the Universe.

EPISTLE TO AUGUSTA

I

My sister! my sweet sister! if a name
Dearer and purer were, it should be thine.
Mountains and seas divide us, but I claim
No tears, but tenderness to answer mine:
Go where I will, to me thou art the same—
A loved regret which I would not resign.
There yet are two things in my destiny,—
A world to roam through, and a home with thee.

II

The first were nothing—had I still the last,
It were the haven of my happiness;
But other claims and other ties thou hast,
And mine is not the wish to make them less.
A strange doom is thy father's son's, and past
Recalling, as it lies beyond redress;
Reversed for him our grandsire's fate of yore,—
He had no rest at sea nor I on shore.

III

If my inheritance of storms hath been
In other elements, and on the rocks
Of perils, overlook'd or unforeseen,
I have sustain'd my share of worldly shocks,
The fault was mine; nor do I seek to screen
My errors with defensive paradox;
I have been cunning in mine overthrow,
The careful pilot of my proper woe.

IV

Mine were my faults, and mine be their reward.
My whole life was a contest, since the day
That gave me being, gave me that which marr'd
The gift,—a fate, or will, that walk'd astray;
And I at times have found the struggle hard,
And thought of shaking off my bonds of clay:
But now I fain would for a time survive,
If but to see what next can well arrive.

Epistle to Augusta

V

Kingdoms and empires in my little day
I have outlived, and yet I am not old;
And when I look on this, the petty spray
Of my own years of trouble, which have roll'd
Like a wild bay of breakers, melts away:
Something—I know not what—does still uphold
A spirit of slight patience;—not in vain,
Even for its own sake, do we purchase pain.

VI

Perhaps the workings of defiance stir
Within me,—or perhaps a cold despair,
Brought on when ills habitually recur,—
Perhaps a kinder clime, or purer air,
(For even to this may change of soul refer,
And with light armour we may learn to bear,)
Have taught me a strange quiet, which was not
The chief companion of a calmer lot.

VII

I feel almost at times as I have felt,
In happy childhood; trees, and flowers, and brooks,
Which do remember me of where I dwelt
Ere my young mind was sacrificed to books,
Come as of yore upon me, and can melt
My heart with recognition of their looks;
And even at moments I could think I see
Some living thing to love—but none like thee.

VIII

Here are the Alpine landscapes which create
A fund for contemplation;—to admire
Is a brief feeling of a trivial date;
But something worthier do such scenes inspire:
Here to be lonely is not desolate,
For much I view which I could most desire,
And, above all, a lake I can behold
Lovelier, not dearer, than our own of old.

IX

Oh that thou wert but with me!—but I grow
The fool of my own wishes, and forget
The solitude which I have vaunted so
Has lost its praise in this but one regret;
There may be others which I less may show;—
I am not of the plaintive mood, and yet
I feel an ebb in my philosophy,
And the tide rising in my alter'd eye.

Epistle to Augusta

X

I did remind thee of our own dear Lake,
By the old Hall which may be mine no more.
Leman's is fair; but think not I forsake
The sweet remembrance of a dearer shore:
Sad havoc Time must with my memory make
Ere *that* or *thou* can fade these eyes before;
Though, like all things which I have loved, they are
Resign'd for ever, or divided far. *80*

XI

The world is all before me; I but ask
Of Nature that with which she will comply—
It is but in her summer's sun to bask,
To mingle with the quiet of her sky,
To see her gentle face without a mask,
And never gaze on it with apathy.
She was my early friend, and now shall be
My sister—till I look again on thee.

XII

I can reduce all feelings but this one;
And that I would not;—for at length I see *90*
Such scenes as those wherein my life begun.
The earliest—even the only paths for me—
Had I but sooner learnt the crowd to shun,
I had been better than I now can be;
The passions which have torn me would have slept;
I had not suffer'd, and *thou* hadst not wept.

XIII

With false Ambition what had I to do?
Little with Love, and least of all with Fame;
And yet they came unsought, and with me grew,
And made me all which they can make—a name. *100*
Yet this was not the end I did pursue;
Surely I once beheld a nobler aim.
But all is over—I am one the more
To baffled millions which have gone before.

XIV

And for the future, this world's future may
From me demand but little of my care;
I have outlived myself by many a day;
Having survived so many things that were;
My years have been no slumber, but the prey
Of ceaseless vigils; for I had the share *110*
Of life which might have fill'd a century,
Before its fourth in time had pass'd me by.

Epistle to Augusta

XV

And for the remnant which may be to come
I am content; and for the past I feel
Not thankless,—for within the crowded sum
Of struggles, happiness at times would steal,
And for the present, I would not benumb
My feelings further.—Nor shall I conceal
That with all this I still can look around
And worship Nature with a thought profound.   *120*

XVI

For thee, my own sweet sister, in thy heart
I know myself secure, as thou in mine;
We were and are—I am, even as thou art—
Beings who ne'er each other can resign;
It is the same, together or apart,
From life's commencement to its slow decline
We are entwined—let death come slow or fast,
The tie which bound the first endures the last!

LINES

ON HEARING THAT LADY BYRON WAS ILL

And thou wert sad—yet I was not with thee:
And thou wert sick, and yet I was not near;
Methought that joy and health alone could be
Where I was not—and pain and sorrow here!
And is it thus?—it is as I foretold,
And shall be more so; for the mind recoils
Upon itself, and the wreck'd heart lies cold,
While heaviness collects the shatter'd spoils.
It is not in the storm nor in the strife
We feel benumb'd, and wish to be no more,   *10*
But in the after-silence on the shore,
When all is lost, except a little life.

I am too well avenged!—but 'twas my right;
Where'er my sins might be, *thou* wert not sent
To be the Nemesis who should requite—
Nor did Heaven choose so near an instrument.
Mercy is for the merciful!—if thou
Hast been of such, 'twill be accorded now.
Thy nights are banish'd from the realms of sleep!—
Yes! they may flatter thee, but thou shalt feel   *20*
A hollow agony which will not heal,
For thou art pillow'd on a curse too deep;
Thou hast sown in my sorrow, and must reap
The bitter harvest in a woe as real!
I have had many foes, but none like thee;
For 'gainst the rest myself I could defend,
And be avenged, or turn them into friend;
But thou in safe implacability
Hadst nought to dread—in thy own weakness shielded,
And in my love, which hath but too much yielded,   *30*
And spared, for thy sake, some I should not spare—
And thus upon the world—trust in thy truth—
And the wild fame of my ungovern'd youth—
On things that were not, and on things that are—
Even upon such a basis hast thou built
A monument, whose cement hath been guilt!
The moral Clytemnestra of thy lord,
And hew'd down, with an unsuspected sword,
Fame, peace, and hope—and all the better life
Which, but for this cold treason of thy heart,   *40*
Might still have risen from out the grave of strife,
And found a nobler duty than to part.
But of thy virtues didst thou make a vice,

So, We'll Go No More A Roving

Trafficking with them in a purpose cold,
For present anger, and for future gold—
And buying other's grief at any price.
And thus once enter'd into crooked ways,
The early truth, which was thy proper praise,
Did not still walk beside thee—but at times,
And with a breast unknowing its own crimes. 50
Deceit, averments incompatible,
Equivocations, and the thoughts which dwell
In Janus-spirits—the significant eye
Which learns to lie with silence—the pretext
Of Prudence, with advantages annex'd—
The acquiescence in all things which tend,
No matter how, to the desired end—
All found a place in thy philosophy.
The means were worthy, and the end is won—
I would not do by thee as thou hast done! 60

SO, WE'LL GO NO MORE A ROVING

I

So, we'll go no more a roving
  So late into the night,
Though the heart be still as loving,
  And the moon be still as bright.

II

For the sword outwears its sheath,
  And the soul wears out the breast,
And the heart must pause to breathe,
  And love itself have rest.

III

Though the night was made for loving,
  And the day returns too soon, 10
Yet we'll go no more a roving
  By the light of the moon.

NOTES

(Notes ascribed to Byron are quoted from those which he himself appended to the poems.)

Childe Harold's Pilgrimage, I and II

Byron started Canto I at Yanina (Ioannina, in Greece) on 31 October 1809 and finished Canto II at Smyrna (Izmir, in Turkey) on 28 March 1810. He brought the manuscript home with him in the summer of 1811 but removed, altered and added stanzas before John Murray published the two cantos together on 10 March 1812. So successful was the volume that Byron could say that he awoke one morning and found himself famous. Edition followed rapidly on edition. The fourth (1812) saw the insertion of the 'Addition to the Preface'; the seventh (1814), of the dedication 'To Ianthe' and ten other stanzas. In the words quoted as an epigraph, Fougeret de Monbron (*d.* 1761) says that experience of other countries has reconciled him to his own, which he used once to hate. Byron had picked up *Le Cosmopolite* (1750) on his travels, and it had become a great favourite with him.

Preface, 22–3. *the appellation 'Childe':* signifying a youth of gentle birth.

Preface, 34. *Dr. Beattie:* James Beattie (1735–1803) is speaking of his principal poem, *The Minstrel*.

Preface, 46. *Ariosto, Thomson:* In *The Castle of Indolence*, James Thomson (1700–48) uses the Spenserian stanza; in *Orlando Furioso*, Lodovico Ariosto (1474–1533) uses the octave stanza (*ottava rima*).

Addition, 12. *besides the anachronism, he is very* unknightly: *The Quarterly Review* for March 1812 complained that Harold was an anachronism in the Spain of the Peninsular War but lacked the gallantry of the Middle Ages.

Addition, 17, 23. *Sainte-Palaye . . . Rolland:* Byron refers to two eighteenth-century authorities on the age of chivalry.

Addition, 26–7. *No waiter, but a knight templar:* The waiter at the Golden Eagle in Weimar, a warrior in disguise, speaks these words in *The Rovers*, a burlesque drama contributed to *The Anti-Jacobin* (1797–8) by George Canning, George Ellis, and John Hookham Frere.

Addition, 34. *its days are over:* Referring in his *Reflections on the Revolution in France* (1790) to the situation of Queen Marie-Antoinette, Edmund Burke (1729–97) 'thought ten thousand swords must have leaped from their scabbards to avenge even a look that threatened her with insult. But the age of chivalry is gone.'

Addition, 37. *Bayard:* Pierre Terrail, Seigneur de Bayard (*c.* 1474–1524), the 'chevalier sans peur et sans reproche', who seemed to embody in himself the ideal of knighthood.

Addition, 37–8. *Sir Joseph Banks:* Botanist and patron of science (1743–1820). He accompanied Cook on his first voyage round the world and later became President of the Royal Society.

Addition, 54–5. *Timon . . . Zeluco:* Shakespeare shows how the ingratitude of Timon's friends makes him a misanthropist; John Moore (1729–1802) shows how a mother's indulgence helps to pervert the character of Zeluco, the eponymous hero-villain of his novel.

To Ianthe: Writing in 1812, Byron addresses Lady Charlotte Harley, the eleven-year-old daughter of his mistress, Lady Oxford.

Notes

11. *unbeseem:* fail in, fall short of.
19. *Peri:* a Persian name for a graceful and beautiful supernatural being.

Canto I
1. *heavenly birth:* The Muses, divinities presiding over the various kinds of poetry, arts, and sciences, were believed in Hellas, or Greece, to be the nine daughters of Zeus and Mnemosyne.
6. *Delphi's long deserted shrine:* This oracular shrine stood on the southern slope of Parnassus, the 'sacred hill' of Apollo and the Muses. Castalia, the 'vaunted rill' was sacred to the same deities.
8. *mote:* may.
10. *Whilome:* once upon a time.
10. *Albion:* England.
11. *ne:* archaic form of the negative.
14. *wight:* creature.
18. *wassailers:* revellers.
19. *hight:* called.
23. *losel:* profligate.
27. *blazon:* glorify.
36. *Eremite:* hermit.
49. *ee:* eye.
55. *his father's hall:* In describing Harold's family home, Byron was evidently thinking of his own Newstead Abbey. (In ll. 39–45 his own frustrated early love for Mary Chaworth may similarly have been in his mind.)
61. *Paphian girls:* courtesans. Paphos was the chief seat of the worship of Aphrodite (Venus).
72. *mote:* might.
77. *lemans:* lovers.
79. *feere:* companion, mate.
99. *Paynim:* pagan; especially, Mohammedan.
99. *Earth's central line:* the equator. Harold does not in fact cross it.
134, 158. *my little page ... my staunch yeoman:* Byron was presumably thinking of Robert Rushton, a handsome boy who accompanied him in 1809 as far as Gibraltar; and of William Fletcher, his valet, who completed the Mediterranean tour and remained in his service until Byron's death.
204. *golden tribute:* small particles of gold in the sands of the River Tagus (Tajo, Tejo).
205. *Lusian:* Portuguese.
215. *Gaul's locust host:* the French invaders.
215. *fellest:* fiercest.
226. *sheening:* glistening.
232. *surtout:* greatcoat, overcoat.
233. *shent:* shamed, disgraced.
241. *bard:* Dante (1265–1321).
242. *Elysium:* heaven.
243. *horrid:* bristling.
255. *of woe:* This should have been 'of the rock', but Byron misunderstood the Portuguese word. 'Below, at some distance,' according to his own note, 'is the Cork Convent, where St Honorius dug his den, over which is his epitaph.'

215

Notes

262. *rude-carved crosses:* Byron mistook the purpose of these; they were guide-posts.
275. *Vathek:* The vastly wealthy William Beckford (1759–1844) is here addressed by the name of his fantastic Oriental tale, *Vathek*. Beckford passed 1794–6 in retirement near Cintra.
288–314. Negotiations after the battle of Vimeiro in 1808 had led to the signing of the Convention of Cintra, which an outraged British public thought unduly lenient to the defeated French.
298. *Marialva's dome:* Byron mistakenly believed that the Convention was signed in the palace of the Marchese Marialva.
305. *Lusitania:* Portugal.
333. *Mafra:* Describing it as the Escurial of Portugal, Byron emphasizes the prodigious extent of Mafra: 'it contains a palace, convent, and most superb church.'
334. *luckless queen:* Maria I, who had long been insane when Byron wrote.
337. *freres:* friars.
338. *Babylonian whore:* Church of Rome.
344. *joyaunce:* delight.
368. *Hispania:* Spain.
388. *standard:* the Cross of Victory, made of Asturian oak, which was said to have fallen from heaven before Pelagio (Pelayo) defeated the Moors at Cangas in A.D. 718.
389. *Cava's traitor-sire:* Count Julian allied himself with the Moorish invaders of Spain in revenge for the violation of his daughter Cava (Caba) by Roderick the Goth.
393. *drove at last:* The Moors were eventually expelled from Spain in 1492, in the reign of Ferdinand and Isabella.
421. *sulphury Siroc:* the sirocco, an oppressively hot wind blowing from North Africa into Southern Europe.
430. *this morn:* The battle of Talavera began on 27 July 1809 and lasted two days. 'Never was there such a Murderous Battle', said the victorious general, later to become Duke of Wellington.
459. *Albuera:* The battle there was fought on 16 May 1811.
463. *meed:* recompense.
484. *Ilion:* Troy.
490. *rebeck:* a kind of fiddle with three strings.
508. *Vivā el Rey:* Byron notes, '"Vivā el Rey Fernando!" Long live King Ferdinand! is the chorus of most of the Spanish patriotic songs. They are chiefly in dispraise of the old King Charles, the Queen, and the Prince of Peace [Godoy, his prime minister and her lover].' These three were held responsible for the betrayal of Spain to the French invaders, and in 1808 Charles IV abdicated in favour of his son Ferdinand VII.
510. *wittol:* contented cuckold.
513–21. Harold recognizes traces of the actions in June and July 1808 which culminated in the defeat of the French by the Spaniards at Baylen. The 'dragon's nest' was a strong point taken in turn by both sides.
523. *badge of crimson hue:* 'The red cockade, with "Fernando Septimo" [Ferdinand VII] in the centre' (Byron).
537. *durance:* confinement.
539. *ball-piled pyramid:* Ammunition was stacked in a pyramidal form at the gun-positions.

Notes

545. *Scourger of the world:* Napoleon I, whom Byron elsewhere views more sympathetically and admiringly.
560. *anlace:* dagger.
566. *Minerva:* sometimes regarded as the goddess of war.
574. *Gorgon:* turning to stone all whom it gazes upon.
576–84. 'Such were the exploits of the Maid of Saragoza, who by her valour elevated herself to the highest rank of heroines' (Byron).
599. *Phoebus:* the sun.
607. *Houries:* nymphs of the Mohammedan Paradise.
612. *Parnassus:* 'These stanzas were written in Castri (Delphos), at the foot of Parnassus' (Byron). The fact that Greece was still under Turkish rule explains the references in the previous stanza.
646. *Daphne's deathless plant:* When Daphne was changed into a laurel, the tree became the favourite of Apollo. Its foliage emblematized distinction in poetry.
651. *Pythian:* The priestess of Apollo at Delphi was called the Pythia.
664. *hydra:* a many-headed monster.
679. *kibes:* Byron means 'heels'; 'kibes' are 'chilblains'.
697. *whiskey:* a light carriage.
706. *Boeotian:* Byron notes that he wrote this at Thebes, the capital of Boeotia, 'where the first riddle was propounded [by the Sphinx] and solved [by Oedipus].'
707. *worship of the solemn Horn:* a mock-ceremony conducted at a tavern at the top of Highgate Hill.
716. *ween:* believe.
733. *featly:* nimbly.
760. *croupe:* used here for 'croupade', a high curvet.
776. *brast:* broken, snapped.
778. *Matadores:* Byron blundered in employing several matadors for a single bull-fight.
781. *conynge:* skilful.
802. *Duenna:* an elderly woman, half-governess, half-companion, who has charge over the girls of a Spanish family.
813. *Lethe:* a river of Hades, which gave forgetfulness to the dead when they drank from it.
854. *Hebrew wanderer:* Ahasuerus, the legendary Wandering Jew.
879. *traitor only fell:* 'Alluding to the conduct and death of Solano, the governor of Cadiz, in May, 1808' (Byron).
884. *Kingless:* Charles IV was an exile, Ferdinand VII a prisoner in France.
890. *War even to the knife:* 'Palafox's answer to the French general at the siege of Saragoza' (Byron).
913–17. The weakness of Spain was the opportunity of her American colonies. Byron sees their liberation ('Columbia's ease') as some compensation for the ruthless subjugation of the Peruvians ('Quito's sons') by Francisco Pizarro (*c.* 1471–1541) and his brothers.
926. *Freedom's stranger-tree:* During the American and French Revolutions it was the custom to plant trees as symbols of growing freedom. None had ever been planted in Spain.
927. *my friend:* 'The Honourable John Wingfield, of the Guards, who died of a fever at Coimbra (May 14, 1811)' (Byron).
945. *fytte:* part.
952. *Eld:* antiquity, the olden time.

Notes

Canto II

1. *maid:* Pallas Athena.
3. *temple:* the Parthenon, on the Athenian Acropolis.
4. *war and wasting fire:* 'Part of the Acropolis was destroyed by the explosion of a magazine during the Venetian siege [in 1687]' (Byron).
16. *stole:* robe.
19. *Son of the morning:* perhaps identifiable with the unmoved Moslem or light Greek of l. 90.
55. *Athena's wisest son:* Socrates (469–399 B.C.).
61. *Acheron:* a river of Hades.
66. *Sadducee:* a member of one of the three sects into which the Jews were divided at the time of Christ. The Sadducees denied the resurrection of the dead.
72. *Bactrian, Samian sage:* Zoroaster and Pythagoras (both sixth century B.C.).
73–81. Evidently an expression of Byron's grief at the death of young John Edleston, or 'Thyrza', to whom he was deeply attached.
84. *thy fav'rite throne:* 'The Temple of Jupiter Olympius, of which sixteen columns, entirely of marble, yet survive' (Byron).
94. *spoiler:* The Earl of Elgin (1766–1841) had recently been removing marbles from the Acropolis, mainly from the frieze and pediment of the Parthenon, and shipping them to England. Byron considered this a desecration. In 1816 the Elgin marbles were placed in the British Museum.
95. *Caledonia:* Scotland. In l. 99, Byron associates Elgin's nationality with his alleged vandalism by calling him 'the modern Pict'.
116. *harpy:* ugly winged predatory monster.
118–22. Alaric, King of the Visigoths, occupied Athens in A.D. 395. Byron refers to the legend that Athena and Achilles ('Peleus' son') frightened him from the Acropolis. The 'Aegis' was the shield of Athena.
123. *Pluto:* the god of the infernal regions.
125. *Stygian shore:* banks of the Styx, a river of Hades.
155. *well-reeved:* roped securely.
155. *netted canopy:* 'To prevent blocks and splinters from falling on deck during action' (Byron).
174. *pennant-bearer:* convoy-leader.
185. *Arion:* a famous poet and musician (*fl.* 600 B.C.), of whom legend says that he once played so beautifully on board a ship that a dolphin subsequently rescued him from drowning.
190. *Calpe:* Gibraltar.
192–8. The moon ('Hecate') being in the southern sky, Spain is in light, Morocco ('Mauritania') in shadow.
209. *Dian:* Diana, goddess of the moon.
236. *Athos:* a Macedonian peninsula rising steeply to a 'giant height' of 6,350 feet. The mountain has been occupied by monks since the Middle Ages.
253–61. When Odysseus was shipwrecked on the island of Calypso, the 'nymph-queen', she fell in love with him. Despite a promise of immortality if he would remain, he continued his journey homewards (*Odyssey*, V). The intervention of the wise Mentor robbed Calypso of Telemachus, the son of Odysseus, too. Byron identified 'Calypso's isles' with Malta and Gozo, the latter of which he thought had been her home.
266. *Florence:* Byron was evidently thinking of Mrs. Spencer Smith, with whom he fell in love at Malta.

Notes

298. *kens:* knows.
322. *ared:* described.
334. *Iskander:* Alexander the Great.
335. *Theme of the young, and beacon of the wise:* whom the young discuss, and the wise take as an example.
336. *namesake:* Scanderbeg (Lord Alexander) (1403–67), a successful champion of Albanian independence.
344. *Where sad Penelope o'erlook'd the wave:* Ithaca, where Penelope awaited the return of her husband Odysseus.
347. *Sappho:* a lyrical poet (*fl.* 610 B.C.) of great genius, said by some to have been a native of Lesbos. Byron accepts the story that unrequited love caused her to destroy herself by leaping into the sea from the Leucadian rock.
356. Actium (31 B.C.), Lepanto (1571), and Trafalgar (1805) were three great naval battles fought in waters over which Harold sails.
371. *Dark Suli's rocks, and Pindus' inland peak:* the mountainous district in the south of the Epirus, and part of the ridge which divided Epirus from Thessaly.
397. *Ambracia's gulf:* where Augustus defeated Antony and Cleopatra in the battle of Actium. In commemoration of his victory he founded the city of Nicopolis, to which Byron refers in l. 402.
407. *Illyria:* an ancient name for the territory on the eastern side of the Adriatic Sea.
410. *Attica:* the division of ancient Greece of which Athens was the capital.
411. *Tempe:* a valley in Thessaly, celebrated for its beauty.
416. *primal city:* Yanina (Ioannina).
418. *Albania's chief:* Ali Pasha (1741–1822), who had made himself despotic ruler of much of what are now Albania and the part of Greece immediately south of it.
421. *daring mountain-band:* The Suliotes held out for many years against Ali Pasha.
424. *Monastic Zitza:* 'The convent and village of Zitza are four hours journey' from Yanina; the situation 'is perhaps the finest in Greece' (Byron).
438. *caloyer:* Greek monk.
453. *Chimaera's alps:* probably the Ceraunian Mountains.
456. *Acheron:* 'Now called Kalamas' (Byron).
466. *capote:* 'Albanese cloak' (Byron).
469. *Dodona:* Dedicated to Zeus (Jove), this was the oldest oracle in Greece. The God declared his will by the rustling of the oak-trees in the wind.
487. *Tomerit:* 'Anciently Mount Tomarus' (Byron).
498. *chief of power:* Ali Pasha.
502. *santons:* Mohammedan monks or hermits.
518. *Delhi:* savage horseman.
519. *glaive:* sword.
532. *Ramazani's fast:* Mohammedans observe Ramadan, the ninth month of their year, by fasting throughout the hours of daylight.
561. *Hafiz:* a famous Persian poet and philosopher (*d. c.* 1390).
562. *the Teian:* Anacreon (*c.* 563–478 B.C.), a famous lyric poet.
593. *fellow-countrymen have stood aloof:* 'Alluding to the wreckers of Cornwall' (Byron).

Notes

602. *Frank:* a name current in the eastern Mediterranean for any person of western nationality.

616. *brand:* torch.

618. *Acarnania:* the most westerly part of Greece; on its east, the River Achelous (Aspropotamo) separates it from Aetolia.

622. *Utraikey:* situated in a deep bay at the south-east corner of the Gulf of Arta ('Ambracia's gulf').

637. *Palikar:* 'a general name for a soldier amongst the Greeks and Albanese . . .: it means, properly, "a lad"' (Byron).

649–92. 'These stanzas are partly taken from different Albanese songs, as far as I was able to make them out' (Byron).

649. *Tambourgi:* drummer.

654. *camese:* fustanella, white kilt.

677. *Previsa:* 'taken by storm from the French [October 1798]' (Byron).

686. Let the Russian infidels behold with dread the insignia that shows him to be a Pasha.

689. *Selictar:* sword-bearer.

695–6. Who now will liberate you from the Turks, as Moses once led the Israelites out of their Egyptian bondage?

699. *Thermopylae:* the pass where a small force under Leonidas, King of Sparta (491–480 B.C.), made an heroic stand against the immense army with which Xerxes, King of Persia, was invading Greece. Leonidas was killed in the battle.

701. *Eurotas:* the river on which Sparta stood.

702–3. Thrasybulus restored democracy to Athens in 403 B.C. In the previous year he had occupied Phyle, which, says Byron, 'commands a beautiful view' of the city.

707. *carle:* churl.

726. *Helots:* the serfs of ancient Sparta.

730. *Othman's race:* the Turks.

731. *Serai:* the palace of the Sultan at Constantinople.

732. *former:* during the period of the Latin Empire of the East (1204–61), which the Venetians and the Crusaders established in Constantinople.

733. *Wahab's rebel brood:* The Wahabees, militant followers of an eighteenth-century Mohammedan reformer, were at the height of their power at the time of Byron's tour. They had recently attacked and ravaged Mecca and Medina.

748. *Stamboul:* Constantinople (Istanbul).

749. *Sophia's shrine:* the church of St Sophia, turned into a mosque after the Turkish conquest of Constantinople (1453).

760. *Queen of tides:* the moon.

765. *caique:* light skiff.

776. *searment:* wrapping.

792. *Lacedemon:* Sparta.

793. *Epaminondas:* Theban general and statesman of the fourth century B.C.

812. *Tritonia:* one of Athena's names. But the temple on Cape Sounion ('Colonna's cliff') was dedicated to Poseidon, god of the sea.

821. *Minerva:* Athena, who gave the olive to Athens.

822. *Hymettus:* a mountain near Athens, renowned for its honey.

826. *Mendeli:* Mount Pentelicus, celebrated for its marble.

836. *Marathon:* the plain near the east coast of Attica where the Athenians defeated the invading Persians in 490 B.C.

Notes

846. *Mede:* Persian.
857. *Ionian blast:* wind from the Ionian Sea.
883. *idlesse:* idleness.
905. *The parent, friend, and now the more than friend:* Mrs. Byron died 1 August 1811; C. S. Matthews died 3 August 1811; and two months later Byron learned that Edleston (see note on ll. 73–81) had died in May. Byron's personal grief for Edleston dominates the whole passage from l. 890.
926. *Eld:* old age.

Childe Harold's Pilgrimage, III

Byron started Canto III early in May 1816 as he crossed Europe after leaving England for the last time. He finished it in Switzerland on 4 July 1816. Publication followed on 18 November 1816. In the words quoted as an epigraph, Frederick the Great prescribes for the recently bereaved D'Alembert (1717–83) a form of activity that will take his mind off his grief.
2. *Ada:* Byron's legitimate daughter, born shortly before he left England. He addresses her again in ll. 1067–1102.
19. *One:* Harold.
48–9. *gaining as we give The life we image:* We impart life to the imagined form, and we receive life from it.
64. *Something too much of this:* Hamlet uses these words when he switches from earnest praise of Horatio to eager planning of the play to be presented before the king (III. ii).
65. *silent seal:* He will say no more of himself. Instead, in ll. 66–135, he outlines Harold's emotional development since Canto II.
72. Only in youth does life seem bright.
74. *he fill'd again:* Like Byron, he married.
99. *fond:* foolish.
118. *Chaldean:* The Chaldeans deeply impressed the Greeks by their skill in astronomy, astrology, occult learning, etc.
145. *an Empire's dust:* The battle of Waterloo, 18 June 1815, brought down the first French Empire, that of Napoleon I. Visiting the field within a year of the event, Byron could not forget that the slain, and much of the débris of the combat, were 'sepulchred below'.
148. *trophied:* decorated with arms taken from the defeated enemy.
158. *pride of place:* Byron explains this as a term of falconry, meaning the highest pitch of flight.
158. *eagle:* used as an ensign and badge by France during the first Empire.
160. *banded nations:* the allies who defeated Napoleon.
162. He who broke the world's chains is now himself confined to the remote island of St Helena.
169–70. Shall the English, who defeated the lion Napoleon, help to reinstate wolfish legitimate monarchs?
171. *prove:* Put it to the test.
180. *Harmodius:* He hid his sword in a myrtle branch when attempting to assassinate the Athenian despot Hippias.
181. *sound of revelry:* 'On the night previous to the action, it is said that a ball was given at Brussels' (Byron). In fact, the Duchess of Richmond gave her famous ball on 15 June 1815. The engagement which followed

221

Notes

closely on it was the battle of Quatre Bras, fought only two days before Waterloo.

200. *Brunswick's fated chieftain:* Frederick William, Duke of Brunswick, who fell at Quatre Bras. His father had been killed earlier in the war: see l. 205.

227. *Albyn:* Scotland.

229. *pibroch:* a series of variations for the bagpipe, chiefly martial, but including dirges.

234. *Evan's, Donald's fame:* Sir Evan Cameron fought against Cromwell; his grandson, Donald Cameron of Lochiel, was wounded at Culloden (1746); his great-great-grandson was mortally wounded at Quatre Bras.

235. *Ardennes:* 'The wood of Soignies is supposed to be a remnant of the forest of Ardennes' (Byron).

261. *Howard:* Major Howard, a relative of Byron's, killed late on the day of Waterloo.

303. *apples on the Dead Sea's shore:* 'The (fabled) apples on the brink of the lake Asphaltites were said to be fair without, and, within, ashes' (Byron).

310. *More than enough:* Waterloo grudged its victims even the threescore years and ten allowed by the Psalmist.

317. *antithetically mixt:* Napoleon I united in himself opposite extremes of character.

366. *Philip's son:* Alexander the Great.

368. *Diogenes:* a Greek cynic philosopher (*c.* 412–323 B.C.), contemporary with Alexander.

369. *sceptred cynics:* Byron described the 'great error' of Napoleon as 'a continued obtrusion on mankind of his want of all community of feeling for or with them'.

420. *battles:* armies.

428. *longer date:* earlier period.

429. '"What wants [lacks] that knave that a king should have?" was King James's question of meeting Johnny Armstrong and his followers in full accoutrements. See the Ballad' (Byron).

476. *one fond breast:* Harold's attachment reflects that of Byron to his half-sister, Augusta Leigh. See 'Epistle to Augusta'.

496. *Drachenfels:* the 'Dragon's Rock', which stands on the Rhine nearly opposite Bonn.

541. *Marceau:* French Revolutionary general (1769–96), killed in combat against the Austrians.

554. *Ehrenbreitstein:* One of the strongest fortresses in Europe, it capitulated to the French in 1799. They dismantled the fortifications when evacuating it in 1801.

567. *vultures:* an allusion to the legend of Prometheus, who was tortured by vultures for having served mankind in defiance of the gods.

601. *Morat:* When the Swiss defeated a Burgundian invasion here in 1476, the bodies of the Burgundians killed were deposited in a charnel-house which the French tore down in 1798.

608. *Cannae:* Hannibal's famous victory over the Romans in 216 B.C.

614. *vice-entail'd Corruption:* corrupt government entailed by the ruler's vices.

616. *Draconic:* Draco was an Athenian lawgiver of the seventh century B.C. His code of laws was exceedingly severe.

Notes

625. *Aventicum:* Only the ruins mentioned in l. 617 survive from the time when this was the Roman capital of Helvetia.

627. *Julia:* 'Julia Alpinula, a young Aventian priestess, died soon after a vain endeavour to save her father, condemned to death as a traitor by Aulus Caecina' (Byron). Julia and her story were in fact the invention of a sixteenth-century forger.

642. *yonder Alpine snow:* 'This is written in the eye of Mont Blanc ... which even at this distance dazzles mine' (Byron).

644. *Lake Leman:* the Lake of Geneva.

673. *blue rushing of the arrowy Rhone:* 'The colour of the Rhone at Geneva is blue, to a depth of tint which I have never seen equalled in water, salt or fresh, except in the Mediterranean and Archipelago' (Byron).

725. *Rousseau:* Jean-Jacques Rousseau (1712–78) made a cult of sentiment, deplored the evils of urban civilization, and advised a simple life in natural surroundings. His writings had profound effects. Immediately, they contributed to the ferment of ideas associated with the French Revolution: see ll. 761–9.

743. *Julie:* the heroine of Rousseau's *La Nouvelle Héloïse* (1761).

745. *memorable kiss:* 'This refers to the account, in his *Confessions*, of his passion for the Comtesse d'Houdetot ..., and his long walk every morning, for the sake of the single kiss which was the common salutation of French acquaintance' (Byron).

786. *eagles:* It was at one time believed that an eagle could gaze at the sun without being blinded.

796. *in one we shall be slower:* The next revolution will do its work more thoroughly.

809. *Jura:* The Jura range lies to the west of the lake.

848. *Cytherea's zone:* the girdle which made Aphrodite (Venus) irresistibly attractive.

851. *early Persian:* a sun-worshipper.

853. *earth-o'ergazing mountains:* 'It is to be recollected, that the most beautiful and impressive doctrines of the divine Founder of Christianity were delivered, not in the *Temple*, but on the *Mount*' (Byron).

861. *storm:* Byron dates this thunderstorm 13 June 1816, 'at midnight'. He adds that he had seen 'none more beautiful'.

900. *knoll:* knell.

923. *Clarens:* scene of love-making in Rousseau's *La Nouvelle Héloïse*. Byron notes the 'peculiar adaptation' of Clarens and its surroundings to the persons and events Rousseau sets there. He comments upon the feeling which invests the whole neighbourhood: 'it is a sense of the existence of love in its most extended and sublime capacity, and of our own participation of its good and of its glory: it is the great principle of the universe'. He is evidently writing under the influence of Shelley.

972. *Psyche:* Cupid's lover, upon whom his mother Aphrodite imposed great hardships. In her endurance of these, she represents the human soul, which is prepared by its ordeals for true happiness.

976. *a couch:* the lake.

977. *Lausanne! and Ferney!:* Edward Gibbon (1737–94) lived at Lausanne from 1783 to 1793; Voltaire (1694–1778) lived at Ferney, near Geneva, from 1758 to 1777. In his *History of the Decline and Fall of the Roman Empire*, Gibbon has occasion to trace the growth of Christianity; he does so with cool irony. Voltaire was the greatest of the French *philosophes*, an

Notes

enemy of superstition, dogmatism, and all else that seemed to him to impede intellectual progress, tolerance, and justice. Like Rousseau's, his writings had profound effects and contributed to the ferment of ideas associated with the French Revolution.

982. *Titan-like:* The Titans' revolt against their father Chronos is often confused with the Giants' rising against Zeus.

986. *The one:* Voltaire.

991. *Proteus:* He had the gift of prophecy but, on being questioned, would assume a variety of shapes to elude his questioner's grasp.

995. *The other:* Gibbon.

1024. *Carthaginian:* Hannibal, who invaded Italy in 218 B.C. See note on l. 608.

1047. *guerdon:* reward.

1057. *filed my mind:* quoted from Shakespeare's *Macbeth* III. i, where 'filed' means 'defiled, corrupted'.

1063–4. 'It is said by Rochefoucault that "there is *always* something in the misfortunes of men's best friends not displeasing to them"' (Byron).

1071. *shadows of far years:* shadows cast now upon distant future years.

Childe Harold's Pilgrimage, IV

Byron started Canto IV at La Mira, near Venice, on 26 June 1817 and finished it by 20 July 1817. It then consisted of 126 stanzas, but he raised the total to 186 by the date of publication, 28 April 1818. In a dedication to his friend J. C. Hobhouse, he announces that in this last canto 'there will be found less of the pilgrim than in any of the preceding, and that little slightly, if at all, separated from the author speaking in his own person. The fact is, that I had become weary of drawing a line which every one seemed determined not to perceive'. The words of Ariosto quoted as an epigraph refer to the extent of the speaker's travels in Northern Italy.

1. *Bridge of Sighs:* a covered bridge, connecting the Doge's Palace with the Venetian state prison.

7. *many a subject land:* Venice had once been a great maritime and commercial power.

8. *winged Lion:* symbol of St. Mark, the patron saint of Venice.

10. *Cybele:* a Phrygian fertility goddess, commonly represented as crowned with towers.

19. *Tasso's echoes:* Gondoliers used once to sing in their own dialect passages from the *Gerusalemme Liberata* of Torquato Tasso (1544–95).

33. *Rialto:* the site of the original city, a district mentioned in *The Merchant of Venice* and *Othello*.

34. *Pierre:* a leading character in *Venice Preserved*, a tragedy by Thomas Otway (1652–85).

75. *it:* the 'inviolate island'(l. 71), Britain.

86. These words are said to have been spoken by the mother of the Spartan general Brasidas who was killed while gaining a brilliant victory over the Athenians in 422 B.C.

91. *spouseless Adriatic:* The Doge of Venice used symbolically to wed the Adriatic each Ascension Day by dropping a ring into the sea. The Bucentaur was the ornamented barge used for this and other state purposes.

Notes

97. *an Emperor:* The Suabian Frederick Barbarossa, who humbled himself before the Pope in Venice in 1177.
100. *the Austrian:* Between 1814 and 1866, Venice was part of the Austrian Empire.
106. *lauwine:* avalanche.
107. *Dandolo:* the aged Doge of Venice who diverted the Fourth Crusade against Byzantium in 1204 and himself led the attack.
111. *Doria's menace:* In 1379, when the Venetians wanted to make peace with their Genoese enemies, Doria, commanding the Genoese navy, replied that there could be no peace until he and his men had bridled the bronze horses standing on the porch of St. Mark's.
118. *Tyre:* For some centuries B.C., this Phoenician city wielded great maritime and commercial power.
119. *by-word:* sobriquet.
124. *Candia:* a town, now called Heraklion, on the north coast of Crete. For twenty-four years (1645–69), the Venetians defended it against the Ottomites, or Turks. The siege of Troy lasted only ten years.
125. *Lepanto's fight:* the great naval victory of the Venetians, in alliance with Spain and the Papacy, over the Turks in 1571. See Canto II, l. 356.
136–44. According to Plutarch, the tragedies of Euripides were so popular with the Sicilians that those among the Athenian prisoners of war taken at Syracuse in 413 B.C. who knew portions of them won the affections of their masters and even gained release from captivity.
156. *water-columns:* waterspouts.
158. *Radcliffe, Schiller:* authors respectively of *The Mysteries of Udolpho* (1794) and *Die Geisterseher* (1789).
172. *tannen:* fir-trees. Byron mistakenly thought that the word referred only to a species 'peculiar to the Alps'.
238. *Friuli's mountains:* north-east of Venice.
240. *Iris:* personification of the rainbow.
242. *Dian's crest:* the horn of the moon in its first quarter.
247. *Rhaetian hill:* west of Venice.
250. *Brenta:* a river.
262. *Arqua:* Petrarch (1304–74), Italian humanist, patriot, and poet, best known today for his sonnets and other poems in honour of Laura, died in Arqua.
269. *tree:* laurel.
307. *Ferrara:* the capital of the ancient ducal family of Este, which patronized Ariosto, Tasso, and other poets.
315. *wreath:* crown of laurel, or bay leaves, conferred upon great poets, such as Dante. See ll. 84, 269.
317. *his cell:* Alfonso II is said to have had Tasso confined as a lunatic.
339. *Cruscan quire:* The Accademia della Crusca (founded 1582) severely criticized *La Gerusalemme Liberata*.
340. *Boileau:* French critic (1636–1711), who dismissed Tasso's poetry as tinsel.
354. *Bards:* Dante, the 'Tuscan father', wrote of Hell; Ariosto, the 'southern Scott', wrote of Chivalry.
359. *Ariosto of the North:* Sir Walter Scott (1771–1832), at this date still best known for his narrative poems.
361 *bust:* surmounting his tomb.

Notes

370–87. In these lines Byron translates, and slightly expands, a sonnet by Vincenzo da Filicaia (1642–1707).

384. *Po:* the river which runs across northern Italy.

389. *Roman friend:* 'The celebrated letter of Servius Sulpicius to Cicero ['Tully'], on the death of his daughter, describes as it then was, and now is, a path which I often traced in Greece, both by sea and land, in different journeys and voyages' (Byron).

425. *Etrurian Athens:* Florence, on the River Arno. Etruria was the ancient name for Tuscany.

433. *Goddess:* the Venus de' Medici, in the Uffizi gallery at Florence.

450. *confirm the Dardan Shepherd's prize:* show that the Trojan Paris was right to give the golden apple, inscribed 'To the fairest', to none other than Venus.

452. *Anchises:* He and Venus were the parents of Aeneas.

454. *Lord of War:* Mars, the husband of Venus.

478. *Santa Croce:* the great church of Florence, in which are buried many of Italy's illustrious dead: for example, the artist Michelangelo (1475–1564), the poet Alfieri (1749–1803), the scientist Galileo (1564–1642), and the political theorist Machiavelli (1469–1527).

495. *Canova:* Italian sculptor (1757–1822).

498. *Bard of Prose:* Giovanni Boccaccio (1313–75), author of 'the Hundred Tales of love', the *Decameron*.

505–22. Dante was buried at Ravenna, Petrarch at Arqua, and Boccaccio at Certaldo, near Florence.

506. *Scipio:* The Roman conqueror of Carthage is said to have spent his last days and been buried at a coast town near Naples.

519–20. *his tomb Uptorn:* This happened in 1783.

525–6. In the pageant decreed by Tiberius Caesar in connection with the public funeral of Junia, wife of Cassius and sister of Brutus, the busts of her husband and brother were conspicuous by their absence.

542. *Arno's dome:* The Cathedral, crowned with Brunelleschi's cupola, here symbolizes Florence.

551. *Thrasimene's lake:* Hannibal defeated the Romans there in 217 B.C. The unnoticed earthquake (ll. 563–7) is mentioned by Livy.

586. *Clitumnus:* a small river in Umbria, springing from a beautiful rock in a grove of cypress trees, where was a sanctuary of the God Clitumnus.

604. *Genius:* guardian spirit.

614. *Velino:* Byron describes this waterfall of the River Velino, near Terni, as 'worth all the cascades and torrents of Switzerland put together'.

620. *Phlegethon:* the flaming river of Hades.

649–69. The Apennines, forming the backbone of the Italian peninsula, seem 'things of lesser dignity' than the mountains Byron saw on the journeys recorded in Cantos III and II. But he makes an exception of Soracte, a mountain north of Rome which 'the lyric Roman' Horace (65 B.C.–8 B.C.) describes as snow-covered.

703. *Niobe:* The mother of six sons and six daughters, she boasted herself superior to Leto, the mother of Apollo and Artemis. For this arrogance, her children were immediately slain, and she was turned into a weeping stone.

707. *The Scipios' tomb:* That of one of the greatest Roman families, it stood on the Appian Way. But see l. 506.

Notes

710. *Tiber:* the river which runs through Rome.
728. *Eureka:* Archimedes' cry of discovery.
732. *Brutus:* He and his fellow-conspirators, as opponents of tyranny, assassinated Julius Caesar in 44 B.C.
734-5. Cicero ('Tully') (106-43 B.C.) was the great orator, Virgil (70-19 B.C.) the great epic poet, and Livy (59 B.C.-A.D. 17) the great historian of ancient Rome.
739-48. In 86 B.C., Sylla's party was overthrown in Italy, but he declined to return until he had subdued Mithridates in Asia Minor. In 81 B.C., he was appointed dictator, and two years later he resigned the office and retired into private life.
757-69. Cromwell, who dismissed a parliament and destroyed a king, was also subject to destiny in that on the same day of the year—3 September—he won Scotland by the battle of Dunbar (1650), secured England by his victory at Worcester (1651), and died (1658).
775. *dread statue:* Byron believed that he was seeing the statue of Pompey at the foot of which Julius Caesar died.
781. *Nemesis:* goddess of retributive justice.
785. *She-wolf:* a bronze statue, damaged perhaps by lightning, of the she-wolf that suckled the infants Romulus and Remus.
800. *one vain man:* Napoleon I.
809. *Alcides:* Hercules, who undertook women's work in the service of Omphale.
811. *came—and saw—and conquer'd:* Julius Caesar's famous boast.
812. *flee:* fly.
828. *rainbow:* sign that there will not be a second universal flood. See Genesis ix. 12-16.
858-63. America ('Columbia'), like Pallas Athena, came into being fully armed. George Washington (1732-99) was her 'champion' and 'child'.
865-7. Byron sees the French Revolutionary Terror (1793-4) as a period of unrestrained licence, like the annual Roman festival of Saturn.
883-927. 'Alluding to the tomb of Cecilia Metella' (Byron) on the Appian Way.
904-5. *Cornelia . . . Egypt's graceful queen:* The virtuous and accomplished matron contrasts with Cleopatra, who had Julius Caesar and Antony in turn as her lovers.
917. *Hesperus:* the evening star.
935. *forth:* from.
951. *Palatine:* This most central of the seven hills of Rome was the site of the palaces of the Caesars.
986-99. The arch of Titus commemorates the capture of Jerusalem in A.D. 70. Trajan's exploits are sculptured in a spiral on his column, but at the top a statue of St Peter has replaced that of Trajan himself and the 'imperial urn' said to hold his ashes. Byron contrasts Trajan, who reigned well from A.D. 98 to 117, with Alexander the Great, a mere conqueror.
1000. *rock of triumph:* Capitoline Hill. Victorious generals drove up it in triumph; condemned criminals were thrown from a part of it called the Tarpeian rock.
1022. *Rienzi:* Cola di Rienzi (1313-54) tried to re-establish the Roman republic.

Notes

1026. *Numa:* the legendary second king of Rome, elected one year after the death of Romulus. He became the lover of the fountain-nymph Egeria, who instructed him in the forms of religious worship which he introduced. Byron goes on to speak of what he supposed to be the Grotto of Egeria.

1030. *Aurora:* goddess of dawn.

1031. *nympholepsy:* possession by a nymph, ecstatic vision.

1129. *upas:* a fabulous Javanese tree, poisonous to all animal and vegetable life for fifteen miles around.

1143. *couch:* remove a cataract.

1147. *Coliseum:* the huge amphitheatre finished in A.D. 80.

1179. *they:* those responsible for Byron's separation from his wife.

1184. *Orestes:* Having avenged his father Agamemnon by killing his mother Clytaemnestra, he was pursued by the fearful goddesses known as Furies.

1221. *Janus glance:* ambiguous glance. Janus was a two-faced god.

1252. *Gladiator:* Byron refers to a well-known statue which is commonly taken to represent a wounded and dying gladiator.

1266. *Dacian:* The Roman province of Dacia occupied roughly the same territory as present-day Romania.

1269. *Goths:* They invaded Italy in the fifth century A.D.

1297-1302. This is recorded by the Venerable Bede (673-735).

1314. *Pantheon:* a celebrated Roman temple which became a Christian church in the seventh century; one of the stateliest buildings in the world.

1320. *sole aperture:* single opening in the crown of the dome.

1324-59. These lines 'allude to the story of the Roman daughter, which is recalled to the traveller by the site, or pretended site, of that adventure, now shown at the Church of St Nicholas *in Carcere*' (Byron).

1341. *Cain was Eve's:* The first son of the first woman was the first murderer.

1351. *starry fable:* that the Milky Way was formed from milk that overflowed when Juno was feeding Hercules.

1360. *Mole which Hadrian rear'd:* 'The castle of St Angelo' (Byron), originally built as a mausoleum—but not in imitation of the Egyptian pyramids.

1369. *dome:* St Peter's, Rome.

1370. *Diana's marvel:* the temple of Diana (Artemis) at Ephesus, one of the seven wonders of the ancient world.

1381. *Zion:* Jerusalem.

1430. *may draw the mind of man:* the mind of man may draw.

1433. *Laocoön:* He and his two sons were killed by two huge serpents which coiled around them (Virgil, *Aeneid*, II). Byron refers to the famous group of statuary disinterred at Rome in the sixteenth century.

1441-67. Byron refers to the statue known as the Apollo Belvedere.

1459. *Prometheus:* He brought down fire from heaven for the use of men. The fire here stands for human longing.

1468. *Pilgrim:* Harold, who has not yet been mentioned in Canto IV.

1494. *fardels:* burdens.

1495-1548. In 1816 Princess Charlotte, only daughter of the Prince Regent, had married Leopold of Saxe-Coburg. In 1817 she died in giving birth to a son, who also died.

Notes

1519. *her Iris:* Charlotte as heir to the throne had inspired some hope in the liberals.
1549. *Nemi:* a lake to the south of Rome which fills the crater of an extinct volcano.
1558. *Albano:* another lake to the south of Rome.
1562. *Arms and the Man:* the opening words of the *Aeneid*, in the latter half of which Virgil describes the 'Epic war' by which Aeneas established himself in Italy.
1564. *Tully reposed:* Cicero had a country house at Tusculum.
1566. *Sabine farm:* belonging to Horace.
1575. *Euxine:* Black Sea. Near its entrance, there were said to be two islands, the 'Symplegades' (l. 1576) which closed together upon ships that tried to pass between them.
1586. *Spirit:* presumably Byron's half-sister Augusta.
1624. *oak leviathans:* warships.
1629. *Armada:* Violent storms completed the destruction of the Spanish Armada after its defeat by the English (1588).
1629. *Trafalgar:* 'The Gale of wind which succeeded the battle of Trafalgar [1805] destroyed the greater part (if not all) of the prizes' (Byron).
1672. *sandal-shoon, and scallop-shell:* showing him to be a pilgrim. 'Shoon' (for 'shoes') is archaic.

The Giaour

Byron wrote this poem between May and November 1813, but during that period it grew by successive interpolations from 407 to 1334 lines. The first edition, containing 685 lines, appeared on 5 June 1813; the seventh, giving the poem in its final shape, appeared about six months later. No doubt the deliberately fragmentary character of the work facilitated its expansion. Byron admitted that the story was based on fact. In Athens, he was said to have interposed on behalf of a girl about to be drowned for a sexual irregularity and to have conveyed her to safety. Without exactly confirming this account, he did communicate it to Moore to let him 'into the origin of *The Giaour*' (letter dated 1 September 1813). 'Giaour' is a term of reproach applied by Turks to Christians and other non-Mohammedans. The lines quoted as an epigraph come from Moore's 'As a beam o'er the face of the waters'.

Advertisement, 7. *Seven Islands:* the Ionian Islands, which Venice ceded to France in 1797.
Advertisement, 9–10. *Russian invasion:* Forces organized by the Russians were operating against the Turks in the Morea (the Peloponnese) in 1770.
3. *tomb:* Supposedly that of Themistocles, the Athenian statesman (c. 514–449 B.C.), it lies not far from the harbour of Piraeus. The Athenian naval victory of Salamis over the Persians in 480 B.C. was due to Themistocles.
9. *Colonna's height:* Cape Sounion, south-east of Athens.
22. *Nightingale:* 'The attachment of the nightingale to the rose is a well-known Persian fable. If I mistake not, the "Bulbul of a thousand tales" is one of his appellations' (Byron).
40. *guitar:* 'the constant amusement of the Greek sailor by night; with a steady fair wind, and during a calm, it is accompanied always by the voice, and often by dancing' (Byron).

Notes

81. *Obstruction:* cessation of the vital functions.
151. *slave:* Byron explains that the governor of Athens was himself subordinate to a higher Turkish official.
171. *Mainote:* Mainote pirates infested the coast of Attica.
177. *Port Leone:* Piraeus.
199. *Othman's sons:* Ottomans or Turks.
212. *ween:* think, believe.
215. *timeless:* untimely, ill-timed.
225. *tophaike:* musket. 'The Bairam [a three-day festival following the fast of Ramadan] is announced by the cannon at sunset: the illumination of the mosques, and the firing of all kind of small arms, loaded with *ball*, proclaim it during the night' (Byron).
251. *jerreed:* 'a blunted Turkish javelin, which is darted from horseback with great force and precision. It is a favourite exercise of the Mussulmans' (Byron).
282. *Simoom:* 'The blast of the desert, fatal to everything living' (Byron).
339. *Fakir:* Mohammedan religious mendicant.
340. *Dervise:* Mohammedan friar.
343. *bread and salt:* 'To partake of food—to break bread and taste salt with your host—ensures the safety of the guest' (Byron, letter dated 3 October 1813).
355. *ataghan:* 'a long dagger' (Byron).
357. *green:* 'the privileged colour of the prophet's numerous pretended descendants' (Byron). 'Emir' is a title of honour borne by such persons.
358. *salam:* salutation, obeisance.
389. *insect-queen:* 'The blue-winged butterfly of Kashmeer, the most rare and beautiful of the species' (Byron).
423. *Scorpion:* It was at one time believed that in an intolerable situation a scorpion would commit suicide.
464. *kiosk:* summer-house, open pavilion.
468. *Phingari:* 'the moon' (Byron).
479. *jewel of Giamschid:* 'The celebrated fabulous ruby of Sultan Giamschid' (Byron).
483. *Al-Sirat:* 'the bridge of breadth narrower than the thread of a famished spider, and sharper than the edge of a sword, over which the Mussulmans must *skate* into Paradise, to which it is the only entrance; but this is not the worst, the river beneath being hell itself' (Byron).
490. *soulless:* 'A vulgar error: the Koran allots at least a third of Paradise to well-behaved women' (Byron).
491. *Muftis:* Mohammedan priests.
496. *hyacinthine:* Several writers have used this word as a poetic epithet of hair. Homer seems to have originated the comparison (*Odyssey*, VI) and to have been thinking of a golden colour.
506. *Franguestan:* land of the Franks, Europe.
522. *arquebuss:* an early type of portable gun.
566. *Liakura:* Parnassus.
568. *Bismillah:* '"In the name of God"; the commencement of all the chapters of the Koran but one [the ninth], and of prayer and thanksgiving' (Byron).
571. *Chiaus:* a Turkish messenger or sergeant.
593. *curl'd his very beard:* 'A phenomenon not uncommon with an angry Mussulman' (Byron).

Notes

603. *Amaun:* 'quarter, pardon' (Byron).
608. *brand:* sword.
666. *palampore:* 'The flowered shawls generally worn by persons of rank' (Byron).
717. *calpac:* 'the solid cap or centre part of the head-dress; the shawl is wound round it, and forms the turban' (Byron).
717. *caftan:* long tunic.
723–8. 'The turban, pillar, and inscriptive verse, decorate the tombs of the Osmanlies, whether in the cemetery or the wilderness' (Byron).
729. *Osmanlie:* Ottoman.
734. *Alla Hu:* 'the concluding words of the Muezzin's call to prayer' (Byron).
748. *Monkir:* 'Monkir and Nekir are the inquisitors of the dead' (Byron).
750. *Eblis:* 'the Oriental Prince of Darkness' (Byron).
784. *Gouls and Afrits:* In Mohammedan mythology, the former are evil spirits that prey on human corpses. the latter are demons.
896. *the Gorgon:* in Greek mythology, one of three sisters with a petrifying gaze; their hair was entwined with serpents.
909. *Saint Francis:* founded the Franciscan order of friars about 1209.
951. *desert-bird:* It was at one time believed that a pelican would wound her own breast in order to feed her young with her blood.
1040. *Nazarene:* Christian.
1058–9. God put a mark on Cain, the first murderer: see Genesis iv. 15.
1076. *Taheer:* During his first visit to Greece, Byron had employed Dervish Tahiri, a Turkish soldier, as a guide.
1102. *Aetna:* the Sicilian volcano.
1273. *symar:* here, 'a shroud' (Byron); normally, a loose light robe.

The Prisoner of Chillon

Byron wrote this poem on 27 and 28 June 1816 at Ouchy, near Lausanne, where he and Shelley were detained in a small inn by the weather. It was published on 5 December 1816. Byron and Shelley had visited the Castle of Chillon, on the Lake of Geneva, on 25 June 1816, and Byron had been deeply impressed by the story of François Bonnivard, a sixteenth-century republican reformer, who had been imprisoned there by order of Duke Charles III of Savoy. Some errors occur in the story as Byron received it.
35. *marsh's meteor lamp:* will-o'-the-wisp, ignis fatuus.
41. *new day:* free life after years of imprisonment.
211. *found him not:* found only his corpse.
339. *town:* Villeneuve.
341. *isle:* Ile de Paix.

Mazeppa

Byron was working on this poem during September 1818 in Venice; it was published on 28 June 1819. Voltaire's *History of Charles XII, King of Sweden* (1731) supplied the basic information about Mazeppa and his ride. In particular, it made the horse carry Mazeppa not to his mansion as in history but to the Ukraine, the horse's own native region.
1. *Pultowa:* King Charles XII, 'the royal Swede' (1682–1718), invaded Russia, defeated Peter the Great at Narva (1700) and was in turn totally

Notes

defeated at Pultowa (Poltava) on 8 July 1709. Mazeppa, Polish hetman or military commander of the Eastern Ukraine, had defected to Charles and now fled to Turkey with him.

10. *year:* 1812, when Napoleon I took Moscow.
23-4. Voltaire records the wounded colonel's self-sacrifice.
34. *agony:* Charles had been shot in the left foot.
57. *outspent:* exhausted.
104. *Bucephalus:* the favourite horse of Alexander the Great.
105. *Scythia:* famous for its cavalry.
116. *Borysthenes:* River Dnieper.
129. *John Casimir:* King of Poland from 1648 to 1668.
155. *Palatine:* local ruler.
157. *salt:* 'This comparison of a "*salt* mine" may, perhaps, be permitted to a Pole, as the wealth of the country consists greatly in the salt mines' (Byron).
178. *passports into heaven:* A cuckold's horns were facetiously said to serve this purpose.
188. *port:* carriage, bearing.
417. Mazeppa is trying to encourage the defeated Charles XII.
428. *northern light:* the Aurora Borealis.
437. *Spahi:* Turkish cavalryman.
533-8. The sensitiveness which made the men of Mazeppa's breed react quickly to sudden attack exposed them to the danger of sinking momentarily beneath accumulated woes.
664. *werst:* A Russian measure of length, equal to about two-thirds of an English mile.

She Walks in Beauty

Byron wrote this lyric in 1814, immediately after seeing for the first time the beautiful Mrs Wilmot. She had appeared in mourning with numerous spangles in her dress. He published the poem in *Hebrew Melodies* (1815).

Oh! Snatch'd Away in Beauty's Bloom

Written before 1815, this is perhaps a final reminiscence of 'Thyrza' (John Edleston). See *Childe Harold's Pilgrimage*, II. 73-81, 890-908. Byron included the lyric in *Hebrew Melodies* (1815).

The Destruction of Sennacherib

Byron wrote this poem early in 1815 with publication in *Hebrew Melodies* (1815) specifically in mind. The events it celebrates are recorded in II Kings xix and Isaiah xxxvii.

21. *Ashur:* Assyria.
22. *Baal:* a god worshipped by the Assyrians and other neighbours of the Hebrews.

Stanzas for Music

These lines were first published in 1816 but may well have been addressed to Edleston some years earlier, perhaps while he was still alive.

Notes

When We Two Parted
Written and published in 1816, this poem was apparently addressed to Lady Frances Wedderburn Webster. Byron had had an inconclusive flirtation with her in 1813. More recently, her name had been slanderously connected with that of the Duke of Wellington.

Darkness
Byron wrote this poem during the earlier part of his stay at the Villa Diodati, near Geneva. He published it later in the same year, 1816. It offers a variant of a prevalent Romantic nightmare; Thomas Campbell and Thomas Hood also wrote 'Last Man' poems.
50. *clung:* shrivelled.

Epistle to Augusta
These stanzas were written at the Villa Diodati in 1816 and sent home to be published if Augusta Leigh should consent. She withheld her permission, and the 'Epistle' did not appear until 1830.
11. *other claims and other ties:* She was a married woman and already had five children.
13. *thy father's son:* Byron. He and Augusta Leigh had the same father but different mothers.
15. *our grandsire:* Admiral Byron (1723–86) sailed so regularly into storms that his men nicknamed him 'Foul-weather Jack'.
73. *our own dear Lake:* at Newstead Abbey ('the old Hall'), where they had known great contentment early in 1814.
81. *The world is all before me:* Byron echoes a clause from the final lines of *Paradise Lost*, in which Milton describes the departure of Adam and Eve from Eden.
112. *fourth:* fourth part, quarter.

Lines on Hearing that Lady Byron Was Ill
Byron wrote this poem in Switzerland in September 1816 after reading a newspaper report of Lady Byron's illness. It was first published in 1832.
31. Byron blamed his mother-in-law and his wife's former governess, Mrs Clermont, for the separation of Lady Byron and himself.
36. *cement:* accented on the first syllable.
37. *Clytemnestra:* Agamemnon's wife, who murdered him on his return from the siege of Troy.
51. *averments:* assertions.

So, We'll Go No More A Roving
Byron wrote this lyric in Venice, immediately after the Carnival of 1817. 'The mumming closed with a masked ball at the Fenice, where I went, as also to most of the ridottos, etc., etc.; and, though I did not dissipate much upon the whole, yet I find "the sword wearing out the scabbard," though I have but just turned the corner of twenty-nine.' Introduced by these words, the poem came to Moore in Byron's letter dated 28 February 1817. Moore published it in his *Letters and Journals of Lord Byron, With Notices of His Life* (1830).
5. *the sword outwears its sheath:* Byron appears to have been the first to use this phrase with the metaphorical application it has here.